BY ORDER OF THE SECRETARY
OF THE AIR FORCE

AIR FORCE INSTRUCTION 16-1202

3 MAY 2001
Certified Current 19 NOVEMBER 2009
Operations Support

PARARESCUE OPERATIONS, TECHNIQUES,
AND PROCEDURES

COMPLIANCE WITH THIS PUBLICATION IS MANDATORY

OPR: HQ USAF/XOOP (CMSgt Miller)

Certified by: HQ USAF/XOO
(Maj Gen Buchanan III)
Pages: 237
Distribution: F

This instruction implements AFPD 16-12, *Pararescue*. This publication outlines procedures and techniques to conduct Pararescue operations. It applies to Air National Guard and United States Air Force Reserve units or members. Send recommended changes, additions, deletions, and any conflict or duplication of other reports to HQ AF/XOOP, Air Force Pentagon, Washington DC 20330-1480, on Air Force (AF) Form 847, **Recommendation for Change of Publication**. MAJCOMs may supplement this instruction. MAJCOMs will send one copy of their printed supplement to HQ AF/XOOP; other organizations send one copy of each-supplement to the next higher headquarters. See Attachment 1 for a glossary of references and supporting information. *NOTE:* This instruction may reference Air Force publications under the old publications scheme (Air Force regulations [AFR] and manuals [AFM]) which remain in force until converted to the new types of publications.

Chapter 1

INTRODUCTION

1.1. Deviations and Waivers. This instruction is directive in nature. Organizations requiring variance from procedures within this instruction require a waiver. Waiver authority for this instruction is MAJCOM/DO.

1.1.1. Waiver requests. Forward waiver requests through the appropriate command channels to MAJCOM/DO with the following information in narrative format:

1.1.1.1. Procedure to be deviated from.

1.1.1.2. Circumstances which necessitate the requirement for waiver.

1.1.1.3. Impact of denial of the waiver.

1.1.1.4. Inclusive dates of the waiver period.

1.1.1.5. Specific location the waiver is to be granted.

1.1.1.6. Units/individuals requiring the waiver.

1.1.2. Deviations occurring during mission execution should be reported to MAJCOM/DO within 24 hours if operationally/tactically feasible with written waiver request submitted as soon as is practical.

1.2. Local Operating Procedures. Units with pararescue combat rescue officer personnel assigned may publish local operating procedures to alter or amend the provision of this instruction to make them more restrictive, if necessary. Units will forward, through channels, an informational copy of local unit operating procedures to MAJCOM/DO.

1.3. Records Disposition. Maintain and dispose of all records created as a result of prescribed processes in this instruction in accordance with (IAW) AFMAN 37-139, Records Disposition Schedule.

Chapter 2

OPERATIONAL/TRAINING RESTRICTIONS

2.1. Safety. The purpose of this chapter is to establish parameters of safety by placing certain restrictions on training and operations.

2.2. Parachuting.

2.2.1. Surface Wind Criteria. During all training jumps, the surface wind velocity criteria established in AFI 13-217 will not be exceeded. The drop zone controller will cancel all training jumps when surface winds exceed these limits.

2.2.2. Specific data for aircraft minimum deployment altitudes and airspeeds are contained in AFI 11-231.

2.2.3. Deployment Altitudes.

2.2.3.1. Operational. Minimum altitudes are based on operational requirements and team experience weighed against the type of equipment utilized.

2.2.3.1.1. Static Line, Parabolic/Round Parachute.

2.2.3.1.1.1. T-10C parachute - 435 feet above ground level (AGL) with a 125 knots indicated air speed (KIAS) minimum airspeed.

2.2.3.1.1.2. MC1-1B/C parachute - 475 feet AGL with a 125 KIAS minimum airspeed.

2.2.3.1.1.3. The minimum deployment for all type aircraft with a drop speed of 90 knots or less is 1500 feet AGL.

2.2.3.1.2. Freefall, Square Parachute. The minimum operational deployment altitude is 2500 feet AGL.

2.2.3.1.3. Static Line, Square Parachute. The minimum deployment for all type aircraft is 1250 feet AGL.

2.2.3.2. Training.

2.2.3.2.1. Static Line, Parabolic/Round Parachute: The minimum fixed-wing aircraft training drop altitude is 1000 feet AGL if weather is a factor, and 800 feet AGL after a Command Decision Risk Assessment has been completed with the time available to activate the reserve parachute, (Table 15.2., TO 14D1-2-1-121), having been reviewed. The minimum training deployment altitude for all type aircraft with a drop speed of 90 KIAS or less is 1500 feet AGL. The minimum drop altitude for aircraft with a 90 to 110 KIAS is 1250 feet AGL.

2.2.3.2.2. Freefall, Square Parachute: The deployment altitude for freefall jumps is determined by the briefed pack opening altitude. The standard training pack opening altitude is 3500 feet AGL. The minimum pack-opening altitude for all training jumps is 2500 feet AGL without an automatic activation device (AAD).

2.2.3.2.3. Static Line, Square Parachute. The standard training pack opening altitude is 3000 feet AGL. The minimum opening altitude for all training jumps is 3000 feet AGL.

2.2.4. Deployment Airspeeds.

2.2.4.1. The minimum deployment airspeed for C-130 aircraft is 130 KIAS.

2.2.4.2. The minimum deployment airspeed for C-141 aircraft is 130 to 135 KIAS. To obtain this slow an operating airspeed C-141s must be able to deploy 75 percent flaps to allow a maximum aircraft paratroop airdrop weight of 204,000 pounds.

2.2.4.3. The minimum deployment airspeed for H-60 aircraft is 65 KIAS indicated and 75 KIAS maximum (optimum 70 KIAS).

2.2.4.4. The minimum deployment airspeed for H-1 aircraft is 50 KIAS indicated and 70 KIAS maximum (optimum 70 KIAS).

2.2.4.5. The minimum deployment airspeed for CH-53 Sea Stallion (USMC) aircraft is 80 KIAS and 110 KIAS maximum (optimum 90 KIAS).

WARNING: MC1-1C parachutes have a maximum deployment airspeed of 135 KIAS. MC1-1C parachutes must not be jumped from aircraft that cannot fly at or below this air speed. This air speed restriction must be emphasized to aircrews during mission planning and briefing.

2.2.4.6. Follow Mission Design Series (MDS) specific instructions for other aircraft deployment airspeeds.

2.2.5. Helicopter parachute operations on HH-60 aircraft will be conducted IAW AFI 11-2HH-60, Volume

2.2.6. Automatic Ripcord Release (ARR).

2.2.6.1. The use of the ARR will be done IAW AFI 11-410.

2.2.6.2. The minimum safe arming altitude for the ARR is 2500 feet above the MSL activation altitude. The normal arming altitude for the ARR is 3000 feet above MSL activation altitude or higher.

2.2.6.3. The ARR will be set for activation 500 feet or more below the briefed main parachute manual activation altitude. However, under no circumstances will the ARR be set to activate below 2500 feet AGL for training jumps utilizing the ARR. Therefore, the minimum safe aircraft training deployment altitude using an ARR is 5000 feet AGL, with a normal safe altitude for deployment being 5500 feet AGL or higher.

WARNING Carabiners (non-locking) and other hook type items (i.e. boots with hook grommets and not eyelet's) will not be worn on the outside of the jumpers equipment or uniform as the possibilities exist for canopy lines to be entangle within the devices preventing cut-away or causing a malfunction. Suggest stowing in fanny pack, pockets, or taping as necessary.

2.2.7. A whistle will be carried on all deployments.

2.2.8. Night Deployments .

2.2.8.1. Strict control of light signals will be maintained at all times as the unnecessary exposure of light may confuse personnel aboard the aircraft. Lights, other than those used for the target, will remain out.

2.2.8.2. In the event injury or an unusual circumstance requires the excessive use of lights, parachute operations will be suspended until a satisfactory light condition can be reestablished.

2.2.8.3. All ground personnel will be cautioned against shining lights in the direction of the descending parachutists until ground contact is made.

2.2.8.4. For night target identification, the target indicator should be readily identifiable by the jumpmaster and all parachutists.

2.2.9. Night Jumper Lighting Requirements.

2.2.9.1. SDU-5/E and MS-2000M strobe light, attached to helmet in accordance with MAJCOM guidance.

2.2.9.2. Chemlites.

2.2.9.2.1. Chemlites will be activated by each jumper on the jumpmaster's command (normally on the "Stand Up" command).

2.2.9.2.2. Front of Jumper. A minimum of one red chemlite will be attached with 80 lb. test tape or a rubber band through the eyelet to the equipment D-ring/large equipment attachment ring. Secure the bottom of the chemlite to the main lift web using a rubber band/retaining band. The chemlite can be attached to either side of the harness so as not to interfere with the jumpmaster's night vision. The minimum of one red chemlite will be moved to the waist band, next to the life preserver unit (LPU) when performing water jumps equipped for harness flotation.

2.2.9.2.3. Back of Jumper. One green chemlite will be attached to the parachute-carrying handle using 80 lb. test tape. Use enough test tape to position the chemlite centered on the protective flap for the reserve ripcord pins. Next, place a rubber band around the protective flap. Secure the chemlite in place underneath the rubber band. Back chemlight is not required for static line jumps.

WARNING: Attempt to use as little 80 lb. test tape as necessary and trim excess tail, to prevent entanglement with reserve bridle cord (in the event of reserve parachute deployment).

2.2.9.2.4. Jumper's Helmet. For night water jumps, an additional green chemlite will be placed on the helmet. One of the following methods of attachment should be utilized:

2.2.9.2.4.1. Run a six-inch piece of 80 lb. test tape through the eyelet of the chemlite. This provides two tails of around three inches that will be taped to the helmet. The chemlight should be taped to the top of the helmet with at least two pieces of duck-tape (tape, pressure sensitive, adhesive, suggested NSN source 7510-00-266-5016), securing the 80 lb. test tape to the helmet.

WARNING: Do not tape over the chemlite, it should be free to tear away at the eyelet in the advent it becomes entangled during parachute deployment sequence.

2.2.9.2.4.2. Attach one green chemiluminescent light, (three inch round, self-adhesive back, 6260-01-334-4272) chemlite to the back of the helmet.

2.2.9.2.5. Chemlite attachment to the altimeter: Tape up a short general-purpose chemlite leaving only a slit for light to escape. The slit should be approximately 1/8 inch wide and run the entire length of the chemlite. Do not tape over the hole at the end of the chemlite. Attach the taped chemlite to your altimeter using rubber bands and/or 80 lb. test tape and duck tape.

Attach the chemlite to the left side of the altimeter between the battery pack and altimeter face with the slit pointing toward the face.

2.2.9.3. Care should be taken on rotary wing aircraft to shield as much light from the cockpit as possible.

2.2.9.4. Additional chemlites for equipment.

2.2.9.4.1. Equipment attached to jumpers should also have separate chemlites for each equipment bundle.

2.2.9.4.2. Use the applicable color for the direction of flight (i.e. red for front mounted loads and green for rear mounted loads).

2.2.9.4.3. When in doubt as to direction of view, use a red chemlite in this instance.

WARNING: Chemlites will be attached in such a manner to allow breaking away from the eyelet or rubber band if entangled by the parachute deployment sequence.

CAUTION: Night lighting, strobe lights, or chemlites should not be worn during day deployments.

2.2.10. Jumpmasters should use a jumpmaster directed drop (JMDD) and/or High Altitude Release Point (HARP) calculation for High Altitude Low Opening (HALO) jumps when the winds at release point altitude are 40 knots or greater, actual or forecasted. (Not required if actual winds are verified lower at time of deployment).

2.2.11. Use of JMDD procedures are restricted to a single aircraft air dropping personnel in visual meteorological conditions (VMC).

2.2.12. Water Jumps.

2.2.12.1. To prevent excessive fluid loss, donning of equipment will be delayed as long as possible without causing a delay in deployment.

2.2.12.2. The water/temperature and the mission being performed will dictate equipment selected. The following information should be used as a guide when deploying:

2.2.12.2.1. A wet suit, dry suit, or maritime thermal protection suit. Suit should be worn on all operational missions when water/air temperatures allow, fuel spills, jellyfish, or coral reefs may be negotiated. Remember that a wet suit doesn't protect from cold air temperature or wind after leaving the water.

2.2.12.2.2. In water temperatures above 70 degree F, it is the team leader's responsibility to ensure adequate protection from physical danger.

2.2.12.2.3. In water temperatures between 60 and 70 degrees F, as a minimum, a wetsuit top will be worn.

2.2.12.2.4. In water temperatures below 60 degree F, a one quarter inch wetsuit or greater should be worn.

 NOTE: To provide the jumper better control of the parachute, non-bulky three or five finger gloves should be worn.

2.2.12.2.5. Dry suits with dry gloves are recommended in water temperatures below 40 degrees F.

NOTE: Dry suit purge valves should be replaced with swimmer valves when no subsurface follow-on operations are planned requiring removal of the parachute harness. DUI AAOPS suits are also useful if no subsurface operations are planned.

2.3. Drop Zones.

2.3.1. During training jumps, every attempt should be made to duplicate conditions encountered during operational missions.

2.3.2. Guidelines for selection and use of drop zones are established in AFI 11-410 and AFI 13-217.

2.3.3. Units will have current and approved drop zone surveys for areas utilized in sufficient quantity / location to provide jumpmasters and aircraft commanders sufficient access to selected drop zone information. Drop zone surveys may be obtained by calling DSN 576-2899 or use the HQ AMC web sight at www.safb.af.mil:81/hqamc/directorates/amcdo/dok/azar.htm.

2.4. Drop Zone (DZ) Operations.
Drop zone operations will be IAW AFI 11-410, AFI 13-217, and operations support squadron training procedures. Additional drop zone guidance is listed below:

2.4.1. During Pararescue (PJ) unilateral operations the Drop Zone Controller (DZC)/Drop Zone Safety Officer (DZSO)/malfunction officer can be one in the same. Personnel will receive training required by AFI 13-217 and AFJI 13-210 prior to conducting jump operations. During Pararescue (PJ) unilateral operations the DZC/DZSO/malfunction officer can be one in the same. Personnel will receive training required by AFI 13-217 and AFJI 13-210 prior to conducting jump operations.

2.4.2. Medical and Evacuation Requirements.

2.4.2.1. A vehicle/boat suitable for evacuating injured jumpers and a driver/boat operator will be adjacent to the drop zone during all fixed wing training jumps. Exception: When the drop zone being utilized is a suitable runway for the drop aircraft and communications will be maintained until conclusion of the jump portion.

2.4.2.2. A vehicle suitable for evacuating injured jumpers and a driver/operator will be adjacent to the drop zone for helicopter jumps if a suitable landing site is not available.

2.4.2.3. Medical equipment may be pre-positioned aboard the helicopter for helicopter deployments if there is a suitable landing site available at the DZ.

2.4.3. Water Drop Zones. The safety swimmer will be appropriately dressed and ready for immediate water entry should an emergency arise.

2.4.4. Drop Zone Communications.

2.4.4.1. The radio, set on approved squadron training frequency, will be the primary method of communication.

2.4.4.2. Air/Ground radio communication is required for all night deployments. The Pararescueman in Charge (PIC) may waive this if procedures in AFI 13-217 and pre-briefed visual DZ markings are used for drop clearance.

2.4.4.3. The term "Cleared to Drop" from the ground party indicates it is safe to jump.

2.4.4.4. The term "No Drop" will be utilized by the ground party to inform the jump aircraft of cancellation of drop clearance IAW Chapter 2, AFI 13-217. If last minute conditions preclude a safe drop and time for proper authentication is not available, the DZC will immediately, and repetitively, transmit cancellation of drop clearance, ("No Drop, No Drop, No Drop,").

2.4.4.5. Training airdrops conducted during IMC or to an unmarked DZ require the DZC to relay drop clearance, ("Cleared to Drop"), to the aircraft by radio or other pre-briefed method.

2.4.5. Alternate Communications.

2.4.5.1. In case of radio failure during day training jumps, alternate ground/water to air signals will be used. The following signals will be briefed to the crew and ground/boat party.

2.4.5.2. CLEAR TO JUMP:

2.4.5.2.1. LAND - Target displayed.

2.4.5.2.2. WATER - Target Displayed. Boat circling off wind line.

2.4.5.3. NO DROP THIS PASS:

2.4.5.3.1. LAND - Target removed and replaced by two streamers forming two parallel bars, placed perpendicular to the line of flight and/or red smoke on the DZ.

2.4.5.3.2. WATER - Boat positioned at target or stationary in water.

2.4.5.4. JUMP CANCELED:

2.4.5.4.1. LAND - Target removed.

2.4.5.4.2. WATER - Target removed.

2.4.5.5. INJURED JUMPER - One (1) MK-13 Flare or similar flare

NOTE: All activities will be directed toward immediate medical care of the injured. This may include the continued deployment of remaining personnel from fixed wing aircraft to assist in treatment or the immediate landing/hovering/low and slow deployment of remaining PJ personnel from rotary wing aircraft.

2.5. Dive Operations.

2.5.1. Wet suit requirements for diving will be IAW paragraph 2.2.12. of this instruction.

2.5.2. Repetitive dives within 12 hours are authorized, provided they fall within the no-decompression limits.

2.5.3. The buddy system is used for all water operations (i.e. minimum of two swimmers or divers per team in the water).

2.5.4. Refer to IAW AFI 11-403 and AFI 11-202V3, Chapter 9 for restrictions to flying after diving.

2.5.5. Altitude dives will not be accomplished above 10,000 feet MSL.

2.6. Team Leader Requirements

2.6.1. It is essential every mission requiring pararescuemen have a designated and qualified Team Leader assigned to evaluate the situation on scene. In order to prosecute a Combat Search and Rescue mission, there must be a pararescue team leader or combat rescue officer on the aircraft.

2.6.2. Team Leaders are broken into the following categories

    2.6.2.1. Rotary Wing – 5 level minimum

    2.6.2.2. Fixed Wing – 7 level mimimum

    2.6.2.3. Special Mission – 7 level minimum

2.6.3. Qualification and upgrade will be in accordance with the Career Field Education and Training Plan

Chapter 3

AIRMANSHIP

3.1. General. Pararescuemen (PJs) may function as mission crewmembers on rescue tasked aircraft. Mission crewmembers are those personnel who enable the aircraft to accomplish the mission. In this role, PJs are an integral part of the rescue crew, and require knowledge of aircrew procedures and aircraft systems. This means they must be able to communicate effectively with the aircrew, integrate team tactics with aircrew tactics, and coordinate deployment/employment. Airmanship is a critical skill PJs bring to the fight and proficiency must be maintained.

3.2. Responsibilities . General responsibilities of a qualified PJ functioning as a mission crewmember are outlined in Figure 3.1.:

Figure 3.1. Mission Crewmember Responsibilities.

Flight Rules
Briefings
Alert Procedures
Individual Equipment
Alert Equipment
Aircraft Configuration
Emergency procedures
      Equipment
Flight duties
    Crew Coordination
        Inter-phone Terminology
        Situational Awareness
    Flight Following
    Scanning
    Parachuting/Jumpmastering
    Aircraft systems
        Radios
        Hoist
        Weapons
        Oxygen
        Flare/Chaff Dispensers
Objective Area

            Employment

            Survivor authentication

            Surface employment

            Survivor evacuation

Egress

            Provide in-flight emergency medical care

            Enroute medical updates/requirements

Post Flight

            Survivor Hand-off/Patient Transfer

            De-briefings

Re-generation

3.3. Crew Coordination/ Duties.

3.3.1. Crew coordination is essential to all flying. PJs must know what their aircraft responsibilities areand how they relate to the rest of the crew. They must also have an awareness of other crewmembers' functions and duties, to increase their own situational awareness (SA).

3.3.2. Interphone.

3.3.2.1. Unnecessary inter-phone conversation must be kept to a minimum. When speaking, talk in shortbursts and half sentences. This allows breaks in which other radios may be heard, or necessary interruptions can be added.

3.3.2.2. All inputs should be accurate, concise; and terminology must be standard.

3.3.2.3. Interphone discussions are prioritized by "Aviate (fly the plane), Navigate (in the right direction),and then Communicate (talking to other airplanes, agencies, etc.)". This implies, for example, it is "OK" to interrupt a pilot talking about navigation waypoints (Navigate) to say "Stop left" (Aviate).

3.4. Enroute Operations.
Immediately after aircraft launch and during the ingress/egress of the objective area (OA), PJs follow route progress of the aircraft on designated, sanitized maps or other electronic/ manual flight following aids, and confirm waypoint passage as applicable. They scan the sky and surface for the presence of air-to-air and ground-to-air threats. Suspected threats are called out to the aircrew. Preparations for aircraft evasive actions commence immediately upon sighting a suspected threat. PJs continue to visually monitor the location and actions of the suspected threat until a no-threat condition is determined. A confirmed threat is reacted to IAW Rules of Engagement (ROE) for the OA and Mission Design Series (MDS) aircraft tactical doctrine.

3.5. Objective Area (OA) Threat Assessment and Control.
The function of assessing the OA threat situation is based primarily on the ability to recognize the threat. A second factor is based largely on ability to quickly associate the type of threat with its correct characteristics and capabilities. From these two factors, a determination can be made regarding the safety or danger to the rescue aircraft and aircrew.

3.5.1. OA Threat Control. OA threat control is the responsibility of all personnel involved in the CombatSearch and Rescue (CSAR). It is a function of location, recognition, communication and action or reaction. There are several methods for assisting with or effecting typical OA threat control measures.

3.5.2. Specific guidance can be found in AFTTP 3-1, (Specific volume for MDS).

3.6. Disabling of Aircraft Systems and Destruction of Classified.

3.6.1. In the event an aircraft has crashed and must be abandoned, all crewmembers must be able toquickly locate and zeroize all electronic radio and navigational encryption equipment. Refer to the MDS-1 series Technical Order (T.O.) for specific instructions.

3.6.2. Crewmembers must be capable of disabling aircraft weapons systems. This may be done by thermate grenades, taking the crash axe to critical soft parts, or disassembling the weapons and scattering/destroying/burying the parts, i.e. firing pins, safety sectors, etc.

3.6.3. Classified materials must be destroyed or retrieved. To effectively accomplish this, all classified material carried on the aircraft must be identified and the exact location known to the entire crew. Identify a crewmember prior to flight, for destruction of classified, or to remind the crew, to retrieve/destroy all the classified, if needed.

Chapter 4

STATIC LINE PARACHUTE OPERATIONS

4.1. Purpose. This chapter outlines technical and procedural information on the use of static line parachutes and jump-related equipment. It includes the operation of the A/P 28S-17/18, MC1-1B, and MC1-1C parachute assembly, parachuting operations, emergency procedures, and description/rigging of specialized equipment

4.2. General.

4.2.1. PJs utilize static line parachuting techniques (day or night) when the threat scenario and/or weatherdictate low altitude airborne insertion, when deploying as part of a joint airborne assault force, and during both land and open sea search, rescue, and recovery missions, PJ teams may be inserted over-the-horizon at sea with an amphibious Combat Rubber Raider Craft, Rigged Alternate Method Zodiac (RAMZ) in support of the Space Shuttle program, kayak, hard hull boat, swimmer/scuba equipment, or on land with all terrain vehicles or other special vehicles to enhance operations. PJ teams are authorized and are required by this instruction to be proficient in the use of Jump Master Directed Drop (JMDD) procedures.

4.2.2. A PJ must be a highly qualified precision parachutist, capable of performing parachute deployments into any type of terrain, into open seas, and during the hours of daylight or darkness. To qualify in these tasks he must be capable of performing the following duties directly associated with precision parachuting:

4.2.2.1. Deployments to restricted or unsurveyed DZs. NOTE: PJs required to deploy to unsurveyed DZsneed advanced parachute skills.

4.2.2.2. Water deployments with and without scuba/RAMZ.

4.2.2.3. Deployments into trees.

4.2.2.4. Deployments onto rough terrain.

4.2.3. DZ Wind Determination. During training deployments the DZC may have a windsock, streamertied to a pole, smoke (not red), or some other device to help indicate ground wind direction to the jumpers. If authorized block letters are used (A, C, J, R, or S), coordinated with the jumpmaster, navigator, and aircraft commander to ensure they are aligned into the wind and not to the DZ axis or aircraft line of flight. All parachutist should make the effort to learn the wind direction while under canopy without the use of drop zone wind direction aids. Parachutist can determine ground winds by:

4.2.3.1. Looking for movement of trees and vegetation on the ground.

4.2.3.2. Watching for noticeable drift of the canopy while toggles up.

4.2.3.3. Looking for smoke or blowing dust or sand.

4.2.3.4. Watching other parachutist landing.

4.2.3.5. Flying an "S" pattern and watching for the difference in drift.

4.3. Parachute Manipulation Using Modified Canopy. To successfully maneuver the parachute to thetarget, a parachutist may have to hold into the wind, run with the wind, and crab to the right or left while holding or running.

4.3.1. Maneuvering Upwind (holding). Hold into the wind line if you are on the wind line and you will overshoot or go past the target. This will decrease your movement across the ground (counteracting the wind drift) without affecting your rate of descent.

4.3.2. Maneuvering Downwind (Running). Run with the wind if you are on the wind line and you will undershoot or fall short of the target. This will increase your movement across the ground giving you the maximum forward speed possible. If the running maneuver is made slightly off the wind line, the final turn into the wind will place the jumper back on the wind line for correct target approach.

4.3.3. Maneuvering While Holding or Running (Crabbing). If your position is to either side of the windline, you will have to perform a quartering or crabbing maneuver. This maneuver will allow you to run toward the target and move towards the wind line or hold into the wind moving towards the target and wind line at the same time.

4.4. Maneuvering to the Target.

4.4.1. Each parachutist must determine the wind line, his distance and direction off the wind line from hisrelease point, his drift rate, and his descent rate.

4.4.2. Wind Line. The wind line is an imaginary line of wind direction passing directly over the intendedtarget. With a variable wind, the average wind direction would be the wind line. The parachutist should attempt to place himself on the wind line with a proper closure rate toward the target.

4.4.3. Release Point. If the parachutist deployed on the correct line-up, he should be on the wind line andat the correct distance from the target. However, the parachutist may have to correct errors in aircraft alignment or for wind shifts in velocity or direction. The normal minimum deployment airspeeds for all types of C-130s are 130 KIAS. The HC-130 aircraft travels 210 feet per second and a delay in exit of one second will cause the PJ to be 210 feet off the exit release point. This distance will be less during helicopter deployments due to the slower drop airspeed (50 to 110 KIAS). Errors to the side or off the wind line caused by wind shifts, exiting the aircraft too soon or too late, or inaccurate alignment of the aircraft, will usually be within the distance a parachutist can make up by maneuvering his canopy. If both the count and the lineup are off, it will be difficult for the parachutist to maneuver to the target.

4.4.4. Drift Rate. Drift rate is the direction and rate of travel (target closure speed),

4.4.5. Direction and Rate of Travel. To determine direction/rate of travel and wind line, attempt to determine movement in relation to the target location. Various methods can be used.

4.4.5.1. Look at the target or some fixed object on the ground and attempt to determine the direction andrate of movement.

4.4.5.2. Sight over your feet at the ground and attempt to determine the direction and rate of movement.

4.4.5.3. Look for the canopies shadow on the ground and observe the shadow's direction and rate of movement.

4.4.5.4. Listen to the noise created by the wind through the suspension lines. High winds can cause the linesto whistle (22 knots).

4.4.6. After parachute opening, the parachutist is normally facing the aircraft flight path. Before initiatinga maneuver, (except to avoid a collision/entanglement with another parachutist), determine the location of the target and make the initial turn towards the target in the direction of the wind line. Determine direction and rate of movement across the ground and maneuver combining, thrust of the canopy, wind velocity, and rate of descent to arrive at the landing site. In effect, a parachutist maneuvers towards a target within an approach cone that is wider at the exit point and progressively narrows as he approaches the target. If the parachutist remains within the approach cone, he should land at the target area. If he allows himself to turn or drift outside the cone (vertically or horizontally), he may not be able to reach the target. The approach cone will vary with wind velocity/direction and the parachutists rate of descent. Approach the target area using a combination of holding, running, or crabbing. A series of left and right running turns allows the jumper to remain in the approach cone varying his movement across the ground reaching the selected target.

4.5. Team Parachuting. Team parachuting ensures all parachutist approach small or restricted targetareas in a controlled manner. Critical to the success of a team deployment is an experienced parachutist leading the team to the intended target area. When making a team deployment, the higher parachutist should follow the lower parachutist mimicking the lower parachutist parachute manipulation, without interfering with the lower parachutist approach to the target area. The parachutist should stagger their approach on the wind line to either side remaining clear of each other during landing.

4.6. Land Parachute Deployment Procedures.

4.6.1. Prepare to Land. Approximately 100 feet above the ground/trees assume a landing attitude. Duringnight deployments , prepare to land at approximately 150 feet above the ground. During night water deployments, prepare to land at approximately 200 feet above the water.

4.6.2. Landing. Most injuries in parachuting result from incorrect landings. The parachute landing fall(PLF) is a precise method of landing which enables the parachutist to distribute the landing shock over his entire body and reduce the possibility of injury. Always be prepared to perform a PLF.

4.6.3. Tree Parachute Deployment Procedures.

4.6.3.1. PJ Tree Suit. The tree suit is designed to minimize possible injury to PJs. Adjustable pads are placedin positions, protecting bony prominences. The jacket is equipped with a high collar to protect the neck and face. The trousers have an adjustable strap running up and down the inside of each leg which is sewn into the trousers to make an inverted "U" at approximately four inches below the crotch to protect the groin area. When deploying in cold climate areas, winter clothing may be worn under the tree suit. Tree suit pads may be removed to accommodate the added bulk of winter clothing. An additional option is to wear only the trousers, with pads removed, to afford the availability of the tape rings and the pockets.

4.6.3.2. Complete PJ tree suit, heavy leather gloves, and appropriate helmet with visor will be worn on allintentional tree parachute deployments . Due to discomfort and body fluid loss incurred when wearing the tree suit for long periods, equipment should not be donned until nearing the deployment area. The tree suit will be donned jacket first with the trousers brought up over the jacket. This will prevent branches from going under the jacket during a descent through the trees. After donning the parachute, the letdown webbing will be threaded IAW Attachment 2 (Figure A2.1.). Secure the end by snapping the snap fastener on the end of the letdown webbing into the right reserve "D" ring. The remainder of the letdown webbing will be coiled into a loose bird's nest and carried in the tree suit pocket. The portion of webbing between the tree suit "D" ring and the suit leg pocket will be secured by the snap cover flap of the knife pocket located on the right leg of the trousers.

4.6.4. Tree Entry Procedures.

4.6.4.1. Pick a tree or close group of trees to land in.

4.6.4.2. Plan the final approach to tree entry so the body enters the tree(s) one-quarter of the way down fromthe top.

4.6.4.3. Before tree contact, place the elbows on top of the reserve parachute and forearms in front of thefaceplate.

4.6.4.4. After tree entry, maintain the tight body position until the parachute is caught in the tree(s) and descent is stopped.

WARNING: The parachute may not catch in the tree, be prepared to perform a PLF.

4.6.4.5. Once descent is stopped, do not bounce in the harness to check the security of the canopy hang-up.

4.6.4.6. Perform the tree letdown procedure immediately.

4.6.5. Letdown Procedures, Using the Letdown Tape Stowed in the Tree Suit Pocket. After hang-up, letdown must be accomplished as expeditiously as possible to reduce the possibility of tearing free and falling. The following procedures will be utilized:

4.6.5.1. Release right side of reserve parachute.

4.6.5.2. Release right side of medical kit or other equipment attached to the reserve "D" ring. If necessary,lower the kit or equipment only if it will make contact with the ground. Caution must be used when lowering to preclude the kit or equipment from tangling.

4.6.5.3. Pull approximately four feet of webbing through letdown "D" ring.

4.6.5.4. Unsnap the end of the letdown webbing, pass through right and left risers twice, and snap onto itself(see Attachment 3, Figure A3.1.). If a secure tree anchor point is readily available, use it instead of the risers.

4.6.5.5. Remove slack from letdown webbing.

4.6.5.6. While holding tension on the letdown webbing with the right hand, apply a brake to the right hiparea and release the safety covers on both releases.

4.6.5.7. Hold head back, face to the opposite side to be released, and actuate the canopy release on the slackside of the risers.

4.6.5.8. While holding head back, face to the opposite side to be released, reach around the letdown tape,release the other side, and descend.

4.6.6. Tree Letdown Tape Manufacture. Letdown tape will be manufactured using 1 inch by 200 feet tubular nylon tape. A static line snap fastener will be sewn to one end IAW T.O. 14D1-2-396, Figure 5-13B titled, "Rework of 23 foot static line".

4.6.7. Equipment will not be released on the lowering line during parachute descent.

4.7. Water Parachute Deployment Procedures. To prevent excessive body fluid loss, donning of equipment will be delayed as long as possible without delaying the deployment.

4.7.1. Minimum equipment worn on water deployments in addition to the parachute assembly (harness,main and reserve):

4.7.1.1. Wet suit/dry suit/uniform as dictated by the water/air temperature.

4.7.1.2. Single Para Scuba Deployment System (SPUDS) with regulator (as required

4.7.1.3. Face mask.

4.7.1.4. Parachutist Flotation Device. Any approved Life Preserver Unit (LPU) system with automatic inflation system, underwater dive team (UDT) vest, or scuba buoyancy compensator may be used in lieu of the B-7 life preserver. Any flotation device placed between harnesses and parachutist must have a safety valve or rigged so as not to injure the parachutist should an inadvertent inflation occur. Standardized wear and procedures will be identified in unit SOPs.

4.7.1.5. Swim fins (on feet using tape or fix-e-palms).

4.7.1.6. Knife or Hook Knife.

4.7.1.7. MK-13/124 flare.

4.7.1.8. Whistle.

4.7.1.9. ML-4 kit (as required).

4.7.1.10. Protective head gear (as required).

4.7.1.11. Gloves (as required).

4.7.1.12. Wrist compass (as required).

4.7.1.13. Carabiner (as required).

4.7.1.14. Snorkel (as required)

4.7.1.15. Fanny Pack (as required).

NOTE: For operational water deployments a full wet suit or dry suit will be worn when water/air temperatures allow, or when fuel spills, jelly fish, or coral reefs must be negotiated.

4.7.2. Water Airborne Descent Procedures.

4.7.2.1. Check canopy.

4.7.2.2. Check other jumpers.

4.7.2.3. Activate Strobe light (as required).

4.7.2.4. Locate target

4.7.3. Pre-water Entry Procedures: Do not start these procedures until the target is in sight and all postopening procedures are accomplished.

4.7.3.1. Release waistband quick-release.

4.7.3.2. Release left side of reserve.

4.7.3.3. Sit well back in harness.

4.7.3.4. Release chest strap.

4.7.3.5. Maneuver to land down drift/wind of the target. NOTE: In high wind conditions, 15 knot or greater,it is recommended to land while crabbing left or right into the wind.

4.7.3.6. Use regulator if SPUDS equipped.

4.7.3.7. Place either hand over the mouthpiece if SPUDS equipped and place other hand over the safetyguard of the riser release.

4.7.3.8. Upon contact with the water, open capewell cover and actuate the canopy release. Actuate the othercanopy release as soon as possible after entrance into the water. (Release only one riser during training operations to prevent loss of the canopy if the recovery boat is nearby).

4.7.4. Emergencies During Descent. In case of an emergency during descent, inflate the LPUs (if worn).This will signal an emergency to the delivery aircraft/recovery boat.

4.7.5. Post Water Entry Procedures.

4.7.5.1. Signal "All OK" (extend arm overhead in the "all OK" signal) or shout "Help", give three blasts onwhistle, deploy MK-13/124 flare, or activate SDU-5/E or MS-2000M strobe light (remains on).

WARNING: Immediately inflate personnel floatation equipment if entangled in the canopy or suspension lines. Some combinations of equipment (i.e. heavy equipment, weapons, ammunition, fatigues versus wet suit) and water conditions (i.e. fresh water provides less buoyancy) will decrease buoyancy.

 NOTE: Immediately after landing, slow down. Do not rush into these steps until breathing has reached a normal rate.

4.7.5.2. Release leg straps.

4.7.5.3. Inflate LPU on parachute waist strap.

4.7.5.4. Swim clear of the canopy.

4.7.5.5. Use facemask (as required).

4.7.5.6. Close canopy releases.

4.7.5.7. Inflate one man raft (as required).

4.7.5.8. Release medical kit or equipment (as required).

4.7.5.9. Swim to objective, recovery boat, or wait for recovery of individual parachute as briefed.

4.8. Water Parachute Deployment Configuration.

4.8.1. Parachute and Equipment Rigging.

4.8.1.1. Ensure parachute harness has an LPU/3P or single bladder of a modified LPU/10P attached to theharness waist strap. Inflate the LPU prior to ditching equipment.

4.8.1.2. A front-mounted fanny pack may be used to store knife, scissors, carabiners, flares, etc.

4.8.1.3. The waist strap is not routed through the reserve and is underneath the D-rings.

4.8.1.4. Route the waist strap under the life preservers and secure with a two to three finger wide quick release.

4.8.1.5. The static line reserve parachute is secured with one safety pin on the right side. The pin should notbe excessively bent to allow easy removal with wet suit gloves on.

4.8.2. SPUDS.

4.8.2.1. Place the scuba cylinder in the MT-1X scuba bottle pocket.

4.8.2.2. Attach the breathing regulator to the scuba cylinder. A regulator with a 34-inch hose will be usedwith the SPUDS system.

4.8.2.3. Stow the excess regulator hose in the scuba bottle pocket.

4.8.2.4. Place the breathing regulator in the regulator pouch with the mouthpiece facing the scuba cylinder.If the regulator is placed in the regulator pouch with the purge valve facing the scuba cylinder, the regulator tends to be difficult to remove from the pouch. Secure the Velcro on the regulator pouch so the regulator hose is against the main pouch.

4.8.2.5. Attach the adjustable belt to the scuba bottle pocket.

4.8.2.6. Don the SPUDS with the belt worn low on the side the scuba cylinder is on, to allow the parachuteleg straps to be fitted properly. When attaching the adjustable belt, route the belt over the friction bar and use only the Velcro to secure the belt.

4.8.2.7. Secure the SPUDS leg strap.

4.8.2.8. Don the remaining parachute equipment using standard donning procedures.

4.9. Night Parachute Deployment Procedures. Night operations present increased hazards over thoseencountered during daylight operations. A closely supervised training program can minimize hazards during night deployments. Terrain, weather, equipment, experience of personnel involved and problems associated with night parachuting are factors requiring consideration.

4.9.1. Dark Adaptation. The eyes require about 30 minutes of dark adaptation before becoming efficientat low levels of illumination. Wearing red lens goggles for 30 minutes is satisfactory. The interior of the aircraft should remain darkened or illuminated with low intensity red light. In spite of dark adaptation, judging the distance to the ground at night is difficult and often misleading.

4.9.2. Night deployment lighting requirements. See Chapter 2, Training Restrictions, paragraph 2.2.9.

4.10. Equipment /Packs/Snowshoe/Ski / Weapon Rigging. The procedures for rigging of equipment forparachute deployments such as packs, snowshoes, skis, and weapons can be found in T.O. 14D1-2-1-121 (Army FM 57-220).

4.11. Equipment Release Procedures.

4.11.1. Release of equipment on a lowering line is optional if it weights 35 pounds or less. Release is recommended if equipment weight is over 35 pounds or a high altitude DZ is used. It is not recommended that equipment be released on land deployments if terrain is rough. When the deployment situation dictates, release of the equipment on the lowering line will be accomplished at approximately 200 feet above the surface.

4.11.2. Use MAJCOM approved procedures for the rigging of all delivery containers with integrated parachute harnesses.

Chapter 5

MILITARY FREEFALL PARACHUT OPERATIONS

5.1. Purpose. This chapter provides specific operating procedures for Pararescue (PJ) military free-fall(MFF) operations. This chapter should be used in conjunction with AFI 11-410, Personnel Parachute Operations, AFI 13-217, Assault Zone Procedures, and Army FM 31-19, Military Freefall Parachuting Tactics, Techniques, and Procedures.

5.2. DZ Wind Determination. During training deployments the DZC may have a windsock, streamer-tied to a pole, smoke (not red), or some other device to help indicate ground wind direction to the parachutists. If authorized block letters are used (A, C, J, R, or S), coordinated with the jumpmaster, navigator, and aircraft commander to ensure they are aligned into the wind and not to the DZ axis or aircraft line of flight. All parachutists should make the effort to learn the wind direction while under canopy without the use of DZ wind direction aids. Parachutists can determine ground winds by:

5.2.1. Looking for movement of trees and vegetation on the ground.

5.2.2. Watching for noticeable drift of the canopy while in deep brakes (not a stall).

5.2.3. Looking for smoke or blowing dust and sand.

5.2.4. Watching other parachutists landing.

5.2.5. Flying a box pattern at 50 percent brakes and watching for the difference in drift.

5.3. Night Deployments.

5.3.1. Aircraft Lighting. Generally, the same procedures utilized in static line parachuting at night applyto night freefall deployments. Any deviations to these procedures that are IAW AFI 11-410 or FM 31-19 may be utilized.

5.3.2. Night Deployment Lighting Requirements. See Chapter 2, Operational/Training Restrictions.

5.3.3. Electro-Luminescent (EL) Lighting. Although part of the canopy purchase, the EL lighting systemis rarely used and may have been removed. Refer to manufactures instructions for proper installation and use.

5.3.4. Night Landings. Even on the darkest nights, parachutist will have an idea when they are descendingclose to the ground. There is normally enough illumination to perform a flared landing except on nights void of moonlight. Landing at night requires more skill than a day landing due to the decrease in depth perception at night.

5.3.4.1. The most desired landing point is just short of the target. It is better to undershoot than to overshootthe lights then land without references.

5.3.4.2. Perform a 50-75 percent braked landing and parachute landing fall (PLF) if any doubt exists as tothe flare point.

5.3.4.3. Notify the DZ controller as soon as possible after landing by shouting "All OK" (extend arm overhead in the "all OK" signal) or shout "Help", give three blasts on whistle, deploy MK-13 flare, or activate SDU-5/E or MS-2000M strobe light (remains on).

5.4. Water Deployment Procedures. Freefall parachuting into the water is different from the standard-freefall to land. The biggest difference, and most important one, is the low altitude with no altimeter or ARR. A good stable exit is essential for three reasons: (1) parachutists must maintain eye contact on the parachutist in front of them, (2) pull ripcord on assigned altitude or delay, and (3) stack their approach to the target to offset target fixation.

5.4.1. Equipment required in addition to the High Glide Ratio Parachute (HGRP) parachute:

5.4.1.1. Wet suit/dry suit/uniform as dictated by the water/air temperature.

5.4.1.2. Scuba mask/goggles.

5.4.1.3. Fins.

5.4.1.4. Knife. (A hook knife can be substituted for the divers knife).

5.4.1.5. Snorkel.

5.4.1.6. Single bladder LPU secured to waist strap on parachute (training use only).

5.4.1.7. Parachutist Flotation device.

WARNING: Any flotation device placed between harness and parachutist must have a safety valve or be rigged in such a manner as to not injure the parachutist should inflation occur.

5.4.1.8. Whistle.

5.4.1.9. Protective headgear (as required).

5.4.1.10. MK-13/124 flare.

5.4.1.11. Gloves (as required).

5.4.1.12. Wrist compass (as required).

5.4.1.13. Carabiner(s) (as required).

5.4.1.14. Fanny pack for additional gear (as required).

5.4.1.15. Alternate loading belt (as required).

5.4.1.16. Survival equipment i.e. ML-4 kit, water, pyro, radio (as required).

5.4.1.17. Equipment lanyard/sling (as required).

5.4.1.18. SPUDS system (as required).

5.4.1.19. Diving regulator (as required).

5.4.1.20. Night lighting (night or as required).

5.4.1.21. Mission Equipment (as required).

NOTE: For operational water deployments a full wet suit or dry suit will be worn when water/air temperatures allow or fuel spills, jelly fish, coral reefs must be negotiated.

5.4.2. Equipment Preparation.

5.4.2.1. Freefall Preparation.

5.4.2.1.1. Place the LPU bladder on the waist strap and secure with 550 cord or route LPU cords/bandsthrough waist strap.

5.4.2.1.2. For night lighting configuration see Chapter 2, Operational/Training Restrictions.

5.4.2.2. Parachutist Equipment Preparation.

5.4.2.2.1. Fins will be on feet and secured with tape or fix-e-palms.

5.4.2.2.2. Parachutist flotation vests will not interfere with activation of any handles.

5.4.3. Pre-water Entry Procedures. Do not start these procedures until the target is in sight and all postopening procedures are accomplished.

5.4.3.1. Release reserve static line system.

5.4.3.2. Sit well back in the harness.

5.4.3.3. Release chest strap and waist strap.

5.4.3.4. Maneuver to land slightly down wind/drift of the target.

5.4.3.5. Fly a normal approach to a flared landing (visibility permitting). If unsure during final approachdue to lack of visual cues, fly final approach into the wind using 50 percent brakes. Hold until water entry.

5.4.3.6. Use regulator (if equipped).

5.4.4. Post Water Entry Procedures.

5.4.4.1. Release the right toggle so the right hand is free to cutaway the main parachute, if being dragged.

5.4.4.2. Signal "All OK" (extend arm overhead in the "all OK" signal) or shout "Help", give three blasts onwhistle, deploy MK-13 flare, or activate SDU-5/E or MS-2000M strobe light (remains on).

WARNING: Immediately inflate personnel floatation equipment if entangled with canopy or suspension lines. Some combinations of equipment (i.e. heavy equipment, weapons, ammunition, fatigues versus wet suit) and water conditions (i.e. fresh water provides less buoyancy) will decrease buoyancy.

 NOTE: Immediately after landing, slow down. Do not rush into these steps until breathing has reached a normal rate.

5.4.4.3. Release leg straps and swim free of harness/chute.

5.4.4.4. Inflate LPU on parachute waist strap.

5.4.4.5. Use face mask/goggles (as required).

5.4.4.6. Inflate one man raft (as required).

5.4.4.7. Release medical kit or equipment (as required).

5.4.4.8. Swim to objective, recovery boat, or wait for recovery of individual parachute as briefed.

5.5. Tree Parachute Deployment Procedures.

5.5.1. PJ tree suit, gloves, and appropriate helmet with visor will be worn on all intentional tree deployments .

5.5.2. PJ Tree Suit.

5.5.2.1. Donning and utilization of the PJ tree suit and let down webbing are identical to those identified inChapter 4 with the following exceptions:

5.5.2.2. The letdown webbing will be coiled into a loose bird's nest and completely stowed in the tree suitpocket. The letdown webbing will not be uncoiled or snapped to the equipment D-rings until after tree let-down is required.

5.5.2.3. Ensure the tree suit pocket zipper is firmly closed to prevent opening in freefall.

5.5.2.4. Remove the shoulder pads (for mobility) and tuck the collar inside the suit and expose the collar onceunder canopy.

5.5.3. Tree Entry Procedures.

5.5.3.1. Pick a tree or close group of trees to land in.

5.5.3.2. Make a steep approach, attempting to put the canopy in the top of the tree(s). The deep brake steepapproach will give you a constant high angle descent into the tree(s).

5.5.3.3. Winds/turbulence may require a moderate brake shallow approach to avoid gust induced stalls. Still, attempt to put the canopy in the top of the tree(s).

WARNING: Do not release equipment on the lowering line during parachute descent.

5.5.3.4. After tree entry, maintain a tight body position until the parachute is caught in the tree(s) and descent is stopped.

WARNING: The parachute may not be solidly entangled in the tree, be prepared to perform a PLF.

5.5.3.5. Once descent is stopped, do not bounce in the harness to check the security of the canopy hang up.

5.5.3.6. Perform the tree letdown immediately.

5.5.3.6.1. Release right side of medical kit or other equipment and if necessary, lower the kit or equipmentonly if it will make contact with the ground. Caution must be used when lowering to preclude the kit or equipment from tangling.

5.5.3.6.2. Route the tree letdown through the "D" rings on the trousers IAW Figure A2.1.

5.5.3.6.3. Pull approximately four feet of webbing through letdown "D" ring.

5.5.3.6.4. Unsnap the end of the letdown webbing, pass through right and left risers twice, and snap onto itselfsee Attachment 3, Figure A3.1.). If a secure tree anchor point is readily available, use it instead of the risers.

5.5.3.6.5. Remove slack from letdown webbing.

5.5.3.6.6. Ensure reserve static line is disconnected.

5.5.3.6.7. While holding tension on the letdown webbing with the right hand, apply a brake to the right hiparea and grasp cut away handle with the left hand.

5.5.3.6.8. Pull cutaway handle.

5.6. Equipment Procedures. The load carried should be as light as possible and consist of only the essential equipment needed until re-supplied. All items of individual combat equipment are normally carried in the rucksack during the deployment. Individual load bearing equipment (LBE) or survival vests may be worn underneath the tree suit or carried in the rucksack or in a small equipment bag separate from the main equipment load. Consider covering Alice packs or similar containers. Rigging for combat pack and equipment containers is explained in Army FM 31-19.

5.7. MFF Grouping and Assembly. A primary consideration of the MFF parachuting insertion technique is to be able to expeditiously assemble once on the ground, either by grouping in the air and landing as a team, or to rendezvous at a predetermined geographic location, organized and ready to accomplish a specific mission.

5.7.1. Team members will exit the aircraft as rapidly as possible at the exit point and maintain heading onan assigned track.

5.7.2. All parachutists will activate their main parachute at a specified altitude.

5.7.3. Parachutists will group in the air, guiding on the team leader, low man, or as briefed. Team integrityis paramount.

5.7.4. Parachutists will attempt to land as close together as possible without interferring with each otherslanding pattern and proceed to a preselected geographical point for rendezvous. Electronic/lighting equipment may be used to facilitate assembly of personnel.

5.8. High Altitude/Oxygen Procedures. (AFI 11-409, High Altitude Airdrop Mission Support Program is the governing AFI for parachuting oxygen requirements)

5.8.1. Airdrops conducted above 3,000 feet AGL are considered high-altitude drops.

5.8.2. Parachutist may operate without supplemental oxygen during un-pressurized flights up to 13,000 feet MSL provided the time above 10,000 feet MSL does not exceed 30 minutes for each sortie. Jumpmasters may operate without supplemental oxygen for an additional 60 minutes within the 10,000-13,000 foot MSL envelope provided their duties do not include parachuting.

5.8.3. Flights above 13,000 feet MSL require supplemental oxygen.

5.8.4. Flights above 18,000 feet MSL will use pre-breathing procedures.

5.8.5. Airdrops above 25,000 feet MSL require a waiver to AFI 11-202, Volume 3 for un-pressurized flight, from HQ AFFSA/XO through the MAJCOM.

5.8.6. Physiological Technician (PT):

5.8.6.1. A minimum of two PTs will be on MFF parachute deployments conducted at 18,000 feet MSL or higher.

5.8.6.2. One PT is required per 16 parachutist, up to a maximum of three PTs.

5.8.7. If a physiological incident occurs:

5.8.7.1. Abort the mission and ensure parachutist/crew member is secured during ramp/door deployments.

5.8.7.2. Begin descent (de-arm ARRs prior to descent).

5.8.7.3. Proceed to nearest base with qualified medical assistance available.

5.8.7.4. Advise the control tower of the emergency and request an ambulance meet the aircraft.

5.8.7.5. Advise attending physician to call Brooks AFB Hyperbaric Medicine (DSN 240-3281/ 3278, commercial (512) 536-3281/3278).

Chapter 6

RAMZ PROCEDURES

6.1. Purpose. The Rigging Alternate Method-Zodiac (RAMZ) is a Pararescue employment system developed for peacetime, military operations other than war, or combat missions to be utilized in any water environment. It can be deployed from rotary or fixed wing aircraft. Parachutists can deploy either static line or freefall configured. The optimal PJ compliment on a RAMZ deployment is three: a team leader and two team members. Any one of the three can serve as the jumpmaster. The minimum personnel requirement for RAMZ deployment is two PJs. Prior to RAMZ deployment training, individuals in RAMZ qualification training will be familiar with the care and procedures of Zodiac watercraft.

6.2. Fuel.

6.2.1. Use any approved fuel container.

6.2.2. Flexible fuel bladders. When using flexible bladders, do not fill over half full. This will allow for expansion of the bladder due to fumes caused by changing temperature and pressures. Purge all trapped air out of fuel bladders.

6.2.3. Rigid Fuel containers. When using rigid fuel containers they must be full; no air can be left in the container.

6.2.4. Mix fuel IAW manufacturers directions. Suggest using high-octane fuel, 91 or greater, or an octane booster. The use of TCW-3 2-stroke oil is recommended. If fuel will be sitting for any length of time, an additive fuel conditioner is also recommended.

6.2.5. Refer to applicable guidance for airlift requirements for shipping fuel.

6.3. Rigging Procedures. Rigging procedures for the RAMZ are contained in T.O. 13C7-51-21, *Airdrop of Supplies and Equipment*. In addition to the rigging procedures, the following equipment should be included in the standard configuration.

6.3.1. Boat Configuration.

6.3.1.1. Fuel Bladders (operational 250 nm)

6.3.1.2. Bow Line (1)

6.3.1.3. Tether/Righting Line attached to the right side main pontoons. (2)

6.3.1.4. Container with contents listed below should be carried on all RAMZ missions. Attachment and location will be IAW unit Standard Operating Procedures (SOPs):

6.3.1.4.1. Carabiner (1)*

6.3.1.4.2. Spark Plugs (2)

6.3.1.4.3. Tool Kit, engine (1)

6.3.1.4.4. Foot Pump W/Hose (1)

6.3.1.4.5. Water Container *

6.3.1.4.6. Cord, 550 pound, 50 feet (1)*

6.3.1.4.7. Tape, OD green, Roll (1)**

6.3.1.4.8. Grease board with pencil (1)*

6.3.1.4.9. Compass (1)**

6.3.1.4.10. Spare Radio/Battery, waterproofed (1)**

6.3.1.4.11. Communications head-set(1)*

6.3.1.4.12. Food*

6.3.1.4.13. Red chemlites, box (1)**

6.3.1.4.14. Green chemlites, box (1)**

6.3.1.4.15. Strobe light with battery (1)**

6.3.1.4.16. Boat repair kit (1)

6.3.1.4.17. Medical Equipment**

6.3.1.4.18. Special Mission Equipment*

*Denotes optional items.

**Denotes items required for operational use.

NOTE: Only 15-foot static lines will be used on the RAMZ cargo parachutes. A 12-foot static line extended to 15-feet will not be used. If personnel deploying by static line are to follow immediately after the RAMZ, their static lines must be 15 feet.

NOTE: Use chemlites on all actuation/release handles during day/night operations.

6.4. Inspection.

6.4.1. IAW AFJI 13-210. 6.4.2. RAMZ Inspection Checklist. Each unit should develop a local inspection checklist. This checklist will be included in the unit SOP.

6.5. RAMZ Static Line Procedures.

6.5.1. Parachutist preparation for static line RAMZ deployments is the same as other static line parachute water deployments.

6.5.2. Conduct static line ramp deployment procedures IAW T.O. 14D1-2-1-121. If parachutists are unable to deploy with the RAMZ off the ramp, then use JMDD moving target procedures after the RAMZ has landed in the water.

6.5.3. Prior to deployment, the JM will:

6.5.3.1. Ensure all applicable checklists are completed.

6.5.3.2. Ensure RAMZ cargo parachutes are secured to the anchor cable.

6.5.3.3. Ensure personnel in the cargo compartment are properly restrained/hooked to the anchor cable. Parachutists and RAMZ static lines will be hooked up to the same anchor cable on the side of the aircraft with a static line retriever.

WARNING: If the RAMZ and parachutists static lines are different lengths they will not be hooked up to the same anchor cable. RAMZ deployment bags (D-bags) must be retrieved before parachutists deploy from the opposite anchor cables. It is recommended if RAMZ and parachutists static lines are different lengths the RAMZ be deployed on one pass and parachutists be deployed on a different pass using moving target procedures.

WARNING: Parachutists must deploy on separate passes if parachutists are using different static lines lengths.

6.5.3.4. Altitude: No lower than 800' Above Water Level (AWL).

6.5.3.5. Airspeed: 130 KIAS. (Or as aircraft requires).

CAUTION: Insure airspeed doesn't exceed parachute limits

6.5.3.6. No more than five degrees nose up attitude.

6.5.3.7. Fly with the wind (optimum).

6.5.3.8. Ensure chemlites/strobe lights/LPUs on the T-10s (For Training Use) are activated.

6.5.3.9. Remove the forward horizontal and vertical axis tie-downs prior to the aircraft turning final for live deployment. Remove the aft horizontal axis tie-down after the aircraft has turned final.

6.5.3.10. Team Positioning:

6.5.3.10.1. JM/TL - Behind the RAMZ.

6.5.3.10.2. #2 parachutist - behind the JM.

6.5.3.10.3. #3 parachutist - behind #2 etc.

6.5.3.11. Deploy the RAMZ first. This allows the team to parachute to the package.

6.5.4. Exit/Deployment Sequence. The pilot will call for the green light backed up by a verbal "green light" call to the loadmaster. This indicates a clear to deploy. The red light/no drop will be used to stop the RAMZ deployment. The loadmaster will cut the load restraint strap (gate), with a verbal "cut the gate" from the JM, unless pre-briefed, otherwise. First parachutist will follow the RAMZ package after a 1second delay, all other parachutists will exit at one-second intervals.

6.6. RAMZ Freefall Procedures.

6.6.1. RAMZ deployments are characterized by low exit altitude without an altimeter and ARR.

6.6.2. Pre-deployment procedures for freefall are the same as static line.

6.6.3. Team Positioning:

6.6.3.1. The TL/JM will be allowed to move freely on the left side of the aircraft (between package and left side of aircraft) to monitor deployment preparations. For actual deployment he will be forward of the package.

6.6.3.2. The #2 parachutist monitors safety and assists the TL/JM as required.

6.6.3.3. The #3 parachutist monitors safety and assists the #2 parachutist and loadmaster as required.

6.6.4. Exit/Deployment Sequence.

6.6.4.1. After the pilot has received an affirmative response to the one-minute call, the pilot will turn on the green light. If the lights fail, a verbal "GO" from the loadmaster will be used as backup. The red light/no drop will be used to stop the RAMZ deployment. The loadmaster will cut the load restraint strap (gate), with a verbal "cut the gate" from the JM, unless pre-briefed, otherwise..

WARNING: The loadmaster must retrieve the RAMZ deployment bags prior to any parachutist exiting. The JM/TL will not initiate deployment until he visually ensures the D Bags have been retrieved. This will preclude any parachutist entanglement with the D bags during the deployment phase.

6.6.4.2. The JM will keep his eyes on the package at all times and ensure the cargo chutes deploy. Approximately six seconds after the RAMZ has successfully deployed at a minimum, the JM will exit, provided the RAMZ static lines have been retrieved within the six second window. The best time is to deploy parachutists is between a 6 to 14 second window, Parachutist exit at one-second intervals. A good stable exit is important for 3 reasons, as it allows the parachutist to: (1) maintain eye contact on the RAMZ and parachutist in front; (2) pull on assigned altitude or delay; (3) maintain proper body position for proper parachute deployment

6.6.4.3. 3500' AWL & above.

6.6.4.3.1. JM - 5 second delay.

6.6.4.3.2. #2 parachutist - 3 second delay.

6.6.4.3.3. Additional parachutists - Clear & Pull.

6.6.4.4. 3000'-3500' AWL. All parachutist: Clear & Pull.

6.6.4.5. Use a stacked approach. During high winds parachutists space along the intended path of the RAMZ, downwind and downdrift.

6.7. De-Rigging Procedures.

6.7.1. Teams should brief alternate downwind landing procedures to intercept a RAMZ being drug by the cargo parachutes. Team leaders and JMs need to be aware of this limitation and consider the using moving target procedures after the RAMZ is deployed.

CAUTION: Use extreme caution to avoid the cargo chutes when the FXC parachute release system has not disengaged the parachutes and the RAMZ is being dragged through the water by the wind and the PJ is attempting a moving intercept of the moving RAMZ package in the water.

CAUTION: During high winds and depending on sea state, the FXC may not release. If the parachutes do not release, place tension on the FXC in attempt to release the device. If the FXC does not release, cut the riser extensions.

6.7.2. Orient the RAMZ to the proper axis for inflation as required.

6.7.3. Container release system:

6.7.4. Release type IV connector.

6.7.5. Release the starboard quick release.

6.7.6. Release the stern quick release.

6.7.7. Remove upper portion of A-22 container diaper from package.

CAUTION: Failure to remove straps before inflation may result in severe damage to the boat.

6.8. Inflation.

6.8.1. Identify compressed air tank valve and turn counterclockwise starting inflation and check for leaks.After three-quarters inflation, disconnect engine strap, clear box, and enter the boat. Inflation time is approximately 1 min 40 sec.

6.8.2. Release air tank quick disconnect.

6.8.3. Tilt engine to remove shock board from between transom and engine.

6.8.4. De-water and start the engine IAW manufacturer's instructions.

WARNING: Ensure propeller is clear prior to starting engine.

6.9. Boat crew duties.

6.9.1. Secure all equipment.

6.9.2. Inflate keel

6.9.3. Turn all valves to the "navigate" position.

6.9.4. Clamp shock-absorbing tubes.

Chapter 7

TREE CLIMBING AND LETDOWN PROCEDURES

7.1. Tree Extraction. The safe extraction of patients and equipment from trees requires each PJ to be proficient in the proper use of tree climbers and procedures for patient evacuation/equipment removal. A thorough understanding of equipment and patient evacuation procedures leads to successful extraction.

7.2. Tree Climbing.

7.2.1. Trees which are completely dead should be approached with extreme caution. Dead trees may lack the support of a sound root system. If dead trees must be climbed to effect a rescue or recovery, then a support/safety line should be used. Hang the line over a sound limb of an adjacent tree while being belayed by a safetyman on the ground. In this case, the adjacent tree must be climbed first to install the safety rope. If this is not possible, then the climber must exercise great caution during the climb, rescue/recovery operation, and during descent.

7.2.2. Do not trust the last 10 feet of any treetop. This part of a tree is very weak and has no hardened core. If the tree is between 60 and 80 feet in height, the weak section might be the last 15 or 20 feet of the treetop. A climber, required to work near the top of a tree, should be secured to a safety line. Run the safety line once around the trunk about 10 to 15 feet below the working area, and then straight to and once around an adjacent tree trunk to the ground-belayer (safetyman).

7.2.3. In addition to the attached safety rope, the climber should be safetied to the tree trunk. Leaning outward or swaying while working in the tree should be avoided; this increases the chance for a fall.

7.3. Using Tree Climbing Equipment.

7.3.1. Tree climbing equipment consists of a pair of spiked "tree climbers" which are strapped to the lower legs and feet, a climbing safety belt which is worn around the waist, gloves, and a helmet.

7.3.2. Tree climbers are worn on the inside of each leg. They are securely strapped to the legs below the knees and to the feet on the outside of the ankles. The spike of each tree climber protrudes downward and at a slight angle inward from the foot. These spikes provide the necessary support for ascent and descent when jammed into the trunk of the tree.

7.3.3. The climber must ensure his knees never get too close to the trunk when using spiked climbing aids; his buttocks should be the farthest part of his body away from the trunk. His arms are either holding onto the trunk, branches, or moving and holding the climbing safety belt.

7.3.4. The climbing safety belt comes in two parts, a leather belt worn around the waist, and a safety belt which is adjustable. Each end of the safety belt snaps to the waist belt. This belt keeps the climber from falling backwards and aids the climber when working to free equipment or personnel. The belt allows the climber to use both hands while working and in case of a fall, keeps the climber close to the trunk.

7.3.5. When used in ascending or descending, the belt should be kept between the head and waist. The length of the belt around the trunk must be adjusted to aid in comfortable climbing.

CAUTION: If the spikes come free of the bark/wood causing a fall, arrest the fall by pinching the tree trunk with the climbing safety belt. Do not try to reset the spikes into the tree until the fall has been arrested.

7.3.6. A short rope or sling can be used in conjunction with the belt. This ensures ascent and descent procedures are safely performed when branches are bypassed. Attach the rope or sling to a solid limb or trunk for additional security.

7.3.7. Caution must be exercised when wearing and using tree-climbers. Unless experienced, individuals may have to look down to observe the spot where the spike is being placed.

7.3.8. Care and caution must be exercised in the transport of spiked tree-climbers. For a tree parachute deployment the tree-climbers can be packed into a container and attached securely parachutist underneath the medical kit or below the parachute on the buttocks.

7.4. Recovery of Personnel Suspended in Trees.

7.4.1. Call to the survivor to check consciousness. If the survivor is conscious, inform them not to move or try to climb down. Ask if they are injured and what type of injuries; then explain your intentions.

7.4.2. Evaluate the situation and coordinate with the team on a plan of action.

7.4.3. One PJ will climb the tree to the patient's location. The climber will carry sufficient equipment to perform a tree let-down and medical supplies to treat life-threatening injuries. Minimum equipment will consist of:

7.4.3.1. Tree climbers and belt (as required).

7.4.3.2. One end of a climbing rope or let-down tape.

7.4.3.3. Three sling ropes.

7.4.3.4. Three locking carabiners.

7.4.3.5. Medical kit.

7.4.4. Initial action upon reaching the patient will depend on the severity of the injuries and security of the parachute hang-up. The PJ should use one sling to secure himself to the tree while working on the survivor. If the tree climbers and belt are used, the belt may be routed above the tree branches to hold the belt from slipping down the tree. If the survivor has a secure hang-up, life-threatening injuries must be treated immediately. However, if the security of the hang-up is in doubt or the possibility of a fall exists, the first action should be to secure the patient to prevent additional injuries. The second sling may be used to secure the patient to the tree. Tie one end of the sling to the tree and the other end to the patients parachute harness. The security of the survivor's harness should be checked to ensure the survivor has not unfastened any of his harness straps. After the patient has been secured, initial medical treatment may be administered.

7.4.5. The survivor letdown is accomplished by a modified belay. The end of the rope or letdown tape is passed through a carabiner secured to a large limb or tree trunk above the survivor, and back to the survivor. The limb or tree trunk must be strong enough to support the weight of the survivor. If a rope is used, a two-loop knot is tied in the end of the rope. A locking carabiner is attached to the main lift-web of the harness above the capewell release on each shoulder. One loop from the knot is clipped into each carabiner. If the letdown tape is used, a figure eight knot is tied approximately six feet from the snap fastener. The snap fastener is routed under one shoulder of the survivor's harness, back up through the figure eight knot, down to and around the other shoulder of the harness and connected back on itself. If a suitable limb is not available to pass the rope over, the third rope sling carried by the climber may be used. One end of the sling may be secured around the main trunk of the tree with a prusik knot safetied with a bowline. The end of the sling will have a figure eight knot with a carabiner clipped into the knot. The rope used to lower the patient will be passed through the carabiner.

7.4.5.1. While one PJ is tending to the survivor, the remaining member will establish a belay system. A rapid belay may be accomplished by passing the standing end of the rope around the base of the tree or the team may use a standard belay used for adverse terrain operations.

7.4.5.2. To lower the survivor, the belayer will take up as much slack as possible and place a brake on the system. The climber will release the capewell on the patient's harness which supports the least weight. If both capewells are under equal tension, release the one further from the tree. Ensure the patient, if conscious, is aware of the procedures used. Release the remaining capewell. As the survivor "drops" free, keep him from slamming into the trunk or large limbs. A short fall will occur when the last capewell is released due to the stretch factor of the rope. This fall may be minimized by holding the harness when releasing the last capewell. The PJ must have tension on his anchor sling for this action to avoid being pulled off the tree.

WARNING: The PJ must ensure his fingers are not caught in the capewell release cable upon release.

7.4.5.3. As the survivor is lowered by the belaying teammate, the PJ in the tree should descend with the survivor and guide him between branches to avoid further injuries. The commands to be used by the climber are "BRAKE" for immediate stop and "SLACK" for continuing a slow descent.

7.4.5.4. If the survivor is unconscious, you should have a litter in place directly below the lowering point. Lower the survivor directly into the litter. Initiate immediate medical care if needed, ensure the patient is on the ground before disconnecting the carabiners and rope.

7.4.5.5. Heavily branched or high trees might require two rescuers to climb the tree while a third remains on the ground as the belayer. One PJ guides and holds the victim's feet and legs, while the other supports the upper body during descent procedures.

Chapter 8

RESCUE JUMPMASTER PROCEDURES

8.1. General. Rescue jumpmaster (JM) procedures are utilized to enable the rapid deployment of personnel and treatment of survivors through precision parachuting. Minimizing the distance to the survivor increases their chance of survival while decreasing the PJs exposure to the elements and the threat. It is the most accurate method of jumpmastering when used with Wind Drift Indicators (WDI), as it is the only method able to accurately determine the actual winds and currents at the time of deployment from surface to parachute activation altitude. It provides rapid control of the incident area, less time to get to the survivor, positive control of the survivor, decreases dispersion of the jumpers, and takes into consideration terrain, weather, and unusual wind conditions.

8.2. Terms and Definitions.

8.2.1. High Glide Ratio Parachute (HGRP): A ram air parachute used in military parachuting for delivery of personnel.

8.2.2. Point of Impact (PI) The point on a drop zone, where the lead jumper or the first bundle of equipment is computed to land.

8.2.3. Opening Point (OP) The point above ground at a specific heading, distance, and altitude from the PI where parachute opening is computed to occur.

8.2.4. Preliminary Release Point (PRP) The point above ground at a specific heading, distance, and altitude from the OP which is computed to be the transition point between forward throw and vertical freefall. This point is used as the release point for slow flying aircraft (less than 80 KIAS) because of negligible forward throw.

8.2.5. Release Point (RP) The point above ground at a specific heading, distance and altitude from the PRP jumper aircraft exit (including the aircraft's forward throw) is computed to occur.

8.3. Jumpmaster Qualification. JMs must be thoroughly knowledgeable in the following: AFI 11-410, AFJI 13-210, AFI 13-217, T.0. 14D1-2-1-121, Army FM 31-19, civilian contract aircraft, and unit SOPs. Previously qualified JMs will be evaluated on their knowledge of rescue JM procedures. This training will be documented in the individual's OJT records. Rescue jumpmaster procedures must be performed on a semi-annual basis to stay proficient.

8.4. Jumpmaster Responsibilities. For operational missions, the JM is either the team leader or is appointed by the team leader. The JM has the authority to delegate any duties, but is responsible for the conduct/completion of those duties.

8.4.1. General Responsibilities.

8.4.1.1. Determine mission requirements and brief all participating parachutist on the following:

8.4.1.2. Aircraft inspection and aircrew coordination.

8.4.1.3. Coordination of support requirements to include transportation, drop zone (DZ), ground party, aircraft utilization, and support equipment requirements.

8.4.1.4. Rigging and inspection of parachutists/equipment.

8.4.1.5. Loading of aircraft.

8.4.1.6. Safety of all parachutist and the completeness of their equipment prior to departure from the aircraft.

8.4.1.7. Ensure all safety standards are complied with and only approved techniques/training operations are conducted.

8.4.1.8. Actions of all parachutist until the deployment is completed.

8.4.1.9. Documentation of all parachute deployment information.

8.4.1.10. Manifest completion and distribution.

8.4.2. Responsibilities at the Unit Area.

8.4.2.1. Check the current situation and gather information.

8.4.2.2. Determine objectives.

8.4.2.3. Coordinate with team leader on JM responsibilities versus team leader responsibilities based on mission tasking.

8.4.2.4. Post Warning Order.

8.4.2.5. Obtain Deployment/DZ information.

8.4.2.5.1. Maps/Charts.

8.4.2.5.2. Photos.

8.4.2.5.3. Surveys.

8.4.2.5.4. Forecasted weather and winds in the DZ area.

8.4.2.5.5. Support available.

8.4.2.5.6. Radio Frequencies.

8.4.2.6. Equipment Requirements: Mission, team, and individual.

8.4.2.7. Assign additional duties.

8.4.2.7.1. Assistant JumpMaster(s)(AJM).

8.4.2.7.2. Safety

8.4.2.7.3. Drop Zone Controller (DZC).

8.4.2.7.4. Drop Zone Safety Officer (DZSO).

8.4.2.7.5. DZ Medic (as required).

8.4.2.8. Coordinate rigging of equipment.

8.4.2.9. Coordinate NOTAMs/Range clearances.

8.4.2.10. Complete Passenger Manifest.

8.4.2.10.1. Primary Jumpmaster (PJM), one copy.

8.4.2.10.2. Aircrew, one copy.

8.4.2.10.3. Unit file, one copy.

8.4.2.11. Coordinate transport to aircraft and to/from DZ.

8.4.2.12. Compute and plot High Altitude Release Point (HARP)/ Computed Air Release Point (CARP) (as required).

8.4.2.13. Compute milibar settings for automatic ripcord release (as required).

8.4.2.14. Coordinate/Brief aircrew.

8.4.2.14.1. Coordinate/Brief the navigator concerning the calculated release point (as required).

8.4.2.14.2. Coordinate/Brief the Safetyman.

8.4.2.15. Coordinate/Brief DZC.

8.4.2.16. Coordinate/Brief DZSO.

8.4.2.17. Coordinate/Brief medical support (as required).

8.4.2.18. Brief team members.

8.4.2.19. Prepare a JM kit.

8.4.2.20. Ensure parachutists have inspected and loaded required equipment items before departure from the work section or staging area.

8.4.2.21. Ensure drying tower is available (as required).

8.4.2.22. Coordinate recompression chamber (as required).

8.4.3. Responsibilities at the Departure Airfield.

8.4.3.1. Ensure show/station times are met.

8.4.3.2. Coordinate/brief with aircraft commander, navigator, and safetyman (if not done previously).

8.4.3.3. Coordinate with aircraft commander and navigator for additional updates.

8.4.3.4. Coordinate/brief with Loadmaster/Flight Engineer Safetyman (if not done previously).

8.4.3.5. Complete JM aircraft inspection.

8.4.3.6. Monitor loading of equipment.

8.4.3.7. Check equipment rigging and security.

8.4.3.8. Update team members (as required).

8.4.3.9. Initiate donning of equipment (as required).

8.4.3.10. Complete Jumpmaster Personnel Inspection (JMPI) on all parachutist (as required).

8.4.3.11. Monitor loading of jumpers.

8.4.4. Responsibilities in Flight.

8.4.4.1. Coordinate parachutist actions with the crew.

8.4.4.2. Recompute HARP/CARP formula (as required).

8.4.4.3. Receive/Update release (navigator).

8.4.4.4. Conduct enroute briefings, providing information on mission progress and any changes.

8.4.4.5. Ensure proper conduct and welfare of team.

8.4.4.6. Alert parachutists to prepare and don parachute and mission equipment and conduct a JMPI on parachutist (if not done previously).

8.4.4.7. Conduct an on-the-scene pre-deployment evaluation (if required) to select and evaluate a DZ and evaluate weather and wind velocity factors.

8.4.4.8. Conduct release point determination procedures.

8.4.4.9. Give time warnings/ deployment commands.

8.4.4.10. Conduct personnel parachute deployment.

8.4.5. Responsibilities on the DZ.

8.4.5.1. Account for all personnel and equipment.

8.4.5.2. Assist injured personnel/coordinate medical treatment.

8.4.5.3. Coordinate transportation back to unit.

8.5. Pre-Deployment Evaluation. A pre-deployment evaluation is conducted at the staging area and on scene. Jumpmasters should make an initial assessment of the proposed DZ area at the unit prior to parachute deployment/operational mission. On-scene evaluation is conducted jointly by the aircraft commander and the JM to evaluate factors in determining the feasibility of a parachute deployment. When the mission team leader/JM determines deployment is required, he will advise the aircraft commander (AC) of his intent. The pre-deployment evaluation is one of the most critical phases in a rescue deployment. Depending on the situation, the deployment aircraft should be flown on as many low-level passes as necessary to accomplish this evaluation. The JM must evaluate all aspects of the conditions and terrain features located around the intended deployment area.

8.5.1. A site evaluation must be conducted. Terrain features and possible hazards at the deployment sites may include; rocks, trees, stumps, snow cover and avalanche/rock slide conditions, streams, lakes, mountains, cliffs, crevasses, frozen ground, or man-made objects. Water hazards may include; temperature vs. time deployed, chill factor, sea state, hazardous marine life, vessel traffic, and channel buoys.

8.5.2. DZ size and location i.e. a small clearing on the side of a hill or deep snow drifts may make it necessary to deploy the parachutists and equipment separately. It may be better to deploy the equipment first, then deploy the team to the equipment.

8.5.3. DZ elevation should be taken into account during a site evaluation. DZ elevation is a factor when parachuting with equipment at elevations as low as 5,000 feet. Taking temperature and density altitude into account; an appreciable increased rate of descent is noticeable at higher elevations. Altitude is not considered a factor for deployments below 14,000 feet MSL without equipment.

8.5.4. The recovery of the team will be considered before deployment. The method of recovery, possible delays in recovery, and hazards involved must be considered.

8.5.5. A weather evaluation must be made to determine on-scene conditions and forecast future conditions.

8.5.5.1. Lower ceilings may prevent the team from using more accurate square parachutes versus static line parachutes.

8.5.5.2. Deployment of back-up kits and housekeeping kits may be mandated with forecasted storms and delays in recovery.

8.5.6. Wind velocity is one of the most important items of evaluation. A maximum allowable velocity will depend on many factors; the experience and ability of the rescue team, type equipment used, and urgency of the mission. Life or death missions may justify a calculated risk.

8.5.7. Wind drift determination is the art of establishing an accurate release/exit point for precision parachuting to a pre-selected impact point. Wind drift determination is critical to accurate target deployment. If the situation allows, the most accurate method of determining wind drift is the WDI. Especially in mountainous terrain, wind and current conditions can change dramatically from the surface to parachute activation altitude. The JM should deploy a minimum of one WDI prior to personnel delivery, with consideration to deploying additional WDIs as necessary for verification. Consider additional WDIs if:

8.5.7.1. Delivery site is restrictive.

8.5.7.2. Wind velocity appears marginal or gusty.

8.5.7.3. Lost sight of, or unsure of the landing location of the previous WDI.

8.5.7.4. Suspect the wind conditions have changed since the last deployment.

8.5.7.5. Any doubt as to delivery conditions.

8.5.8. Wind Drift Indicators and Configurations. The AF/B 28J-1 Wind Drift Determination Parachute (with MK6 MOD 3 Smoke/Flare, MK 58 MOD 1 Smoke/Flare, or a 16-21 pound weight), crepe paper streamers with ¾ of one ounce weight, or the Search and Rescue Light are the only devices authorized for determining wind drift.

8.5.8.1. AF/B 28J-1, Wind Drift Determination Parachute. When using the AF/B28J-1 parachute, use the 16-21 pound weight provided with the parachute, a MK 6 Mod 3, or a MK-58 Mod 1. When the AF/B 28J-1 is used in conjunction with MK 6 Mod 3 smoke/flare, it will be configured by installing two MK 6 Mod 3 Suspension Bands (NSN 1370-00-069-9946) four inches from the weighted end of the MK 6 Mod 3, with the attaching rings at 90 degree angles to each other and tightened sufficiently to prevent separation during delivery. Same procedures apply when using the MK 58 Mod 1 except MK 58 Mod 1 suspension bands (round instead of square), will be used. Chemlite or strobe lights will be attached to the AF/B 28J-1 risers for night land deployments. The strobe lights should be upright on one side and inverted on the other side of the single portion of the risers above the weight/MK 6 Mod 3/MK 58 Mod 1. Use tape and 80 lb. test tape to secure the strobe lights. For night water deployments, attach chemlites to the AF/B 28J-1 risers to aid in recovery of the wind drift chute in case the MK 6 Mod 3/MK 58 Mod 1 malfunctions. The MK 6 Mod 3/MK 58 Mod 1 signal may also be used for land deployments when a fire hazard does not exist, (i.e. snow covered terrain). The signal will be easier to see than a streamer or wind drift parachute.

8.5.8.2. Crepe Paper Streamers. The crepe paper streamer is 20 feet long and 10 inches wide. The metal rod is 10 inches long and weighing ¾ of one ounce. For night deployments the metal rod will be replaced with two six-inch long high intensity chemlites. Crepe paper streamers can be procured assembled or assembled from locally obtained materials. They can be made of any color crepe paper, but should be of a color that contrasts with the terrain. Caution must be taken to prevent squeezing the rolled streamers prior to delivery. The paper may compress causing the streamer not to unroll to its full extent. A number of streamers should be deployed simultaneously on each release point determination pass to provide a better reference. Ensure the tape has been broken and one or two feet pulled from the roll prior to deployment.

8.5.8.3. Search and Rescue Light (SRL): The SRL is a durable light sphere used during search and rescue missions carried out at night. The lights are used to mark targets, landing sites, and to indicate wind drift. The SRL is currently produced in white, red, green, and yellow colors. The SRL has either a steady or flashing mode, selected by a three-position recessed toggle switch recessed into the outer surface of each half of the ball. A steel band wraps around the sphere, providing a secure anchor for a standard drag chute and provides a watertight seal. When the SRL is used to assess wind drift, it is deployed from the aircraft using a drift parachute NSN 1670-21-812-7369. (The SRL is locally purchased through Quantaflex Canada Inc. NATO Stock Number 6230-21-910-3387 White, 6230-21-910-5796 Red, 6230-21-910-3386 Green, and 6230-21-910-5797 Yellow).

8.6. Airdrop Release Methods.

8.6.1. Computed Air Release Point (CARP). CARP is the most often used method to deploy conventional airborne forces. CARP is computed by the aircrew (navigator). Procedures for calculating the CARP are found in AFI 11-231. The navigator uses updated winds obtained from the aircraft instrumentation/forecasted winds on the DZ to calculate the release point. CARP is also referred to as a "navigator release". When a CARP deployment is performed the aircrew takes responsibility for the accuracy of the deployment. However, the JM has "No Drop" authority and can prevent an incorrect release. Close coordination between the aircraft navigator and JM is essential to ensure deployment over the correct spot. Prior to exit on navigator release deployments, the JM and aircraft navigator should separately determine the release point, compare their results, and resolve any differences. All parachutists will be briefed on selected exit and opening points.

NOTE: Suspended equipment weights greater than 35 pounds increases the rate of descent and may require adjusting the constant value to a lower number i.e., a constant value of 25 for a 35-pound load to 18 for a 115-pound load.

8.6.2. High Altitude Release Point (HARP). HARP is similar to CARP but is used for obtaining the release point for a HAHO or HALO deployment. HARP takes into account the amount of drift of the parachutist in freefall plus the drift from canopy opening to landing. This method may be used for both JM or navigator release jumps. JMs may learn how to perform a HARP calculation by consulting FM 31-19, Appendix B, as compared to the updated aircrew version found in AFI 11-231. When performing a navigator release HARP deployment, the JM should also accomplish a separate HARP and compared his results with the navigator for accuracy.

8.6.3. Ground Marking Release System (GMRS). GMRS is computed by the Drop Zone Support Team Leader (DZSTL) and determines the release point from the ground by placing panels/lights in strategic locations for visual identification/release point by the deployment aircraft. It is most often used by Special Forces teams for insertion of personnel and equipment from low altitudes to small DZs.

8.6.4. Verbally Initiated Release System (VIRS). VIRS is used by the Army and USMC to deploy small numbers of personnel from rotary or small fixed wing aircraft to small DZs. The release point is indicated by an oral command from the DZ to the deployment aircraft. VIRS is only performed by qualified CCT or TALO personnel.

8.6.5. Wind Streamer Vector Count (WSVC). WSVC is a JMDD utilizing streamers and count for establishing the release point from the air. This is the method most often utilized by PJs as it is the most accurate method for inserting small teams into confined or unprepared areas utilizing both static line/freefall canopies.

8.6.6. The U.S. Air Force has developed other airdrop methods utilizing radar systems in conjunction with navigator release airdrops for Instrument Meteorological Conditions. Some examples of these are Adverse Weather Aerial Delivery System (AWADS), Radar Beacon Airdrops, Ground Radar Aerial Delivery System (GRADS), Ground Control Approach/Computers Aerial Delivery System (GCA/CADS), Self Contained Navigation System (SCNS)/Station Keeping Equipment (SKE)/Zone Marker (ZM) Airdrops.

8.7. Jumpmaster Directed Drops (JMDD).

8.7.1. Sight Alignment. Sight alignment is the method utilized by the JM to obtain an accurate sight picture from the aircraft to the target. The sight picture from each aircraft will be different and requires an understanding of the principles involved and training in a variety of aircraft.

8.7.1.1. The JM should be in a position that affords him the best opportunity to determine whether the aircraft is flying the correct track. The head should not be too far inside or too far outside the aircraft. Improper head alignment can cause the JM to align the aircraft right or left of the track. Proper sight alignment should be parallel to the ground directly over the intended track.

8.7.1.2. When the JM changes position from the prone or kneeling position to standing position, it is imperative that the proper sight alignment be maintained.

WARNING: For all aircraft, parachute ripcord handles will be guarded to prevent accidental deployment.

8.7.2. The JM must be able to inform the pilot of the location of an object in the air or on the ground, i.e., wind drift device, equipment, parachutist , etc. The JM can use two methods. One method is to identify the object's position in respect to the aircraft giving a clock position, distance, and altitude. The other method uses the PI and heading of "last final flown" to provide reference information only for locating an object on the ground. The direction of the "last final flown" will always be identified as 12 o'clock. Any reference using this method should include the word PI in the statement and should be stated as follows: "The streamer landed at the PI's 5 o'clock position, 300 meters."

8.7.3. For fixed wing aircraft utilizing JMDD instead of a CARP/HARP (navigator release) drop, the aircrew will allow the JM to begin spotting at a minimum of two minutes out. The green light will be turned on one minute prior to the calculated release point. This will still allow the aircrew the use of the red light for stopping the deployment . Do not confuse a JMDD with a CARP deployment , (i.e. going on the green light), as this will result in an early release and probably an off-DZ landing. Parachutists will not exit the aircraft if the green light is not illuminated or a no drop condition exists.

8.7.4. Fixed (Normal) Target Pattern (Attachment 4, Figure A4.1. and Figure A4.2.). The fixed target pattern/normal flight pattern will be a rectangular or racetrack pattern with the final approach from WDI to target. Each leg of the pattern must be long enough to allow the JM and parachutists preparation time needed prior to deployment. The legs of the pattern, in order, are crosswind, downwind, base, and final.

8.7.4.1. A pattern with crosswind and base legs of not over one half minute and with downwind and final legs of 1 to 1 ½ minutes will allow time for heading corrections on final and keep the objective area in sight. This also permits the JM and aircrew to observe the descent of parachutists or WDI.

8.7.4.2. The turn to the crosswind leg will be made as soon as possible after the WDI is released. This ensures JM doesn't lose sight of the WDI. If necessary, request the pilot to lift a wing or turn more left or right as necessary to keep the WDI in sight. Relay directions to the pilot to allow him to sight the WDI. If a delay is expected, another full pattern should be flown, as opposed to extending the downwind leg or performing a 360 degree turn on final, this maintains the aircraft close to the area for continued evaluation. This pattern will place the aircraft a maximum of five minutes from the site at any one time.

8.7.4.3. The aircraft will be flown over the target at a predetermined altitude and airspeed. When directly over the target or PI, a minimum of one WDI will be dropped. The WDI will be deployed at the planned parachute opening altitude. The JM and aircrew will make every effort to keep the WDI in sight from release to impact with the ground/water. Over land, the pilot may have to circle over the WDI to ensure the location of, or orientation from the impact point of the WDI to the target/intended PI of the jumpers. After the first WDI has reached the ground and its position noted, the aircraft will return to the normal pattern. The final approach should pass directly over the WDI and the intended target. This pattern automatically aligns the final approach of the aircraft into the wind.

8.7.4.4. A right or left hand pattern may be flown depending on terrain and aircraft configuration. The aircraft will be flown in this pattern with minor course corrections on final. As the aircraft passes directly over the first WDI, the JM will start a uniform count to measure the time from the WDI to the target. When the aircraft is over the target, the count will be stopped and immediately a new count will begin, when that count equals the first, the second WDI or jumper will be deployed. The count will measure the same distance past the target with the accuracy of the deployment dependent upon the JMs alignment and uniformity of the count.

8.7.4.5. If subsequent passes or sticks of jumpers are necessary, the JM should have noted the release point of the first jumpers. See "Spotting Techniques" below.

8.7.5. Moving target pattern (Attachment 5, Figure A5.1.). Deployment procedures to a moving target are similar to those employed for a stationary target. The moving target procedures takes into consideration target drift and will place the team on the downdrift line of the moving target and not necessarily on the target. It is always better to land downwind/downdrift of the target to allow the target to drift towards PJ team rather than land upwind/updrift forcing the PJ team to swim/chase after the target in the water. Attention should be paid to the following items:

8.7.5.1. The pattern must be adjusted so the initial pattern over the target after WDI deployment will return over the intended release point not less than five minutes and not more than nine minutes, seven minutes being ideal. If the initial pattern requires more than nine minutes, the team will be too far downdrift/downwind and with a high target drift rate may not be able to locate the target visually. Less than five minutes may put the team upwind/updrift of the target depending on the target's drift rate. Although a target can be moved by the ocean current, wind will affect a stationary object to travel a greater distance. When the wind and current are heading in the same direction, the target may be moving at a greater speed than the PJ will be able to make up with fins alone.

8.7.5.2. On the initial pass after the WDI deployment, an accurate count can be obtained by the JM and the heading noted by both the JM and pilot. All subsequent passes will be made on this initial heading using the count obtained on the first pass. No attempt should be made to recheck the count or change the initial heading because the target will have drifted.

NOTE: On subsequent passes requiring a course correction to place the aircraft over the target, ensure the pilot corrects back to original heading.

8.7.6. Crosswind pattern (Attachment 6, Figure A6.1.). This involves deploying the team in a crosswind direction, 90 degrees to the known wind line. A crosswind pattern may be required due to terrain or sun reflection on the surface of the water preventing a desirable release into the wind. The pilot and JM must accurately judge the upwind distance from the target in order for this technique to be effective. The easiest method for obtaining an accurate upwind distance is the utilization of a reference/ release point. Judging distance over water is more demanding due to the lack of fixed reference points and tests the distance judging of the JM (see "Spotting Techniques" below). The JM must ensure the spot is at a right angle from the heading of the initial pass. Error towards the target if in doubt. Consider throwing a check streamer if heading cannot be determined to verify the spot is downwind and downdrift. This will ensure a downwind impact point. It is imperative the parachutists are deployed prior to reaching the reference point due to the forward throw of the parachutist in the direction of aircraft travel. The object is to place the reference point at the center of the stick after forward throw is considered.

8.7.7. Spotting Techniques.

8.7.7.1. Reference points should be used on all JMDD, CARP, and HARP land deployments. The utilization of reference points will increase the JM's accuracy in determining the proper release point. An established reference/release point will allow the aircraft to fly in any direction as long as it will pass over the reference/release point.

8.7.7.2. Approaching from a different flight heading may confuse the parachutist with the actual wind line. However, the parachutist may find the direction of the wind line while under canopy by drawing a straight line from their release point to the target/PI, then course correcting onto the proper wind line.

8.7.7.3. Finding and Using a Reference Point.

8.7.7.3.1. Upon completion of the initial pass over the target for WDI deployment, establish the impact location of the WDI.

8.7.7.3.2. Pick out a spot that is an equal distance on the opposite side of the target as the WDI. This spot can be any readily identifiable feature, i.e. discolored ground, bushes, trees, etc. Back up this location using the JM count from the first deployment and by looking at the ground after releasing the first stick of parachutists. Fix that location in your memory. For water deployments, you will just have to trust in finding the correct distance equal to the WDI to target distance for your release point.

8.7.7.3.3. The JM should pass the reference/release point to the pilot to assure both are utilizing the same point.

8.7.8. Voice Terminology and Hand Signals. During JM directed airdrops, the JM must use clear and concise communications with the aircrew.

8.7.8.1. If the JM is wearing a helmet for communications, he will ensure the chin strap is fastened. If unable to wear a helmet, such as during water operations or prior to the JM's own exit, the JM will communicate using hand signals.

8.7.8.2. When communicating with the aircrew, the JM will use standard voice terminology and hand signals. Refer to T.O. 14D1-2-1-121 for standard static line deployment commands and signals. Refer to FM 31-19 for standard freefall deployment commands and signals.

8.7.8.3. In addition to the standard visual/verbal commands listed for CARP deployments, JMDD requires visual/verbal deployment commands for directing the aircraft over the intended RP. These hand and voice signals are normally relayed to the pilot over intercom and when necessary, to the safetyman for relay to the pilot when the JM is off intercom.

8.7.8.3.1. "STEADY" - A voice or hand signal indicating the present direction of flight is satisfactory. The hand signal is an "open hand", palm vertical pointing the fingers toward the flight deck.

8.7.8.3.2. "LEFT"/"RIGHT" - A voice or hand signal indicating the direction of flight should be changed to the left or right five degrees. The hand signal is a "closed fist, thumb extended" lateral hand movement with the thumb pointing to the left or right side of the aircraft.

8.7.8.3.3. "LEFT/RIGHT X DEGREES" - A voice or hand signal indicating a change of flight direction required in excess of five degrees. The hand signal is the LEFT/RIGHT hand signal from above followed by indicating the desired number of degrees. Multiple hand movements will indicate directional changes in five-degree increments.

8.7.8.3.4. "THUMBS UP" - A hand signal from the safetyman indicating the aircraft commander has given the "Clear to Jump" command. This is to be used by safetymen for the JM who is off intercom. Do not confuse this hand signal with the JM's thumbs up for "Standby" to the jumpers.

8.7.8.3.5. "NO DROP" - A voice, hand, or light signal indicating an unsafe condition exists and all jump activities will cease until the unsafe condition is corrected. The hand signal is a "clenched fist" held in front of the face. If a jumper is in the door, the "clenched fist" will be placed in front of his face. The "red" jump light (if used/available) is turned on as the light signal. The JM or any crewmember noting an unsafe condition will immediately call or signal a "NO DROP". The standard Army freefall hand signal is a shaking head from left to right without any hand movement. US Army personnel may also use the term "Abort" to mean "No Drop". These signals may also be used by the JM, but ideally, within the Air Force, the "No Drop" signals for static line and freefall use should be standardized to avoid confusion.

WARNING: If the parachutist is exiting the aircraft, do not attempt to physically restrain/stop him.

8.8. General Jumpmaster Information/Requirements.

8.8.1. Specific aircraft parachute deployment procedures are contained in each aircraft MDS, specific AFIs, or MCI, Volume 3, and amended as necessary by MAJCOM/Wing Supplements, Flight Crew Information Files (FCIFs), and unit Flight Crew Bulletins (FCBs

8.8.2. JMs should be familiar with and review the paradrop procedures used by the deployment aircraft.

8.8.3. All JMs and assistant jumpmasters (AJMs) should review the applicable portions of the FCB of the flying organizations routinely supporting PJ parachute operations.

8.8.4. Chief, Standardization Certifier/Evaluator (Stan/Eval) Responsibilities.

8.8.4.1. It is the responsibility of the PJ unit Chief, Standardization Certifier/Evaluator to monitor/be on distribution for those FCBs of flying units supporting PJ parachute operations on four or more separate occasions per year. Multiple paradrops accomplished during a single exercise may constitute a single occasion.

8.8.4.2. The Chief, Standardization Certifier/Evaluator is responsible to inform unit assigned JMs and AJMs of a change to an FCB or MDS specific volume 3 affecting procedures used for parachute operations.

8.8.5. It is still the individual JM's' responsibility to keep abreast of all changes.

8.8.6. Deployment airspeeds and altitudes for general aircraft types are listed in Chapter 2, Operational/Training Restrictions and AFI 11-231.

8.9. Static Line Aircraft Deployment Procedures.

8.9.1. General guidance on how to JM specific aircraft types is found in TO 14D1-2-1-121.

8.9.2. As paradrop procedures rarely change, some of the more important procedures (as well as some general JM tips), of the more common jump platforms, are provided in this section.

8.9.3. HH-60 Aircraft.

8.9.3.1. Parachute Delivery Procedures.

8.9.3.1.1. Delivery will be made from straight and level flight. Without internal auxiliary tanks installed the maximum number of parachutists is four per door per pass.

8.9.3.1.2. With the twin 185 auxiliary fuel tanks installed, only two parachutists with equipment per door may be deployed on a single pass. Without equipment, three parachutists per door may be deployed on a single pass.

8.9.3.1.3. Parachutist deployments will be accomplished at one second intervals. Order of deployment of parachutist is from the left rear parachutist forward.

8.9.3.1.4. The right door will not be used for static line parachuting if the internal hoist has been installed.

8.9.3.1.5. The deployment position for the H-60 aircraft is sitting on the cargo floor with the legs outside the aircraft.

8.9.3.1.6. At the "Standby" command the parachutists place both hands, palm down, on the cargo floor alongside their thighs. On the "Go" command the parachutist pushes himself out and grasps his reserve, performing normal procedures.

8.9.3.2. Doors/Exits.

8.9.3.2.1. Double door exits are authorized. On double door exits, the first parachutist of the second stick will exit one second after he visually observes the exit of the last parachutist from the opposite side.

8.9.3.2.2. The opposite door should be closed during single door parachute operations. It may be opened for JM spotting training in concurrence with an actual deployment.

8.9.3.2.3. Doors may be opened or closed in flight as necessary with the pilot's approval.

8.9.3.2.4. JM duties may be performed from any position in either door.

8.9.3.3. Configuration.

8.9.3.3.1. Passenger seats will be removed from the cargo compartment.

8.9.3.3.2. Tape sharp edges, cargo floor troop seat and tie-down fitting wells, and door jambs that could cut or fray static lines or snag parachutists' equipment.

8.9.3.3.3. Tape must not interfere with closing or opening the doors in flight.

8.9.3.3.4. Seat belts/personnel restraint devices will be used for all parachutist for take-off and cruise flight.

8.9.3.3.5. Safetyman/JM, when secured with a gunner's belt, will be attached to a location on the airframe that will not interfere with parachutist exit.

8.9.3.4. JM Responsibilities.

8.9.3.4.1. Seat belts will not be removed until the aircraft is at 1000 feet AGL or higher. The aircraft commander should be informed before seat belt removal.

8.9.3.4.2. Parachutists will not remove seat belts unless wearing a manual release (reserve or HGRP) type parachute.

8.9.3.4.3. The static lines of the parachutists seated in the left and right doors should be routed directly behind them and down to the anchor line. Ensure any excess static line slack is stowed in the pack tray retainer band.

8.9.3.4.4. The static line anchor line cable is never rigged to the cargo doors or overhead rappelling rings, since training D-bags might foul the main rotor system.

8.9.3.4.5. The pilot must maintain the aircraft in level flight and airdrop speed during D-bag retrieval to preclude D-bag entanglement with the cargo doors. The aircraft will not be "clear to turn" until the D-bags have been retrieved.

8.9.3.4.6. The D-bags will be retrieved before disconnecting the static lines.

8.9.3.4.7. When parachutists assume a door position, the pilot will be advised of delivery status.

8.9.3.4.8. The JM may perform wind drift determination before or after the parachutists assume a door position.

8.9.3.4.9. The wind drift chute, if used, will be attached on the anchor line cable aft of the first parachutist in the first stick and delivered on the JM's signal.

8.9.3.5. JM Sight Alignment. The H-60 sight alignment is accomplished by sighting along the edge of the aircraft. When the PI reaches a position directly below the JM, on the edge of the floor, an over the PI position has been reached. The JM can accomplish this from the kneeling or deployment position.

8.9.3.6. Inflight Visual/Verbal Signals.

8.9.3.6.1. The pilot will normally give 10, 5, and 1minute warnings.

8.9.3.6.2. After turning "final," the JM will advise the pilot when the target is in sight and when going off intercom. The pilot will call one minute prior to drop and will acknowledge "Clear to Drop" after he receives "Target In Sight, Safetyman Check Completed." If the JM is not on intercom, the safetyman will relay the "Clear to Drop" to the JM.

8.9.3.6.3. The words "No Drop" over the intercom, or a "Clenched Fist" visual signal by any person will serve as notification to terminate parachute operations until the situation is resolved.

NOTE: The term "No Drop" instead of "Abort" should be briefed to the pilot before parachute operations are conducted.

WARNING: When parachutists are in the door, ensure the aircraft clears terrain at the minimum safe deployment altitude.

8.9.3.6.4. The JM will acknowledge all calls from the pilot.

8.9.3.7. Safetyman Responsibilities. Flight engineers/aerial gunners may be used as safetymen and will relay hand signals between the JM and pilot.

8.9.3.8. Parachutists Responsibilities.

8.9.3.8.1. Seat belts will be adjusted to ensure the connection is above the reserve parachute.

8.9.3.8.2. Crowded conditions inside the cargo compartment make accidental activation of the reserve parachute more likely. During movement inside the aircraft, parachutists must protect their ripcord.

8.9.4. C-130 Aircraft.

8.9.4.1. Configuration.

8.9.4.1.1. Personnel required to be mobile in the cargo compartment during low-level phases will wear protective headgear, as a minimum, from the start of the pre-slowdown checklist until the completion of the deployment checklist. (Exception: Personnel performing day water jumps).

8.9.4.1.2. During an airdrop, occupants in the cargo compartment will either have a seat belt fastened, wear a restraint harness, or wear a parachute before doors are opened.

8.9.4.1.3. Static lines are attached to the anchor cables before doors are opened. (Exception: Parachutists exiting on subsequent passes may stand and hook up with doors open if they are forward of the aft edge of the wheel wells (Flight Station [FS] 617).

8.9.4.2. Doors/Exits.

8.9.4.2.1. When parachuting the paratroop doors the ramp will be closed.

8.9.4.2.2. The aircraft must be at or above drop altitude and stable no later than one minute out (two minutes out for JM directed drops) to allow the JM access to the paratroop door.

8.9.4.2.3. At no time will both paratroop doors be opened for paratroop drops if only one loadmaster is on board.

8.9.4.2.4. When more than 20 static line parachutists are dropped on a single pass, the paratroop doors will be used.

8.9.4.3. JM Responsibilities.

8.9.4.3.1. JMDD releases will not be mixed with any other type of airdrop method, i.e., GMRS, VIRS, or standard CARP deployments .

8.9.4.3.2. Checklist times may be compressed during racetrack patterns, but the one-minute advisory is never compressed and is always given on time.

8.9.4.4. JM Sight Alignment.

8.9.4.4.1. The JM should use the forward edge of the deployment platform support and the forward edge of the air deflector door to obtain his sight alignment. The target should pass from the "V" in the air deflection door to the leading edge of the deployment platform. When the PI reaches the leading edge of the deployment platform, a direct over the PI position has been attained. The JM can be in a kneeling, prone, or standing position during sight alignment. This sight alignment may have to be modified if the aircraft is required to crab to maintain proper ground track. It is especially valuable to have the ground reference point when this situation occurs. For ramp procedures ensure paratroop doors are closed. JM will place himself in a position to visualize the target and exit point. He will make course corrections to the aircraft alignment until the aircraft flies directly over the exit point.

8.9.5. HC-130 Aircraft.

8.9.5.1. Parachute Deployment Procedures. Same as above.

8.9.5.2. Doors/Exits. The authorized exits for static line parachuting from an HC-130 aircraft are the left and right paratroop doors and ramp exits if the aircraft is configured IAW the applicable T.O. Standard static line delivery procedures are single door exits. Double door exits require a qualified safetyman to be available for each door. Single or multiple exits are authorized from either door.

8.9.5.3. Configuration. Standard configuration for the HC-130 requires deployment platform(s) to be extended when using the paratroop doors. If an air-to-air recovery system (ATAR) is installed, static line parachuting is restricted to the right paratroop door. Further, the ATAR cover plate and hydraulic lines must be removed to gain parachutist access to the right door. In order to preclude damage to the parachutists parachute canopy by contact with the Overhead Delivery System (ODS) rails during the opening sequence, the aircraft cargo door must be open during parachute deployments. The only authorized parachute static line hook-up point is the installed anchor line cables. During WDI delivery, the door not being used will be closed unless a PJ trainer or certifier elects to have it open to conduct training or evaluations. All aircraft seats aft of FS 617 will be stowed on the side of the aircraft being deployed from prior to starting the PJ Pre-Deployment Checklist.

8.9.5.4. JM Responsibilities. JM duties can be performed from any position in either parachute door. It is recommended the JM use the right door for right-hand patterns and the left door for left-hand patterns. The safetyman will be hooked up to the personnel restraint system. The JM will use either a personnel parachute or the personnel restraint system. When using a parachute, the JM will hook-up his static line forward of the center overhead anchor line cable support. A static line restrainer will be used to hold the JM's static line (if the JM is not the first parachutist) to the rear against the overhead anchor line cable support and clear of exiting parachutists. The static line restrainer will be looped around the support at FS 770 below the cargo door uplock manual release lever, and hooked to the anchor cable forward of static lines to be restrained. If the parachutists are to exit using a JM selected exit point, the team leader may elect to have a JM who will not deploy, but stay with the aircraft. This will preclude a parachutist who is suited up with cumbersome gear from having to perform JM duties.

WARNING: Prior to opening the ramp, cargo door, or paratroop door, all personnel aft of FS 617 will be wearing a restraint harness with the safety line properly attached to the aircraft, a parachute with the static line attached to the anchor cable, or a seat belt when seated in a troop seat. Exception: Parachutists with reserve parachutes properly installed may proceed aft of FS 617 for the sole purpose of hooking their static lines to the anchor line cable. Parachutists wearing freefall parachutes may proceed aft of FS 617, if the aircraft is 1000 AGL or above, to perform jump duties.

8.9.5.5. Inflight Visual/Verbal Signals. The JM will visually relay steering signals to the loadmaster, who will verbally relay the signals to the pilot. The JM may spot from the aircraft ramp or paratroop door. If exit of jumpers becomes unsafe (aircraft emergency or similar circumstances), the aircrew will turn on the red light and the loadmaster will direct the JM to stop remaining parachutists. After turning "final," the JM will advise the pilot when the PI is in sight and when he is going off intercom. One minute prior to the navigator's release point, the copilot will indicate "Clear to Drop" by turning on the "green" jump light. When the JM is not the first parachutist to exit, he will move to the aft edge of the door and signal the first parachutist to assume his deployment door position by slapping the deployment platform with his hand. The JM will move clear of the door to give clear access to the deploying Parachutists. Parachutist will not exit the aircraft unless the "green" light is illuminated.

 NOTE: During scuba/SPUDS/oversized equipment parachute deployments, parachutists fully mission equipped may remain seated with seatbelts fastened until the wind drift device has been deployed. Seating should be opposite the deployment exit. All equipment including the reserve parachute should be worn while seated to preclude unnecessary delays. Parachutists will stand up, hook up, and be checked prior to final approach.

8.9.5.6. Safetyman Responsibilities. The safetyman is responsible for monitoring the JM's static line until he exits, and each following parachutist's static line after they approach the door to exit and pass the static line to him. When the JM is not deploying first, he will determine who (himself or the safetyman) has responsibility for monitoring the parachutists static lines as they exit. During instruction or evaluation, the safetyman may be required to monitor a PJ trainers' or certifiers' static line when they are aiding or observing the JM's duty performance. The trainer/certifier may assist by monitoring the JM's static line. The safetyman will relay all hand signals given by the JM. The safetyman will assist in the delivery of supporting equipment. He will recover the deployment bags of deployed parachutists. If the JM did not deploy , he must monitor his own static line during deployment bag recovery.

8.9.5.7. Parachutists Responsibilities. When two or more parachutists are to be deployed, each parachutist is responsible for monitoring his own static line. Once the static line is hooked to the anchor line cable, parachutists will remain standing and avoid movement away from the anchor line cable except to jump. The parachutists will line up from the paratroop door forward either in file or slightly staggered paralleling the side of the aircraft and the respective anchor line cable. This is necessary to avoid excessive static line from playing out which would create an exit hazard to the parachutists. By staggering the file, as many as six fully mission-equipped parachutists can be safely lined up in the space between the paratroop door and the Benson fuel tank. Three fully equipped scuba parachutists can fit in the same space. When parachuting from the left door, the parachutist's static line will be over the left shoulder and held in the left hand. When parachuting from the right door, the parachutist's static line will be over the right shoulder and held in the right hand. The parachutist will form a bight in the static line of approximately four to six inches and hold it to his front. The remainder of the static line will be carried over the shoulder with all excess stowed in the static line retainer bands to reduce any possibility of entanglement.

WARNING: Parachutists must exercise caution as they approach and prepare to exit the door to avoid becoming entangled with their own static line or the static lines of proceeding parachutists. To preclude entanglement; as much static line as possible will be stowed in the retainer bands; parachutists will pass, not throw their static lines to the safetyman; and each parachutist must use caution to ensure other static lines do not entangle his hand.

8.9.5.8. Towed Parachutist . Towed parachutists on an actual tactical mission will be recovered into the aircraft. By the time the parachutist could be identified as towed, conscious and capable of deploying a usable reserve, the aircraft would be off the DZ. If cut away, the towed parachutist could compromise the security of the team and the mission. Plan for a safe area for cut-away of a towed parachutist if retrieval is not possible. These procedures must be briefed to the aircraft commander prior to flight.

8.10. Freefall Deployment Procedures.

8.10.1. General guidance on how to jumpmaster specific aircraft types is found in Army FM 31-19. All static line parachute procedures apply to freefall except as noted here and in Army FM 31-19 and AFI 11-410.

8.10.2. C-130 Aircraft.

8.10.2.1. The ramp or paratroop doors (single or double door) may be used for deployment for freefall parachutists. Deployment platforms are not necessary.

8.10.2.2. Loadmaster Requirements.

8.10.2.2.1. Two loadmasters will be used on actual equipment deployments utilizing the ramp and door.

8.10.2.2.2. Two loadmasters will be used on all HALO personnel deployments (13,000 feet MSL and above).

8.10.2.2.3. One loadmaster may be used on HALO personnel deployments (up to 13,000 feet MSL) when utilizing the ramp and door, or only one paratroop door.

8.10.3. H-1 Aircraft. Freefall parachutists may use either door or both doors simultaneously for deployment. When opened, the doors will be pinned in the open position.

8.10.4. H-60 Aircraft. Freefall parachutists may use either door or both doors simultaneously for deployment. Parachutist will use caution when exiting the right door if the internal rescue hoist is installed. Deployment position may be standing (bent over at the waist).

8.10.5. Other Aircraft. When using aircraft other than those listed for deployment of freefall parachutists, the procedures outlined in TO 14D1-2-1-121, unit OI's for contract use of civilian aircraft, and the appropriate operations regulations will be used.

8.10.6. VMC Restrictions. All freefall parachute deployments using wind drift devices for wind drift determination will be restricted to VMC weather conditions at deployment altitude. When the target is obscured, the JM can deploy himself or other parachutists if he has at least two known points in sight for cross-reference and is familiar with the DZ.

8.11. Deployment to a Vessel. The many factors affecting the decision to deploy a team to vessels at sea preclude the establishment of a single procedure that will apply to all situations. In all cases, thorough pre-deployment planning and coordination with the recovery vessel is vital to a safe and successful operation. The following will provide guidelines and considerations:

8.11.1. In sea conditions other than calm, it is essential that large vessels, where boarding may be difficult, have a small motorized launch in the water prior to team deployment. Alternatively, if deploying a boat, the team should inform and coordinate the boat and personnel requirements with the captain of the vessel.

8.11.2. Positioning/maneuvering of the ship and the launch is the captain's decision. However when possible, the rescue team should coordinate with the captain prior to deployment. The PJ Team Leader should consider the following:

8.11.2.1. Can the vessel/ship remain stationary in the water?

8.11.2.2. Will the vessel/ship be steered into the wind, crosswind, or other direction?

8.11.2.3. Where will the launch be positioned?

8.11.2.4. What are the procedures for boarding the vessel from the launch?

8.11.2.5. If deploying a boat with the team, can the boat safely be brought along side for boarding and can it be moored or retrieved?

8.11.3. The JM should deploy the team to the launch. The launch should remain in position during the deployment pattern. A marking device may be dropped in the water to mark the intended DZ and the launch requested to position itself upwind of the marker.

8.11.4. The method of recovering the team from a launch to the vessel is the vessel captains decision. However, the PJ team will ensure that a suitable means of boarding is available.

WARNING: Any time a team member is in the water alongside a vessel, the vessel's propellers should be shut down or placed in neutral.

8.11.5. In the rare case a decision is made to deploy the team without the use of a motorized launch, the team should land upwind and drift/swim to the vessel. An alternative/extra safety measure, may be to have the ship put a raft/launch on a securing line to the stern of the vessel and pick-up the parachutist similar to the method a water-skier is retrieved/given a line in recreational boating.

8.11.6. Other items to be considered by the JM include:

8.11.6.1. Does the mission require SCUBA/SPUDS tanks? SCUBA/SPUDS should always be considered as an option as it enhances parachutists safety in the water and allows the PJ to work on the RAMZ package underwater if required.

8.11.6.2. Do low visibility conditions require additional parachutist /bundle lighting?

8.11.6.3. Is an additional life raft needed for PJ equipment? This may prevent the unnecessary loss of equipment.

8.11.6.4. What action is to be taken if ship boarding is not possible after deployment?

8.12. Parachute Deployment Documentation.

8.12.1. AF Form 922, Individual Jump Record provides a certified record of parachute deployment qualification and experience, and is the prime document in the Jump Record Folder. This form is maintained IAW instructions found in AFI 11-401, Flight Management and AFI 11-410, Personnel Parachute Operations.

8.12.2. For all assigned parachutists the following definitions for jump types and deployment conditions will be utilized, until incorporated in AFI 11-410, when completing the AF Form 922:

8.12.2.1. Deployment Types:

8.12.2.1.1. Administrative (A) - Any non-tactical or non-operational parachute deployment accomplished only for proficiency pay purposes.

8.12.2.1.2. High Altitude High Opening (H) - Any freefall deployment from medium or high altitude with a parachute opening of medium or high altitude.

8.12.2.1.3. Ejection Seat (J) - Any parachute deployment performed from an ejection seat bailout.

8.12.2.1.4. High Altitude Low Opening (L) - Any freefall deployment without the use of a static line.

8.12.2.1.5. Mass Tactical (M) - Any parachute deployment which includes more than one parachutist per pass and the parachutists are deploying on an actual operation/mission or on a training mission in which a tactical event is included.

8.12.2.1.6. Tactical (T) - Any parachute deployment with one parachutist per pass and the parachutist is deploying on an actual operation/mission or on a training mission in which a tactical event is included.

8.12.2.1.7. Experimental or Test (X) - Any parachute deployment performed as part of an official Air Force test or experiment of parachute systems/equipment.

8.12.2.1.8. Other (Y) - Any parachute deployment that does not meet the requirements of any other deployment type.

8.12.2.2. Deployment Conditions:

8.12.2.2.1. Combat (C)- Any parachute deployment performed under actual combat conditions.

8.12.2.2.2. Equipment (E) - Any parachute deployment performed where the parachutist deploys with mission equipment.

8.12.2.2.3. Freefall (F) - Any parachute deployment performed without the use of a static line.

8.12.2.2.4. Night (N) - Any parachute deployment performed between the start of evening civil twilight and the end of morning civil twilight in which the center of the sun's disk is less than six degrees below the horizon.

8.12.2.2.5. Oxygen (O) - Any parachute deployment performed with the use of an oxygen mask and oxygen equipment.

8.12.2.2.6. Scuba (S) - Any parachute deployment performed with the use of an underwater breathing apparatus.

8.12.2.2.7. Water (W) - Any intentional parachute deployment performed into a body of water.

Chapter 9

ALTERNATE INSERTION AND EXTRACTION METHODS

9.1. Purpose. This section establishes the general guidelines and procedures for insertion and extraction by rotary wing aircraft. The diversity of missions, organizations, and theater of operations require this section to be general in nature to cover all aspects of insertion and extraction. Specific procedures such as anchor points and altitude restrictions are contained in the Model Design Series (MDS). Insertion and extraction is normally accomplished using the air-land method. Other methods of insertion and extraction may be necessary to accomplish the mission and are sometimes referred to as alternate insertion and extraction (AIE). The techniques described in this chapter may be accomplished day or night. The information contained in this chapter is not all-inclusive.

9.2. Qualification and Training. Pararescuemen will train and qualify IAW this section, unit SOPs, and applicable references. Prior to participating in specific insertion and extraction operations, personnel will be thoroughly briefed and trained on the method, purpose, capabilities, limitations, and emergency procedures. The briefing will include duties and responsibilities of the Aircraft Commander (AC), the Person In-Charge (PIC) of the specific deployment method, AIE Master, PJ team leader, and team member responsibilities.

9.2.1. Initial/Familiarization Training. Initial training should be IAW with the objectives defined in the CFETP. Prior to conducting actual aircraft operations, it is recommended a training tower be used. Personnel qualified in AIE methods that are newly assigned, or have not conducted training on unit specific aircraft should receive familiarization training.

 NOTE: Any object/structure may be used as a training tower for AIE operations as long as: (1) base Real Property/Safety personnel, Pararescue unit commanders, and PJ Superintendents have approved objects/structures use as an AIE training tower IAW AFI safety requirements. (2) proper installation of anchor system is accomplished and inspected IAW inspection requirements, and (3) all personnel are properly trained in the safe use of AIE training tower for AIE operations.

9.3. AIE Master Responsibilities. Use standard certification to document (AF Form 803, Report of Task Evaluations) AIE Master qualification. As a minimum, the AIE master is responsible for:

9.3.1. Obtaining and inspecting necessary equipment.

9.3.2. Aircraft inspection/preparation.

9.3.3. Installation of equipment.

9.3.4. Command and signal.

9.3.5. Briefing aircrew on:

9.3.5.1. Type of operation.

9.3.5.2. Location of Insertion/Extraction point

9.3.5.3. Direction of approach.

9.3.5.4. Altitude.

9.3.5.5. Actual Combat Load (ACL).

9.3.5.6. Number of iterations required/personnel involved.

9.3.5.7. Station/load time.

9.3.5.8. Interphone/communication requirements.

9.3.5.9. Cabin configuration (day/night).

9.3.5.10. Aircraft lighting.

9.3.5.11. Hand and arm signals.

9.3.5.12. Assistance required.

9.3.5.13. Emergency procedures.

9.4. Planning Considerations.

9.4.1. Determining if an AIE is necessary is a critical factor in pre-mission planning. The team should determine if the increased difficulty of performing an AIE is justified, when compared with the risks or benefits of moving the survivor to a new location. Performing an AIE requires additional power available, demands greater crew coordination, increases exposure time, and is more hazardous and difficult for the survivor. However, in certain situations, moving the survivor may be impractical or more hazardous than an AIE would be to the crew.

9.4.2. Alternate Loading Operations. Alternate loading procedures are normally used during contingency operations and tactical training missions when standard passenger seating reduces the crew's ability to accomplish the mission effectively. The cabin floor itself is defined as the seat and either a seatbelt or personal restraint device restrains the occupants. Alternate loading expedites team deployment/recovery, maximizes cabin space, and allows maneuverability of the team during mission execution. Restrain all personnel by the safest means possible for the type mission flown. Restraints may be removed upon landing in the landing zone (LZ) or while taxiing to the off-load point. For hover operations (including water ops), restraint devices are removed as required.

9.4.3. Restraining Devices. Troop seats are the primary method of securing personnel. The primary alternate load method used by most teams is the alternate load belt. The secondary alternate load method is fastening the troop seat seatbelts to the floor tiedown rings. The least desired alternate load method uses a cargo tiedown strap. The tiedown strap is fastened to the floor tiedown rings and run across the lap. When using this method, it is best to be facing forward to absorb the most common displacement of aircraft maneuvering or a crash landing.

9.4.4. Equipment. The team leader/AIE is responsible for coordinating with the mission support aircraft to determine the equipment necessary to conduct the operation and will coordinate with the aircrew on installation and inspection of the system(s) prior to use. Aircraft space requirements must be pre-coordinated to facilitate the removal of aircraft seats or equipment. Equipment will be serviceable and meet safety requirements. Equipment required for each specific AIE will be addressed in the procedure section of this section.

NOTE: A helmet is required for all land AIEs where multiple iterations are planned. If the intent of the mission is to perform and AIE and move to an objective, then a helmet is not required. Helmet should always be considered for training when evaluating ORM. When the AIE is accomplished in the water and you are not wearing a helmet, lighting may be attached to your personal floatation device in a manner that will not interfere with inflation.

9.4.5. Ensure intercom cords are clear of pathways. Route them up the walls, along ceilings, and down from above to the safetyman. The team leader's cord should only be long enough for necessary movements. Ensure gunner belts are clear of personnel and paths of travel. The V-Blade knife or other similar tool should be readily available to use if the ropes need to be cut during aircraft emergencies or rope entanglement. If overhead support straps are required, the straps are cargo tiedown straps or locally produced straps hooked to the overhead litter strap rings to help balance the deploying individuals. When using floor straps and seats are removed, rig according to appropriate alternate loading procedures.

9.4.6. To facilitate night insertion/extraction operations, the chemlight configurations listed in Table 9.1. are recommended. Activate chemlite attached to insertion/extraction equipment at or prior to the five-minute out call. Remember that blue chemlites are hard to see under NVGs and should not be used to mark your location on the ground or in the water during night helicopter operations.

Table 9.1. Chemlight Configurations.

Operation	Chemlight Configuration ,
Rappel	1 green stick on the top of the drop sack
Fast Rope	2 red sticks at the bottom of the rope 1 red stick 10 feet from the bottom 1 green or blue stick at the top of the rope
Rope Ladder	1 red stick on each side of the ladder at the bottom and 5 feet up from the bottom of the ladder. Note: Chemlites should be placed perpendicular on the lateral sides of the ladder
Hoist	1 red stick on bottom of each forest penetrator paddle
Stokes Litter	2 red sticks on head, one on foot
SPIE	2 red sticks at the bottom of the rope and 1 red stick 3 feet from the first set of D-rings

9.4.7. Ensure the aircrew keeps the team informed of position and distance to the LZ. Standard announcements of "time remaining to the LZ" at the 20, 10, 5, and 1minute out points greatly aids in preparation for the AIE. Employ these calls regardless of the specific type of AIE.

9.5. General Contingencies/Emergency Procedures.

9.5.1. When unsafe conditions are encountered, stop any additional team members deploying from the aircraft using appropriate hand signals. Make no attempt to physically stop a person in the act of deploying as this may cause the person to lose grip of the rope and increase the probability of injury to the team member.

9.5.2. If the helicopter experiences an engine malfunction or other critical emergency during any AIE operation, the team should descend as rapidly as possible and move from beneath the helicopter. Normally personnel move away from the deploying side of the helicopter (terrain permitting). The helicopter should move away from the team to a safe area. If the aircraft gains altitude or starts to fly away, the ropers attempt to reach the ground and dismount. If the team cannot dismount the device, personnel should stop their descent and lock-in. When terrain does not permit flying out with the team attached, the aircraft commander must make the call whether to cut the ropes free.

9.5.3. If the aircraft comes under fire, the deploying team may consider securing themselves to the device so the aircraft can depart the immediate area. The aircraft will accomplish slow forward flight to a safe area if flight characteristics and power requirements allow.

WARNING: The team leader should conduct a thorough briefing on team security procedures to prevent individuals manning aircraft weapons systems from inadvertently firing on the team.

NOTE: Procedures for recall must be pre-briefed and understood by all members of the crew and team.

9.6. Rope/Rappel/Cast Master. The rope/rappel/cast master is the deploying team leader, and is responsible for making the final determination on the safety of the deployment. During operations where the rope master cannot safely determine operational parameters (aircraft altitude, drift, obstacles, and rope position), the rope master should coordinate with the safetyman for assistance.

9.7. Air Land Operations. Air land operations provide the fastest and most desirable means of all rotary wing insertion and extraction methods. This method limits exposure to threat from enemy observation and engagement due to relatively short time periods in the area. Security and safety of the team is usually enhanced.

9.7.1. Rotary wing tactical off-loads. Proper tactical on-load planning and procedures improves speed, efficiency, and safety during tactical on-loads. Rotary wing procedures for planning, alternate load, and off-load, all follow the same general guidance as fixed wing. Differences are in the vehicle tiedown procedures and what can fit where.

9.7.1.1. Vehicles. Vehicles are normally secured with a minimum of four tiedown straps. For larger aircraft, occupy the off-load vehicle and start engine at the one-minute call. After landing, the scanners remove the tiedown straps from vehicle, ensure the ramp is down, and clear you for deployment. For smaller aircraft, offloading the vehicles prior to starting engines may be required.

9.7.1.2. All Terrain Vehicle (ATVs). For H-53 helicopters, a total of 6 ATVs (two ATVs fit side by side) in the cargo compartment (possibly 7 with one in the center of the cabin next to the avionics rack). With the HH-60, 2 ATVs fit side by side, depending on mission and cabin space. Ensure ramps are available for off-load of ATVs from the HH-60 door.9.7.1.3. Motorcycles. Depending on the room available, secure motorcycles along the sides of the aircraft cabin wall. Secure motorcycle with a minimum of one tiedown strap. Tighten the tiedown strap so the motorcycle suspension is completely compressed.

9.7.2. Rotary Wing Tactical On Loads. Proper tactical on-load planning and procedures improves speed, efficiency, and safety during tactical on-loads.

9.7.2.1. Load location selection.

9.7.2.1.1. The load location for remote, unimproved surface helicopter landing zones (HLZs), is usually the touchdown point. When loading litter patients or other heavy items, ground marshaling to move the aircraft from the touchdown point to the load can expedite exfil. Load locations on improved surfaces can take place at the touchdown point or at predetermined parking/load locations.

9.7.2.1.2. Designated HLZs for multiple aircraft landings must be strictly controlled to ensure proper aircraft separation, approach, and landing. Aircraft may be required to clear the HLZ immediately for follow-on landings of additional aircraft. When this is required, aircraft either taxi on their own or are marshalled to their parking/load locations.

9.7.2.1.3. Personnel Accountability. When conducting on-load operations, the team leader is usually the first to arrive at the aircraft. Upon arrival he should immediately connect into the aircraft interphone system and advise the pilot on any critical information about the area. Afterwards he conducts a head-count of embarking personnel. Once all personnel are accounted for he loads onto the aircraft and notifies the crew in preparation for takeoff.

9.7.2.1.4. Aircraft entry and securing equipment/personnel.

9.7.2.1.4.1. A special consideration for helicopter entry is the hazard associated with the main and tail rotor clearance. A sloped HLZ can drastically reduce rotor clearance on the up hillside while most tail rotors are already low enough to be a direct hazard.

9.7.2.1.4.2. Before entering under the rotor plane wait for a signal by a crewmember to ensure the aircraft is settled and ready to receive you. Approach the aircraft with weapons pointed down and on safe. Radio antennas must be collapsed to avoid contact with the rotors. If troop seats are unavailable, use alternate load methods.

9.7.3. HLZ Operations. Within their range limitations, helicopters provide an excellent means of insertion, extraction, and evacuation from operational areas. Their advantages include landing in relatively small areas, discharge of personnel and cargo without landing and the ability to fly safely and efficiently at low altitudes. Some unfavorable characteristics of helicopters are noise, rotor induced dust, snow, water clouds may compromise security of location, and changes in atmospheric conditions affect the lift capability of the aircraft. PJ duties during HLZ operations may include selecting the site, securing the perimeter, clearing obstacles, building a landing pad, establishing the appropriate landing signals, establishing radio communications with the aircraft, and giving landing clearance or go around information to the pilot. When the type of extraction aircraft is known, review HLZ criteria for the specific MDS aircraft. The following information provides general rules and guidelines for HLZ operations.

9.7.3.1. HLZ Selection. HLZ selection requires consideration of many factors. HLZ surface, size, or other criteria is based on helicopter MDS, use the following only as guidelines when no other documentation exists or type of aircraft is unknown. The tactical situation limits extraction locations by preventing aircraft access. Placement of the HLZ should provide the aircraft with the best opportunity for success.

9.7.3.1.1. HLZ size is determined by the space required for the touch down point and rotor clearance of the aircraft. Touch down point refers to the area required for the landing gear arrangement of the specific model aircraft. This area can be quite small relative to the total aircraft size but should include an additional 10 feet each direction for safety. A suitable touchdown point should be cleared to the ground and be firm enough to prevent the aircraft from becoming bogged down. It will also need to be free of loose dirt or snow that can be blown into a dense cloud around the aircraft when its rotor wash hits it.

9.7.3.1.2. HLZ surfaces should be as close to level as possible. The surface should be relatively level and free of obstructions such as rocks, logs, tall grass, ditches, and fences. Heavy dust or loose snow can interfere with pilot vision just before touchdown. Ground slope must be considered and must be firm enough to support the aircraft. A sloping grade of greater than seven percent becomes difficult for the pilot and should be avoided. A 15 percent grade is beyond most helicopter landing capabilities. Leveling or building a landing pad may be required. Helicopters without the use of special flotation equipment may land in water provided: the water depth does not exceed 12 inches; a firm bottom such as gravel or sand exists; and submerged objects can not penetrate the tires of fuselage. When considering how long the approach/take-off path should be, use the climb ratio of 1:5.

9.7.3.1.3. Clearance for the aircraft's body and rotors requires a much larger area than does the landing gear. The standard minimum size criteria for a landing area is two rotor diameters. All vegetation or obstacles should be cleared to a maximum of 3 feet above ground level. Multi-ship operations require the addition of at least one rotor disc spacing between the helicopters. Remove any lightweight materials in and around the HLZ that might be blown by the rotor wash. This will reduce the possibility of damage to the aircraft or injury to team/personnel on the ground.. Below is a list of rotor spans for some commonly used helicopters.

Table 9.2. Helicopter Rotor Spans.

AIRCRAFT	ROTOR SPAN (FEET)
AH-6 "LITTLE BIRD"	27
AH-64 APACHE	46
AH-I COBRA	48
UH-1 HUEY	48
UH-60 BLACKHAWK	54
MH-53 PAVELOW	67
CH-47 CHINOOK	60 X 99

9.7.3.1.4. Far recognition signal. Prepare a far recognition signal to alert the aircraft to your location. Typical far recognition signals include but are not limited to; signal mirrors, smoke, strobe lights, bright colored panels, etc. Alerting an aircraft to your position can also be accomplished with radio vectoring.

9.7.3.1.5. Near recognition signal. Helicopter operations can be conducted with little or no HLZ markings; however, marking is suggested for rapid exfil. Near recognition signals are often used for team authentication and giving the aircraft a reference point for landing. Near recognition signals can be as simple as standing in front of the intended HLZ or using a HLZ pattern. You can assist the aircraft further by providing wind direction with your near signal by using smoke/streamers. If smoke is used to assist in HLZ recognition/wind determination, place it to the side or downwind of the landing area so as not to interfere with the pilot's visibility during the approach or landing.

9.7.3.1.6. HLZ patterns. Marking an HLZ with a LZ pattern informs the pilot of the prevailing winds, the best area for touchdown, and whether the approach path they are taking is correct. Because LZ patterns present a specific landing location, their use can prevent a delayed on-load. Night HLZ marking is not required for NVG operations, but like day operations, it is advisable. Lights can also provide HLZ authentication, identify the touchdown area, and aid the pilot in his approach. The standard marking patterns are the "Inverted Y" pattern, and the "T" pattern.

9.8. Hoist Operations. Hoist operations provide a controlled means of descent as well as ascent. There are many different ways to employ the hoist. Capabilities and limitations of the hoist are dependent on the manufacturer. Prior to conducting operations, it is the responsibility of each PJ to understand the capabilities and limitations of the type hoist being used. As a minimum, they must know the maximum load, cable shear procedures, general control and function, and emergency procedures. The primary hoist operator is the flight engineer; however, a PJ may be designated when the mission dictates. During live hoist training/exercises, personnel should wear goggles and a helmet when riding the hoist. The aircrew or PROTEC-type helmet may be used.

9.8.1. Rescue Devices. The PJ team and crew determine which device to use.

NOTE: Rescue devices used for hoist training will be identical to and configured the same as operational equipment. If live hoist training is to be conducted, only operational equipment will be used.

9.8.1.1. Climbing Harness. The climbing or body harness is the method of choice for hoist insert into all environments. A Swiss seat, climbing harness, or body harness provides a secure attachment point for hoist operations in lieu of other devices.

9.8.1.2. Forest Penetrator. The forest penetrator is used for single or multiple recoveries from land or water. Description and maintenance instructions are found in TO 14S6-3-1 and TO 00-25-245, Section 4.

9.8.1.3. Stokes Litter. The stokes litter is constructed of mesh and lightweight steel tubing that holds a survivor immobile in a supine position. The sides of the litter protect the survivor from bumping against obstructions or the side of the helicopter during retrieval. The stokes litter should be configured with sling, flotation devices (if required), and three restraining belts when stowed on the aircraft. A tag line should be available if the stokes is used. Construction, modification, inspection, and maintenance instructions are contained in TO 00-75-5.

9.8.1.3.1. Tag Line. The tag line is a rope of varied construction and length with the purpose of being deployed to surface personnel in confined or obstructed areas. It is used to prevent pendulum or spinning motion of the rescue device caused by rotor wash during hoisting. It may also be used to guide the rescue device or survivor to or from confined areas, such as ships, trees, or canyon areas. The tag line may aid the pilot during water operations by reducing time required to hover directly over small watercraft without a reference.

9.8.1.3.2. A weight should be attached to the end of the tag line without the weak link. This keeps it from being blown about by the rotor wash and gives the crewmember better control delivering the line to a confined or restricted surface position. The weak link end of the tag line may be fastened to the hoist hook or the rescue device, before the device goes out the door.

NOTE: The weak link is created using a single loop of gutted 550 cord or two wraps of 80 pound test tape between the rope end and carabiner

NOTE: A pair of leather work gloves should be provided with the tag line for personnel other than the team.

9.8.1.3.3. To deliver the tag line to a large vessel with a restricted pickup area, the tag line should be lowered after the helicopter is in a hover over the vessel.

9.8.1.3.4. Once the tag line is on the ground/vessel and the team/boat crew is tending it, the hoist operator will direct the pilot clear of the survivor/vessel while paying out slack in the tag line. The tag line weak link will be attached to the rescue device. When the pilot can again see the survivor/vessel, the hoist operator begins to lower the hoist. At this point the team/ship-board personnel use the tag line to guide the rescue device into the desired location.

9.8.1.3.5. When the rescue device is on the ground/vessel's deck and the survivor is ready for hoisting, the hoist operator gives directions to position the helicopter back over the survivor/deck. Retrieving the rescue device vertically may not always be possible. Be aware of this and be prepared to recover the rescue device at an angle. However, when conditions permit, recover the rescue device vertically. As soon as the survivor is clear of the deck or obstructions, the hoist operator clears the helicopter away from the obstacles/vessel, usually left or back. The crew maintains this position until the survivor is in the cabin and the tag line is either retrieved or discarded, and the crewmember has reported ready for forward flight.

9.8.1.3.6. The tag line may be used in lieu of the hoist cable to lower small items to a boat. The item to be lowered will be attached to the snap link with a weight. Use the same procedure for delivery of the tag line to small and large vessels. The weak link end of the tag line will be attached to a cabin tiedown ring.

9.8.1.4. Tag Line Procedures. Tag line procedures should always be used to prevent and control spinning, pendulums, and/or and oscillation. There are times when use of a tag line may be impractical (i.e. night water hoist missions). When used in these situations, always ensure a weak link has been installed at the stokes litter attachment point.

9.8.1.4.1. For aircraft with skis installed, attach the tag line to the head of litter, as opposed to the foot This allows the tag line attendant to avoid the worst of the helicopters rotor wash. When PJs utilize the barrelman technique for survivor rescue and recovery, PJs are able to ensure the tag line does not become entangled with the skis.

NOTE: The use of the tag line should be considered carefully for its benefits against spinning, pendulum, and oscillation over having to move the tag line attendant into the rotor wash or having the line becoming entangled with PJs in the water, trees, skis, etc.

9.8.1.4.2. When rappelling the PJs in prior to the stokes litter, the rappel rope can then be quickly used as a tag line provided, a carabiner with a weak link has been attached to the foot or head end of the stokes litter

9.8.1.5. Rescue Net. The rescue net is constructed of stainless steel tube frame and 5/16-inch polypropylene netting. The net weighs approximately 20 pounds. A sea anchor drogue is provided to position and stabilize the net and allow for flight path corrections. The sea anchor drogue may be replaced by a 10-foot line with a 3- to 5-pound bag of shot for stability. The rescue net is particularly useful for recovery of personnel not familiar with the forest penetrator or rescue strop. Because entry is easier and more rapid for a survivor than a forest penetrator, it is perhaps the best device for recovery of survivors from frigid waters. The disadvantage is the size of the device.

9.8.1.6. Rescue Strap (Horse Collar). The survivor's sling is a buoyant device constructed of a fiber filling encased in a waterproof cover. Webbing, woven through the cover with both ends terminating in two v-rings, is used to attach the sling to the hoist hook. Two retainer straps, one long with a quick ejector snap, and one short with a v-ring, are provided for personnel security. Information on the rescue strap is found in NAVAIR 13-1-1-6.5. The strap can be used to lower a rescuer, as well as raise a survivor over land or water. The rescue strap is useful in all environments except the forest or jungle where it can get snagged on branches stopping its deployment.

WARNING: This is not a good device for injured or questionable survivors that could accidentally slip out of the device.

9.8.2. Execution. If possible, establish a right-hand rectangular pattern with the final approach oriented into the wind. This aids in keeping the survivor in sight while preparing for pickup. The pilot should keep the crew informed of the helicopter's position in the pattern and the hoist operator advises the pilot when ready to deploy smokes or accomplish the pickup.

9.8.2.1. Hoist retrievals from trees must be slow enough to allow survivors to fend off branches and prevent cable entanglement. Radio communication or pre-briefed signals for lost visual procedures should be briefed prior to deployment. It may be possible for a crewmember on the hoist to recover the survivor without disconnecting from the device. Maximum loading of the hoist cable should not occur unless critical to mission accomplishment.

9.8.2.2. Crew briefings should include actions to be taken in the event of equipment malfunctions or impending failures. During training missions, terminate live hoisting immediately at the first indication of equipment malfunction. Existing circumstances will dictate actions to be taken, if required, the individual may be returned to the surface by lowering the aircraft.

9.8.2.3. Ensure cable slack is held to the minimum necessary to perform the recovery. Excessive slack can be especially dangerous during water recovery when the hoist operator cannot see the cable.

CAUTION: Exercise caution to keep from anchoring the hoist hook or cable around an immovable object.

9.8.2.4. Cable shock loading can occur when the cable is subjected to a sudden heavy loads (i.e., entanglement, stokes litter being caught by waves, or weights being rapidly applied). The effects of shock loading are worse when the device is close to the full up position when the loading occurs.

WARNING: Cables suspected of shock loading will be reported to the crew and replaced IAW published directives.

9.8.2.5. The hoist should be grounded prior to pickup to discharge static electricity to prevent being shocked. To preclude ignition of fuel, the hoist should not be grounded near spilled fuel from damaged aircraft or vehicles.

9.8.2.6. Severe oscillations/pendulum may occur when the hoist cable is raised and lowered without a weight attached. Be prepared to be lowered or the aircraft to transition to forward flight to correct.

9.8.2.7. When pulling the survivor into the helicopter, the easiest method is to turn the survivor's back to the helicopter and pull in. This reduces the possibility of semiconscious or injured survivor fighting the hoist operator.

9.8.3. Water Hoist Operations.

9.8.3.1. Day Water Hoist. While in the water, prepare a signaling device to assist the aircraft in locating your position and don a facemask to shield your eyes from the rotor wash. After sighting you, the aircraft will maneuver to approximately 100 feet downwind and make a low reconnaissance pass over your position. Once past you, the pilot may initiate a climbing right turn and deploy a sea dye or smoke marker to act as a hover reference during the hoist operation. The pick-up will normally be on the following pass, depending on the hover reference device

9.8.3.2. Night Water Hoist.

9.8.3.2.1. The aircraft may deploy chemlites to mark survivor/PJ location and provide them an approach pattern and hover references. This will also ensure you can be reacquired if the hoist pattern is flown wider than intended. You can also mark your position with an IR strobe, chemlights, or a flashlight.

9.8.3.2.2. NVG water operations are more difficult for the aircrew to accomplish than other hoist operations because of reduced light, lack of hover references, and reduced field of vision from NVGs. You will have difficulty seeing due to the darkness and rotor wash. Be on alert for the hoist devices to prevent injury to you or the survivor. Be aware of the hoist cable around you and the survivor in the water to prevent entanglement.

9.8.3.2.3. Signals From Swimmer to Helicopter. For successful night water extraction, pre-brief swimmer to helicopter signals that indicate ready for pickup and for immediate emergency extraction. One method used in night operations is for the PJs to turn on strobe lights when ready for pickup. Once the rescue device starts its decent the PJs turn off their strobes. Another method used during heavy seas or periods of low visibility is for the PJs to leave their strobe lights on once deployed. This will aid the crew in maintaining your position. Indicate ready to be picked up by turning off the strobes for a brief period, then follow the procedures listed above.

9.8.4. Forest Penetrator:

9.8.4.1. Fold the seat paddles and stow safety straps before lowering the penetrator through trees or dense foliage.

WARNING: The aircraft may depart the area with you still suspended on the cable. When conducting hoist operations using the Forest penetrator, keep arms down, elbows locked against the body, and do not attempt to grab the cable or weighted snap link above the device.

 NOTE: If the penetrator strap is not used (bulky equipment), use an alternate means of securing (i.e. chest strap, alternate load belt.)

9.8.4.2. For water recoveries, install the flotation collar before lowering the penetrator. Place at least one seat paddle in the down position and remove one safety strap from the stowed position. Do not unhook the safety strap fastener from the penetrator. If the penetrator is left to assist the survivor, fold the seat paddles and stow the safety straps so they will not snag on obstructions if the helicopter moves or the hoist cable has to be retrieved.

9.8.5. Stokes Litter:

9.8.5.1. To lower the stokes litter, attach the stokes litter to the cable, maneuver it outside the aircraft foot end first and then parallel to the side of the helicopter. The FE/PJ may be required to lean out of the door to maneuver the stokes litter.

 NOTE: An alternate method of lowering the stokes litter is to connect the hook to the head of the stokes litter so it hangs vertical during lowering.

9.8.5.2. Lower the stokes litter to the survivor after the helicopter is established in a hover. When raising or lowering an empty stokes litter for water recoveries, the use of the cable safety/retaining pin is not required.

9.8.5.3. Once the stokes litter is on the surface, the hoist operator should provide you slack in the hoist cable allowing you to disconnect it from the stokes litter. The aircraft can then move to a holding position while you secure the patient or hover above you. In a low threat environment it is advisable to have the helicopter move away so you can complete a patient assessment and secure the patient in the stokes litter without the added burden of noise and rotor wash.

9.8.5.4. After the survivor is secured in the stokes litter and ready for hoisting, the team reconnects the hoist cable ensuring the rescue hook safety pin and carabiner locking sleeves are properly positioned/secured. Ensure the survivor is securely strapped in the stokes litter prior to hoisting. For small patients, the belt can be routed directly across the patient. For large patients, the belt can be routed outside and over the top bar before securing the patient to the stokes litter.

9.8.5.5. Consider tag line procedures to prevent or control common problems during hoisting like pendulum, spinning, and oscillation. After the patient is secured in the stokes litter and is ready for hoisting, reconnect the hoist cable and reinstall the rescue hook safety pin. A stokes litter attendant may be required. The stokes litter attendant will hook directly into the cable hook. Always move yourself to the far side of the stokes litter from the helicopter so it is not pulled into you when it is lifted off the ground. Signal the aircraft for the pick-up.

NOTE: Installation of the snow shield on the stokes litter may result in uncontrollable spinning. Consideration should be given to the use of a tag line when the snow shield is installed.

9.8.6. Barrelman Hoist Technique

9.8.6.1. The barrelman hoist technique is a method for trained PJ personnel to attach directly to the hoist hook using a climbing harness and sling with carabiner. This method was first developed and has been in use for some time by civilian SAR agencies, primarily for having a litter attendant ride up the hoist with a stokes litter.

9.8.6.2. Equipment:

9.8.6.2.1. Climbing Harness. The PJ is securely connected to the hoist cable with an approved harness.

9.8.6.2.1.1. The climbing harness and barrelman technique can be used for both land and water. If used in water operations it is recommended a separate climbing harness be used and marked "For Water Use Only". Like all operations requiring the use of a climbing harness, inspect the harness for suitability, paying particular attention to the metal areas for corrosion and stitched areas for wear and tear. When selecting a harness for water use, the simpler the better. Continuous loop harnesses remain strong even with a single point failure.

NOTE: All sit harnesses used during salt water training will be thoroughly soaked and rinsed in fresh water immediately upon return from training.

9.8.6.2.1.2. Sit Harness. The harness should ride high on the waist area and be adjustable to fit over bulky clothing or wet/dry suits. This allows the harness to handle the bulk of the load and is the primary attachment point for the retaining strap.

9.8.6.2.1.3. Chest Harness. A chest harness may be used but is not always necessary. It is advisable to use a chest harness when performing stokes litter pick-ups or when carrying a pack or other equipment in which a PJ can become inverted. The chest harness functions primarily as a balance point, as most of the load is on the sit harness, and also prevents the PJ from becoming inverted. Substituting a carabiner through the front LBE or Pack straps is an alternative to wearing a commercial chest harness.

9.8.6.2.1.4. Retaining Strap. The primary anchor line used to attach the PJ from the sit harness to the hoist hook. Various types of retaining straps and methods are described below. Which type of retaining strap, method, or combination of retaining strap/chest harness used, will depend on the availability of equipment and type of pick-up operation that will be performed.

NOTE: The retaining strap may be used as an alternate loading belt provided a separate Pelican hook is attached to one end.

WARNING: Do not use "Pelican hooks", non-locking carabiners, or similar quick release devices on your primary anchor line/retaining strap.

9.8.6.2.1.4.1. Retaining Strap Methods and Types

9.8.6.2.1.4.1.1. Simple Tubular Nylon Strap. The retaining strap is constructed of one inch tubular nylon (or equivalent) and locking carabiners (Auto-lock recommended).

Figure 9.1. Harness Set Up.

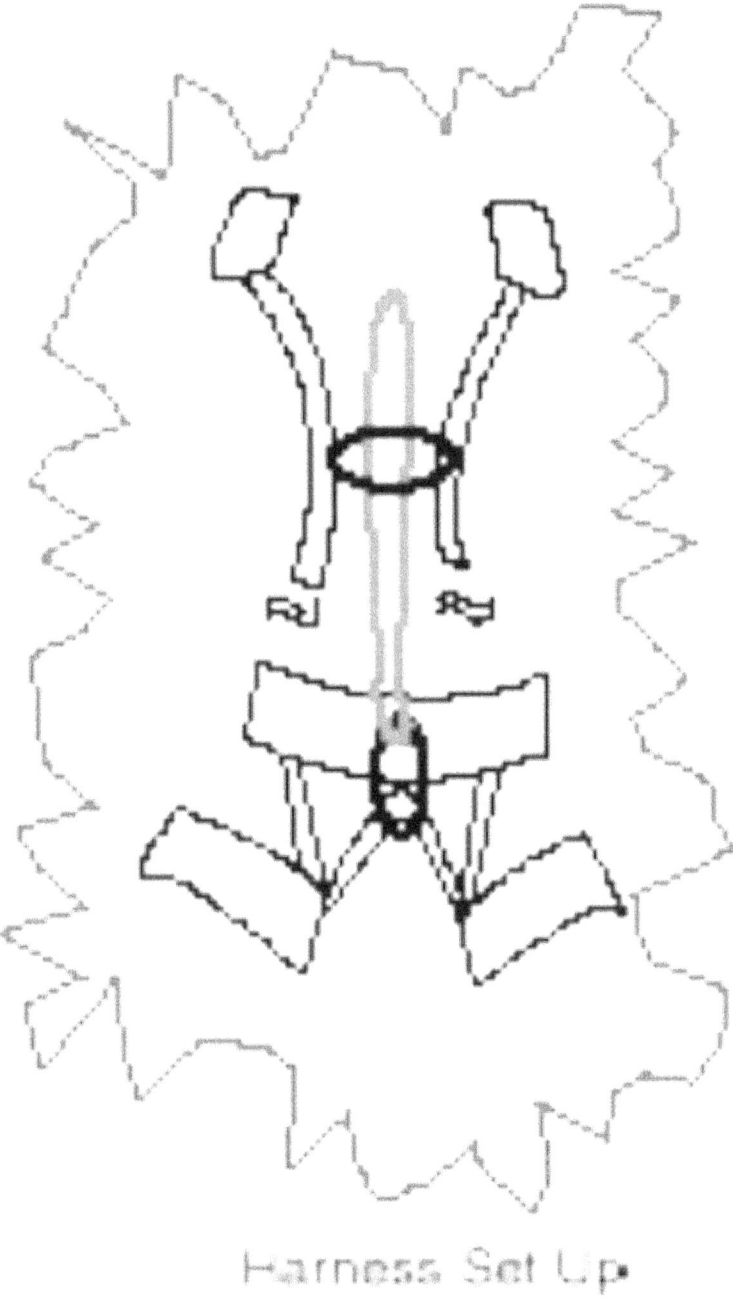

Harness Set Up

9.8.6.2.1.4.1.1.1. Typically the ends of the strap are connected to the sit harness by carabiner leaving a short loop from between the chest to chin level
depending on the PJ's body size. This allows the strap to be placed onto the
hook end of the hoist using a carabiner, or by itself, while maintaining the
proper distance once the sit-harness slack is pulled up. The strap must be
adjusted to place the PJ approximately "belly button" level to the stokes litter.
This is the desirable distance as the length of the strap is normally fixed and it

is a comfortable distance for using the strap as an alternate loading belt. The PJ may not have time to re-adjust the length.

9.8.6.2.1.4.1.1.2. Careful attention must be made to ensure the strap is the correct length prior to the operation being conducted. If the strap is too long, the PJ may be below the level of the cabin floor. If the strap is too short, the PJ's legs will not be able to reach the floor underneath the stokes litter. Size your strap on a static aircraft with the stokes litter on the ground first. If necessary, the strap may need to be adjusted after the first hoist mission to find a better position of comfort and control.

9.8.6.2.1.4.1.1.3. Running the tubular nylon strap through a carabiner attached to the LBE, chest harness, or backpack provides a balance point for stokes litter pick-ups when the backpack is worn.

9.8.6.2.1.4.1.2. Daisy Chain Strap. A daisy chain may be used instead of a tubular nylon strap. The main advantage of using a daisy chain strap is the ability to quickly size the strap for the operation involved. Additionally, the daisy chain strap provides a fixed loop for a chest area carabiner when performing stokes litter pick up while wearing a backpack.

9.8.6.2.1.4.1.2.1. Attach the daisy chain strap to the sit harness either with a looped bight through itself or a locking carabiner in one end.

9.8.6.2.1.4.1.2.2. Place a locking carabiner the correct length as determined above.

9.8.6.2.1.4.1.2.3. Attach a carabiner to the chest harness, LBE, or backpack to provide an upright position of comfort and control. It is helpful to mark these loops for future reference.

Figure 9.2. Daisy Chain Chest and Sit Harness.

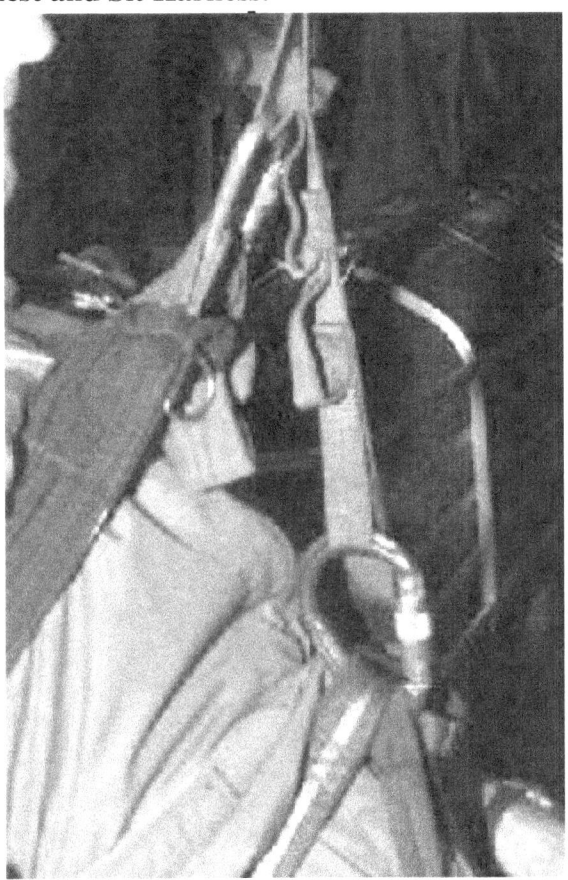

Figure 9.3. Daisy Chain to Hoist Cable Attachment.

CAUTION: All figures are shown only to show procedures and hook-up points, full safety gear must be worn

9.8.6.2.1.4.1.3. Rope Strap (Kernmantle/Perlon/Dynamic) or (Mountain-lay/Hawser-laid/Gold Line/Static) with Ascender. This is more complicated than daisy chain straps or the tubular nylon strap, but may be useful if daisy chain and tubular nylon straps are in short supply or movement inside the helicopter is desired. The ascender also facilitates quick strap length sizing in situations where proper static sizing could not be accomplished prior to the operations commencing. The rope strap may be used with or without the Jumar/Ascender instead of a tubular nylon or daisy chain straps.

9.8.6.2.1.4.1.3.1. Method of attachment is the same for the rope strap as the tubular nylon, however a separate line is necessary for hoists when the chest sling is required. The ascender is attached to the same carabiner on the sit harness as the rope strap.

9.8.6.2.1.4.1.3.2. The ascender may quickly be disconnected once inside the helicopter, while still allowing the PJ to be connected to the aircraft via the hoist hook. This allows greater freedom of movement once inside to assist in strapping the stokes and securing oneself or others prior to forward flight.

Figure 9.4.   Rope Strap with Jumar Ascender.

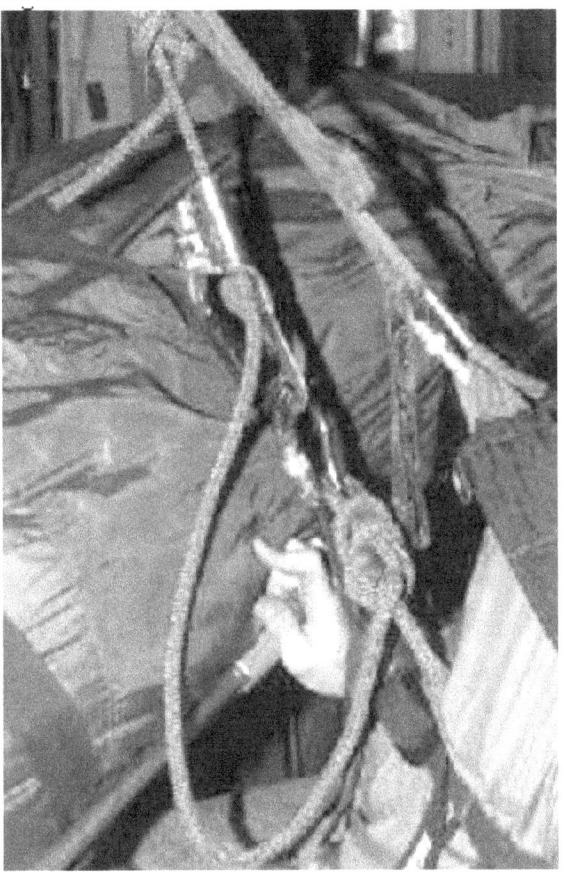

Figure 9.5. Prusik Strap.

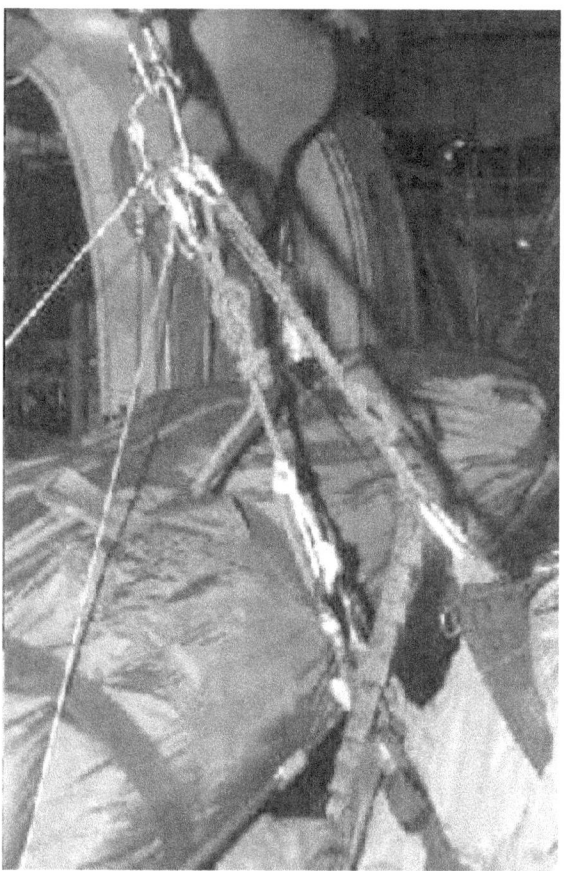

CAUTION: All figures are shown only to show procedures and hook-up points, full safety gear must be worn

9.8.6.2.1.4.1.4. Prussik Strap. Method and use is the same as for the Rope Strap Other types of friction knots may be utilized, i.e. (climb heist, double Prussik, etc.).

9.8.6.3. Procedures

9.8.6.3.1. Hoisting. Hoisting using the climbing harness is relatively simple. Place the strap/ carabiner through the rescue hoist hook. Ensure the pin is in the hook and the gates are locked on the carabiners. The rescue hoist hook should have a chemlight secured to it for night/NVG operations to facilitate the FE/Crew knowing where it is. Use standard signals and detach once reaching the ground

9.8.6.3.2. One-Man Pick-up. Hoisting one man using the barrelman technique is the simplest and fastest method for hoist retrieval. Perform the pickup using the above methods of attachment to the hoist.

9.8.6.3.2.1. Because the PJs' hands and feet are free, he can freely use his arms and legs to counter spinning, fend off obstacles, and prepare for a controlled landing. He does not require any assistance to enter the helicopter on his own except when injured, bringing up a survivor or other objects, or during water pick-ups where the PJ has not removed his fins.

9.8.6.3.2.2.   Any retaining strap method described above may be utilized. The chest harness/backpack strap/LBE balancing point/strap is not needed if the PJ is without a pack and is able to keep himself from becoming inverted.

9.8.6.3.2.3.   When entering the cabin, place your feet on the hoist bumper bar and then the aircraft floor and grab the ceiling strap, H-bar, FRIES bar, or airframe as necessary to facilitate entry into the helicopter. Do not grab any cables, wires, or the FE. Be cautious of taking hold of the forward edge of the door as you may inadvertently move/depress switches and wheels attached to the FE's hoist cabin control panel (CCP).

9.8.6.3.3.   Two-man Pick-up. The two-man pick-up is similar to the one-man in both restrictions and methods.

9.8.6.3.3.1.   It is easier to enter the cabin if both PJs, or a PJ plus the survivor, are eye level with each other as opposed to having one higher or lower.

9.8.6.3.3.2.   When picking up a survivor using the rescue strap ensure you are at a comfortable height to control the survivor. Ensure the survivor does not remove himself from the device or attempt to grab cables, wires, or the FE.

9.8.6.3.3.3.   If the survivor is incapacitated, maneuver the survivor to enter the cabin first toward the FE.

9.8.6.3.4.   Stokes Litter Deployement. Hoisting using the stokes is also simple, however a few techniques will help make it more successful. Although deploying the stokes litter using barrelman techniques is quicker and simpler than previous methods, serious consideration should be given to the tactical threat before deploying a stokes litter at all. It was learned late in the Vietnam War that deploying the stokes was a greater threat to the rescue mission than picking up a survivor with a back injury using a penetrator strap (without paddles) or the rescue strap . The practice of deploying the stokes litter and two PJs during CSAR missions was discontinued due to this. The amount of risk in longer hover periods has to be weighed against the probable reaction time and capability of the enemy. There is still a viable use for this technique in non or low tactical threat scenarios/operations.

Figure 9.6. Two-Man Leaving Aircraft.

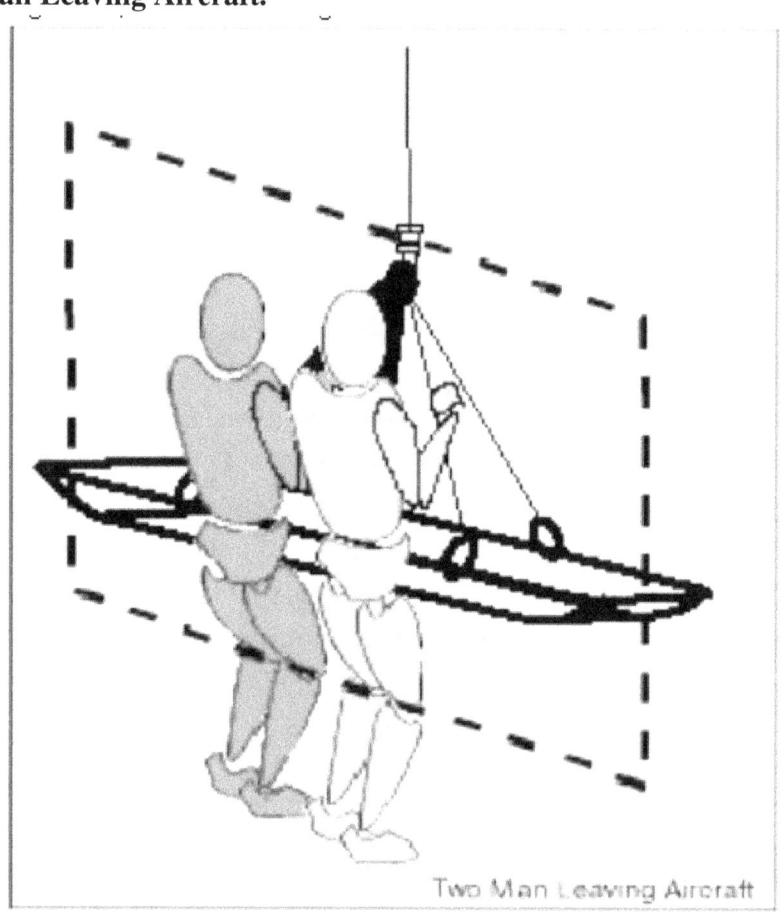

9.8.6.3.4.1. Horizontal Stokes Litter Deployment. One or two PJs and the stokes may deploy from the door. During insertion, PJs connect to the rescue hoist hook along with the stokes. The stokes litter is positioned on the outside of the cabin and the two PJ's position themselves in the door. Do not wear backpacks. Either secure them in the stokes litter or remove them. Move the stokes out the door first, slowly place your weight on the straps, and once PJ/PJ team is ready, give the hoist operator the signal to begin lowering. PJs should stabilize themselves and "fend" off the aircraft until below aircraft ensuring stokes litter does not become entangled/caught on anything in cabin doorway. Once the stokes litter and PJs are on the ground and secure they detach from the rescue hook The stokes is lowered to the ground and personnel detach from the device.

 NOTE: PJ/FE should ensure the combined pick-up weight of PJs and survivor do not exceed the hoist "up" maximum weight.

9.8.6.3.4.2. Vertical Stokes Litter Deployment. An alternate method is to deploy the stokes litter vertically. This may be useful for deployment into wooded areas and is a better method to control the litter during the descent. Attach yourself to the rescue hoist hook in the normal manner. Place a carabiner on the head (or foot) end of the stokes litter. Then attach a large Pelican hook to the carabiner. The Pelican hook is then attached to the rescue hoist hook. The Pelican hook gives the PJ the ability to cut the litter away should he needed during the descent. The FE then (using the hoist) pulls the PJ(s) and the litter toward, and out, the cabin door.

CAUTION: Use care when utilizing this method from altitudes higher than 25 feet above the ground. As there is no tag line, it is possible uncontrolled spinning, pendulums, and oscillations could occur. For training hoist work , either stick to low altitudes or have a monitored tag line on the ground. Unless the situation warrants, consider rappelling the PJs in first, and then using the rappel rope as a tag line for the hoist.

9.8.6.3.4.3. Aircraft with Skis Installed. Deploy the stokes litter vertically (as described above) rather than horizontally when skis are installed. If deploying the litter horizontally, the forward PJ maneuvers the head-end of the stokes litter around the skis, while the rear-most PJ maneuvers the foot-end of the stokes litter from the door. This last sentence needs to be re-written. Should be written in the same manner as 9.8.6.3.4.1.

9.8.6.3.5. Stokes Litter Pick-up.

9.8.6.3.5.1. When using the stokes litter, ensure the patient is securely strapped into the stokes litter prior to hoisting. Ensure the carabiner locking sleeves are positioned towards the inside of the stokes litter. After the patient is secured in the stokes litter and is ready for hoisting, reconnect the rescue hoist hook to the stokes litter cables and reinstall the rescue hoist hook safety pin.

9.8.6.3.5.2. Pararescue Barrelman on the Outside. This is the normal position for the barrelman or PJ ?? and is the only method allowable for aircraft with skis installed.

9.8.6.3.5.2.1. Always move yourself to the far side of the stokes litter from the helicopter so it is not pulled into you when lifted off the ground. PJs with short legs may have to adjust their retaining straps lower than the "belly button".

9.8.6.3.5.2.2. When nearing the aircraft, the PJ maneuvers to place the stokes litter towards the inside . He places his feet on the hoist bumper. If aircraft has skis installed, the PJ should use his forward foot to maneuver the stokes litter outside the skis. He may place his foot on the ski, tire, or bumper as necessary to clear the stokes litter from the aircraft.

9.8.6.3.5.2.3. As the FE raises the hoist cable, the PJ will maneuver the head of the stokes litter inside the helicopter (overhead straps greatly facilitate the hoist entry). After the PJ has his feet on the cabin floor, the FE will begin to lower the hoist while the PJ pulls/pushes the litter inside. If done correctly, the FE should not have to assist the PJ in pulling the litter inside the aircraft.

Figure 9.7. Foot Placement.

CAUTION: All figures are shown only to show procedures and hook-up points, full safety gear must be worn.

Figure 9.8. Maneuvering the Head Inside on the Way.

CAUTION: All figures are shown only to show procedures and hook-up points, full safety gear must be worn.

Figure 9.9. Swing In.

Figure 9.10. Pull In.

CAUTION: All figures are shown only to show procedures and hook-up points, full safety gear must be worn

9.8.6.3.5.3. Pararescue Barrelman or PJ on the Inside. This may be necessary, for example, on a hoist pick-up over water when the PJ has not been able to removed his fins. The disadvantages are the PJ is actually coming up under the floor of the helicopter and the stokes litter must be turned to the outside. Patient and PJ individual size are the primary considerations when using this technique.

9.8.6.3.5.3.1. Always move yourself to the far side of the stokes litter from the helicopter so it is not pulled into you when lifted off the ground. When nearing the aircraft the barrelman or PJ maneuvers to place the stokes litter towards the outside. He enters the aircraft first and then maneuvers the stokes litter inside.

9.8.6.3.5.3.2. The hoist operator may assist by turning both the stokes litter and the barrelman or PJ sideways in order to maneuver them into aircraft. The stokes litter is pulled inside and secured (normally head first). The hook is then sent down to retrieve the other PJ.

9.8.7. Rescue Net:

9.8.7.1. The net will be lowered to the water short of the survivor at an approximate ground speed of 3-5 knots and raised as soon as the last person enters. There is no requirement for hand signals.

Due to the size of the net, the survivor must be removed from the net before bringing the net into the helicopter.

WARNING: The rescue net must be secured against the helicopter while the survivor or PJ departs the net to prevent falling.

9.8.8. Rescue Strap/Horse Collar. The procedures for the use of the rescue strop are the same as those described for the Forest Penetrator with the exception of the obvious differences between the two devices. Up to three slings may be lifted at one time, not to exceed hoist weight limitations.

WARNING: Improper donning of the rescue strap may result in a fall. Before use, consult manufacturer operating instructions for type device used.

9.8.9. Hoisting From Vessels. Some general planning considerations include estimating the amount of time you will operate over the vessel, translator requirements, and communications. The common tendency is to underestimate the time required for the pick-up. Normally, it takes more time to recover a survivor in a stokes litter than using any other hoisting device. If a translator is required, send the translator on the HC- 130 due to space limitations on the helicopter. PJs deploy with radio's in order to communicate and expedite the recovery. This will also allow the aircraft to depart the hover operation and conserve fuel.

9.8.9.1. Check the vessels selected extraction area for poles, antennas, cables, smoke stacks, or any other possible hazards to the aircraft/hoist operation. Usually the most stable part of a ship for hoist operations is the superstructure amidships. Smaller boats don't have a "stable area" but they often have a clear area at the aft end adequate for hoist operations. Confirm the location for extraction with the ships Captain and request a better one if hazards are present.

9.8.9.2. Helicopter approaches to survivors in a raft should be done carefully in order to minimize potential for survivors being blown or flipped from the raft. If the survivor is attached to a parachute, offset approach an adequate distance to prevent the rotor wash from billowing the parachute and dragging the survivor. If in doubt use an offset approach and deploy PJs low and slow in order for them to swim to the survivor's location. Upon reaching the raft, deploy the sea anchor if not already deployed. Partially deflate the raft and fill it with water so it does not get blown away by the rotor wash. PJs assist survivors in positioning/securing to rescue device used. As a last resort, the raft may be knifed. Upon reaching survivor attached to a parachute release both risers and deflate canopy. Ensure canopy is completely deflated and either rolled or submerged before calling in helicopter for pick-up.

9.8.9.3. To aid the aircraft, direct the vessels Captain to maneuver his vessel to a position so the wind is 30 degrees off the port (left) bow. This may have to be varied depending on available hover references. The surface vessel should maintain minimum forward speed (idle or steerageway speed) in calm areas.

9.8.9.4. Slightly higher vessel speeds are required in higher seas.

9.8.9.5. Night water hoist pickups may be complicated by inadequate lighting of mast, booms, or rigging. If possible, direct the vessel Captain to illuminate these obstacles prior to the arrival of the aircraft.

9.8.9.6. When conducting stokes litter operations, disconnect the stokes litter from the rescue hoist hook for survivor loading. This will eliminate potential injury to survivor, PJs and other personnel from the stokes litter lifting off the deck prematurely. Assign someone to hold the rescue hoist hook and monitor the cable. The FE may want to retract cable until signaled by PJ to lower for pickup.

NOTE: Use of tag line should be considered when raising and lowering rescue cable and hoist hook.

WARNING: Do not allow the hoist cable to be secured to the vessel or taken below decks.

9.8.9.7. Ensure proper cable management to prevent inadvertent entanglement. Excessive amounts of cable may be spooled out when conducting hoist operations leading to possible entanglement of personnel or equipment. Communication between team members, aircraft, and vessel personnel is critical.

9.8.9.8. If no radio communication is available, visually signal the hoist operator when ready for pick-up. A "thumbs up" or vigorously shaking the cable from side to side is the standard signal.

9.9. Freefall Swimmer Deployment . Also known as Low and Slow or freefall swimmer deployments provides an effective method of delivering PJs, stokes litter(s), or equipment (boat delivery) to a defined objective in the water by flying the aircraft low and slow enough to allow PJs to deploy from the aircraft into the water.

9.9.1. Required Equipment.

9.9.1.1. Alternate loading belt.

9.9.1.2. Carabiner.

9.9.1.3. Mask.

9.9.1.4. Fins.

9.9.1.5. Snorkel.

9.9.1.6. Emergency signaling device.

9.9.1.7. Lighting (as required)

9.9.1.8. Knife.

9.9.1.9. Personal Flotation Device.

9.9.1.10. Wet/dry suit (as required).

9.9.1.11. Stokes litter with flotation/tag line (as required)

9.9.1.12. Recommended Equipment.

9.9.1.12.1. Helmet .

9.9.1.12.2. Sit Harness/Improvised harness.

9.9.1.12.3. Single Para-Scuba Utility Deployment System (SPUDS).

9.9.1.12.4. Fanny pack

9.9.2. Predeployment Considerations. The flight path of the aircraft should not pass directly over the survivor until the hoist pickup phase to reduce rotor wash over the objective . Determine the wind direction prior to delivery. Set up for a delivery downwind and downdrift of the survivor allowing the survivor to drift to your position. At the intended insertion point, the aircraft should be flying at a maximum of 10 Knots Indicated Air Speed (KIAS) and maximum 10 feet Above Water Level (AWL).

When mission circumstances warrant, you may be delivered upwind or off-wind. If this is the case, be prepared to swim hard to reach survivor . In heavy winds/seas or during low light conditions, delivery away from the survivor may complicate procedures due to team separation, and/or loss of contact with the survivor.

9.9.3. Aircraft Procedures. Deployment procedures vary depending on the airframe, number of personnel, and special equipment being deployed. The H-60 or a similar platform can allow the deploying team members to sit in the door in the order of deployment. Since the aircraft is in forward flight the order of deployment starts at the rear of the aircraft and moves forward. This should limit the chance of team members deploying on top of one another.

9.9.4. When deploying from a larger airframe like the H-53, the team lines up as if it is performing a static line parachute deployment and everyone follows the first man out. Spacing should be one second between team members. If the team is deploying from the aircraft crew entrance door and the ramp simultaneously , deploy all aft team members first before team members deploy from the crew entrance door. This avoids deploying teams on top of each other.

9.9.5. Last minute corrections of the flight path are made by the FE/PJ Team Leader . The PJ Team Leader passes hand signals for aircraft up, down, left, and right, by moving the open palm of the hand in the direction desired. Continue signals until reaching intended deployment location.

9.9.6. During high seas, the aircraft flies 10 feet above the wave crests. Time your exit to land on or near the wave crest. Team deployments in high seas usually require deploying no more than two team members per wave crest in order to avoid some members deploying the additional distance into the trough of the wave. During high sea states consider using the fast rope for deployment.

9.9.7. Deployment Procedures.

9.9.7.1. The team leader should be in a position to view the objective area at approximately 50 feet AWL. All deploying exits will be open at 50 feet AWL and below. Deploying personnel will be secured until established on final approach. The "thumbs up" from the safetyman to the deploying team on final indicates 10 feet AWL and 10 knots is confirmed, and the team is cleared to deploy at the team leader's discretion. Deploying at night with non-NVG equipped crewmembers may require a non-IR chemlight at night attached to each individual deploying. Personnel exit the aircraft in a position that reduces possibility of entanglement and expedites delivery of personnel and equipment. The exit maneuver should not be forceful. Exit by stepping off or pushing away from the aircraft. After the exit, bring your legs together with the fins pointed upward so the heels contact the water first. It is required to take/wear a facemask with snorkel for water operations. When wearing a facemask during deployment, use one or both hands to prevent the mask from coming off, hold it in your hand, or securing it in a cargo pocket. Once in the water, deploying team members surface with raised clinched fist over head and immediately locate other team members. Team members indicate a "thumbs up" signal after water entry to indicate they are "OK" and have not sustained injuries.

9.9.7.2. Deploying with scuba tanks can provide a tremendous advantage for search and recovery operations. If deploying with scuba tanks, grab the tanks support strap just behind the hip and hold it firmly down and against the back. This technique prevents the tank manifold from rising and striking the head. Holding the tank tight against the back also prevents a water surge between the tank and the back that could injure you or damage equipment.

9.9.7.3. When you deploy to an injured survivor, always consider deploying with a stokes litter. This saves time and keeps the helicopter, with its rotor wash, away until the survivor is packaged and ready for the pick up. To ensure you maintain control of the stokes litter, deploy the stokes litter between number 1 and number 2PJ with number 2 deploying stokes litter. Number 2 PJ must ensure number 1 PJ is clear before deployment.

9.9.8. Safety Procedures.

9.9.8.1. When you deploy from the H-53 crew entrance door, caution should be exercised to avoid contacting main landing gear. 9.9.8.2. When your team conducts freefall swimmer deployment training, a safety boat or second hoist-equipped helicopter should be present at the water-training site.

9.10. Rappel.

9.10.1. Rappelling allows direct control of descent and precise placement of the team into the objective area. Rappelling has also been historically proven to be a successful backup for insertion if the hoist fails. Deploying personnel are responsible for aircraft rigging, proper anchor hookup,, and team leader is responsible for providing the safetyman checks prior to deployments.. Rappelling may reduce aircraft exposure in a tactical environment; however, it requires more specialized equipment and preparation than a fast rope.

9.10.2. Equipment Description.

9.10.2.1. Rappel ropes should be static.

9.10.2.2. Personal equipment is similar to standard climbing equipment.

9.10.2.3. Rappel lines are best deployed from the aircraft with the use of a rappel deployment bag. Back coil the rappel rope into the rappel deployment bag until only 2-3 feet are left out of the bag. Tighten the top (opening) of the rappel deployment bag so the rope feeds out freely but is contained within the bag. Use the rope coming out the top of the bag to attach to the anchor point in the aircraft. As the bag is deployed, the rope will feed out only the amount needed to reach the ground. This method keeps positive control of the rope in the aircraft, during deployment, and on the ground.

9.10.3. Required Equipment.

9.10.3.1. Rope, minimum 9mm (double rope 9mm or greater, single 11 mm may be used for heavy loads) back-coiled in rappel deployment bag (weighted).

9.10.3.2. Carabiners to attach rope to the aircraft anchor points.

9.10.3.3. Alternate loading belt.

9.10.3.4. Flight gloves.

9.10.3.5. Leather work gloves.

9.10.3.6. Descending device.

9.10.3.7. Sit Harness (commercial/improvised). NOTE: Improvised sit harnesses must be properly tied, safetied with the correct knots, and inspected prior to rappel deployment.

9.10.3.8. Eye protection.

9.10.3.9. Lighting (as required)

9.10.3.10. Helmet (as required). NOTE: Helmet required on all training rappel deployments

9.10.4. Cabin Configuration.

9.10.4.1. Anchor point installation varies depending on the aircraft. Any hoist-equipped aircraft can support rappel anchoring at the hoist hook.

NOTE: Aircraft 781's should be reviewed prior to all rappel deployments to ensure no write-ups are on any aircraft anchor points/systems.

9.10.4.2. Installation. Aircraft seats will be removed from the deployment area. Cargo compartment doors will be placed in the locked-open position before final approach. Pad/tape any sharp edges that could damage ropes. Ropes will be attached to the anchor points using locking carabiners. Refer to MDS publications for detailed information.

9.10.5. Time Warnings. Timing is critical to optimize the success of the mission (speed and surprise). When the aircraft arrives at the insertion point (IP), the deploying team(s) need to be prepared to exit immediately. To accomplish this, standard time warnings are used to ensure both the deploying team and the crew are ready. Standard time warnings of 20, 10, 5, and 1 minute are announced by the aircrew based upon their calculated arrival Time on Target (TOT). Rappellers should be ready for deployment and the team leader should inspect all team members prior to the 5-minute warning.

9.10.6. Deployment Procedures. Standard deployment procedures are used to enhance both crew coordination and team actions during rappel operations. The following items explain the standard procedures you will use.

9.10.6.1. The safetyman will monitor intercom and be secured with a crewman's harness. Once hooked to the rappelling equipment, personnel may release other restraints in preparation for exit. On short final, personnel may position themselves to facilitate immediate deployment. The safetyman will confirm the deployment location and direct the rappelling when a hover is established. Do not deploy ropes until the aircraft is in a stable hover over the intended deployment area. As the aircraft comes to a hover, the pilot gives the command "ROPES, ROPES, ROPES". The safetyman ensures the ropes reach the ground At this time, the safetyman relays the signal by yelling "ROPES" and pointing out the door. The safetyman coordinates with the pilot to ensure the aircraft maintains a hover altitude that keeps the ropes in contact with the ground. After the last rappeller is off the rope, the safetyman releases or retrieves the ropes. Aircraft release ropes before they land or commence forward flight. Have a V-blade knife or other similar tool readily available to cut ropes during emergencies or rope entanglement.

WARNING: The safetyman will ensure the ropes reach the ground prior to final positioning of rappellers for deployment. The safetyman will coordinate with the pilot to ensure the aircraft maintains a hover altitude keeping the ropes in contact with the ground.

9.10.6.2. Individual Procedures.

9.10.6.2.1. Don an approved rappel sit-harness and place a carabiner on or through primary harness attachment point. Grasp the rappel rope from the anchor side (in between rappeller and the anchor point), route the rope through descending device, and attach to rappel sit-harness carabiner ensuring locking gate is locked and backed off a quarter turn. Have only enough slack in the rope to attach the descender to primary sit-harness carabiner. Take-in all slack in the rope until rappellers weight is supported by the anchor. Rappeller establishes brake hand with right/left hand gripping the rope and positioned against right/left hip. Rapeller holds the deployment bag with left/right hand.

9.10.6.2.2. Upon safety check after hook-up to anchor system and rapeller's brake hand is established, rappeller is cleared to release aircraft restraint in preparation for the exit. On short final (normally 50 ft and 50 KIAS and after the one minute call), rappellers position in doorway for pre-briefed deployment sequence. The designated aircrew member will relay the deployment command from the pilot by shouting "ROPES" and pointing out the door. Do not deploy the rope until the aircraft is in a stable hover over the intended deployment area. To deploy the rope, merely drop the deployment bag, upright, outside the aircraft. The rappel rope will simply uncoil as the deployment bag falls away.

9.10.6.2.3. Exit Procedures: Rappellers stand with the balls of their feet on the edge of the aircraft, place tension on the rappel rope with full body weight keep guide hand relaxed with brake hand gripping the rope and positioned on your hip, and then push-off with enough force to clear the aircraft doorway simultaneously releasing the brake hand grip to allow rope to feed through brake hand in order to begin rappel descent. The force upon exit depends on many factors such as anchor point, the amount of equipment carried, and the specific method used for rappelling. Rappellers ensure their exit is forceful enough to properly clear them from contacting aircraft or possibly entangling with other rappellers. Common mistakes are weak exits causing rappellers to swing back into the side of the aircraft , and too strong an exit causing you to entangle with other rappellers or swing into the bottom of the aircraft.

NOTE: To facilitate rappelling through obstacles (i.e., trees, ships masts), rappels may be accomplished using rappel deployment bags attached to the lower leg of the rappeller. If this procedure is used, the rope should be at least 50 ft. longer than the intended deployment altitude with the weights removed. The rope will be secured to the inside of the rope bag using a figure eight knot to ensure the rappeller cannot rappel off the end of the rope.

9.10.6.3. Night Procedures. Use chemlights to mark the rappel deployment bag so it can be easily retrieved/seen after the deployment.

9.10.6.4. Safety Procedures.

9.10.6.4.1. If the helicopter experiences an emergency during rappelling, the rappellers on the rope must descend as rapidly as possible, run "off" the rope if possible, and move out from beneath the helicopter.

9.10.6.4.2. If the helicopter gains altitude above the length of the rope, the rappeller immediately brakes and if necessary ties off. Wait for the helicopter to descend to a safe rappelling altitude before continuing.

9.10.6.4.3. When using a rappel deployment bag, fasten weights to the inside bottom of the bag.

9.10.6.4.4. In the event the rappel deployment bag is not used (not recommended), the rappel rope should be daisy chained and/or weighted to prevent contact with rotors.

9.10.6.4.5. Ensure a "V" blade knife is readily available in the event the aircraft must depart and rappellers are still attached to the rope(s). Rope(s) are cut free once all personnel are known to be on the ground.

9.11. Fast Rope.

9.11.1. Fast rope technique allows the rapid insertion of personnel, limiting aircraft, and personnel exposure time. The inherent simplicity and speed of fast rope operations constitute its greatest attributes. The main disadvantage of using a fast rope is once deployed there is no expedient method for immediate extraction Fast ropes are typically used for hovers at 50'and below and do not provide the descent control of deploying personnel that rappels do. Since fast roping does not incorporate mechanical fasteners or friction devices, it is unsuitable for delivering equipment unless the equipment is attached to personnel conducting fast rope operations. Normally, the deploying team is responsible for providing and inspecting the ropes.

9.11.2. Aircraft Capabilities. Most military helicopters can be configured for fast rope operations, provided (1) anchor system (either already in place or installed) can support the weight of personnel/equipment, and (2) helicopter crew is properly trained in the safe execution of fast rope operations. Use a location that ensures the ropers will not become entangled with the aircraft and it can hold the suspended weight of the ropers being deployed. Hoist equipped aircraft can be used for fast rope operations by connecting the rope to the pendent. When using the hoist as an attachment point, do not exceed the rated suspended weight. Refer to specific MDS publications for detailed installation.

9.11.3. Aircrew Responsibilities.

9.11.3.1. The aircrew will install the fast ropes and inspect attaching points. Note: The team leader or AIE Master should always inspect the equipment and attaching points. Ropes can be attached at any time before or during the flight. All fast ropes should be in their deployment position prior to the five minute call.

9.11.3.2. On final, the pilot maneuvers the aircraft over the target and establishes a hover. Do not deploy the fast rope until the aircrew confirms the deployment signal. At the completion of the approach, the aircraft should be in a stabilized hover at the designated altitude for deployment. If requested, the aircraft can maintain a 3-5 knot forward ground speed. This can assist the deploying team members by spacing them out upon landing.

9.11.3.3. The pilot signals clearance to deploy the ropes with the call, "ROPES, ROPES, ROPES" when he has ensured the aircraft is at the correct altitude. The appropriate scanners give the hand signal for rope deployment (a sweeping motion of the hand with the index finger extended toward the exit).

9.11.4. Cabin Configuration. Coil and secure fast ropes with a cargo tiedown strap or seat belt next to the deployment location to be used. Coil the ropes toe to head and tie them down with the bottom of the rope (toe) on the bottom of the coil and the attachment point (head) on top. This method of securing the ropes allows them the best opportunity for trouble-free deployment.

9.11.5. Personnel Equipment Preparation.

9.11.5.1. Secure all equipment snugly to your body to avoid any center of gravity shifts that could cause balance problems during deployment. Keep the body front body clear of items that may interfere with your grip on the fast rope. Secure communication cords and loose clothing before fast rope deployment. Sling weapon over the shoulder and across the back or secure it in a ready position by a quick release system like a bungee cord. In all cases, secure the weapon from movement and position it away from the rope. Pad all shock sensitive equipment.

9.11.5.2. Always wear leather gloves for fast rope operations. Sliding down a fast rope causes a tremendous amount of friction heat. Without the proper hand protection, such a slide can seriously burn your hands. Using flight gloves (or any suitable insert) in conjunction with the leather gloves provides additional padding/insulation. Fast rope lengths of 90 feet and greater often require a combination of three gloves to provide enough protection from the friction heat buildup.

WARNING: Fast rope personnel must ensure they can securely grip the fast rope when 2-3 gloves are worn.

9.11.5.3. Required Equipment, Land:

9.11.5.3.1. Fast rope.

9.11.5.3.2. Alternate loading belt.

9.11.5.3.3. Flight gloves.

9.11.5.3.4. Leather work gloves.

9.11.5.3.5. Carabiners (2 each).

9.11.5.3.6. Eye protection.

9.11.5.3.7. Lighting (as required)

9.11.5.3.8. Helmet (as required)

9.11.5.3.9. Required Equipment, Water:

9.11.5.3.9.1. Fast rope.

9.11.5.3.9.2. Alternate loading belt.

9.11.5.3.9.3. Leather work/dive gloves. NOTE: Use leather gloves over the dive gloves as long as a good grip can be maintained.
9.11.5.3.9.3. Carabiners (2 each).

9.11.5.3.9.4. Mask.

9.11.5.3.9.5. Fins

9.11.5.3.9.6. Snorkel.

9.11.5.3.9.7. Emergency signaling device.

9.11.5.3.9.8. Lighting (as required)

9.11.5.3.9.9. Knife.

9.11.5.3.9.10. Personal Floatation Device.

9.11.5.3.9.11. Recommended Equipment.

9.11.5.3.9.11.1. Helmet (water)

9.11.5.3.9.11.2. Wet/dry suit as needed for water ops.

9.11.5.3.9.11.3. Quick release sling (Stokes Litter).

9.11.6. Time Warnings. Because fast rope operations are designed to be tactical infiltrations, timing is critical to optimize the success of the mission (speed and surprise). When the aircraft arrives at the insertion point, the deploying team needs to be prepared to exit immediately. To accomplish this, standard time warnings are used to ensure both the deploying team and the crew are ready. Standard time warnings of 20, 10, 5, and 1 minute are announced by the aircrew based upon their calculated arrival, Time on Target (TOT).

9.11.6.1. The rope master may require more than the minimum time calls and should be on intercom until at least the 5-minute call. The 20 and 10 minute time warnings are designed to inform you of the approaching TOT; usually no actions are required.

9.11.6.2. The following lists the actions to be taken from the 20-minute time warning, to the deployment.

9.11.6.2.1. At the "20-minute" call, all personnel should begin preparations for deployment and receive final instructions from the team leader.

9.11.6.2.2. At the " 10-minute" call, personnel inspect equipment and complete final preparations for deployment.

9.11.6.2.3. At the "5-minute" call, move to the exit point. The safetyman or designated team member disconnects the fast rope from its storage point and prepares it for deployment by handing it to the first man out of each stick or by setting it up on the edge of the exit. Ensure it is back-coiled and held secure. Activate chemlights for night deployments.

9.11.6.2.4. At the "1-minute" call, the safetyman checks should be done and all team members move into position for deployment at the door or ramp. It is recommended the team do not disconnect from their alternate loading device until the aircraft is on short final (50 feet/50 knots).

9.11.6.2.5. As the aircraft comes to its hover, the pilot flying will give the command "ROPES, ROPES, ROPES". At the command "ROPES" or the signal (the designated crewmember pointing out the exit), the first man of each team kicks out the rope, determines the rope is on the ground, then exits the aircraft. Off the aft ramp, deploy the rope at a 45-degree angle away from the rear of the aircraft.

9.11.7. Night Deployments. Procedures remain the same as for day. Use chemlights to identify ropes and exits. Use a minimum of four chemlight on each fast rope. Tape two at the bottom, one 10 feet from the bottom and one at the top of the rope to identify where to place your hands. The chemlight 10 feet from the bottom ensures at least 10 feet of rope is on the ground. A chemlight may also be taped horizontally just above the crew entrance door in line with the rope. Tape over the chemlights to provide enough light for the team to ensure the rope is on the ground.

9.11.8. NVG Over Water Operations. With the exception of the final approach, the fast rope pattern is the same as the hoist pattern for the aircrew. On final, the aircraft descends to intended hove height while decelerating to the deployment ground speed. The fast rope is deployed as the aircraft enters the insertion zone. Depending on the mission profile, you may request a slow forward movement of the aircraft. This can assist deploying personnel by spacing them apart upon water entry. When fast roping into the water, wet/dry suit material may be vulnerable to damage from rope friction. Duct tape wet/ dry suit . on locations where rope may come in contact with suit.

WARNING: Multiple rope iterations into the water will have an affect on your descent speed if your gloves are wet.

9.12. Extractions using Fast Rope Insertion Extraction System (FRIES).

9.12.1. "Attach only two people per personnel attaching loop on the FRIES. Use the top and bottom loops when extracting four personnel. When extracting an odd number of personnel, position the odd man on the higher personnel attaching loop. Attach any combat equipment to the last bridle loop so it will be lower than the personnel.

9.12.2. As the aircraft approaches the pickup point, the ropes will be deployed from the aircraft. After the ropes have been deployed, the personnel to be extracted will move under the helicopter and secure themselves. Personnel to be extracted will face into the direction of travel of the helicopter, ensuring that none of the connections and ropes are crossed or entangled, and squat side by side. Personnel being extracted will interlock arms or grasp harnesses. This will prevent collisions between personnel while airborne. Extraction is limited to an altitude to permit terrain/obstacle clearance of at least 100 feet. Maximum forward speed is 80 KIAS.

9.13. Rope Ladder.

9.13.1. The use of a rope ladder provides a quick method for recovering team personnel from the surface when an LZ is unavailable or for rapid extraction of large teams. The decision to use a rope ladder must be weighed against the difficulty of personnel climbing the ladder with equipment and time constraints. The rope ladder is not a suitable method of recovering injured personnel or personnel who are not familiar with the device or do not have the proper strength to safely climb the device. The rope ladder can also be used simultaneously with hoist operations allowing a patient/survivor a secure extraction strapped onto a hoist device while your team climbs the ladder.

9.13.2. Required Equipment, Land.

   9.13.2.1. Rope ladder.

   9.13.2.2. Alternate loading belt.

   9.13.2.3. Eye protection.

   9.13.2.4. Carabiner.

   9.13.2.5. Lighting (as required)

   9.13.2.6. Helmet (as required)

   9.13.2.7. Required Equipment. Water.

      9.13.2.7.1. Rope ladder.

      9.13.2.7.2. Alternate loading belt.

      9.13.2.7.3. Carabiner

      9.13.2.7.4. Mask.

      9.13.2.7.5. Fins.

      9.13.2.7.6. Snorkel.

      9.13.2.7.7. Emergency signaling device.

      9.13.2.7.8. Knife.

      9.13.2.7.9. Personal Flotation Device.

9.13.2.7.10. Lighting (as required)

9.13.2.8. Recommended Equipment. Sit harness/Improvised harness.

9.13.3. Aircraft/Ladder Capabilities and Limitations.

9.13.3.1. Rope ladder operations are limited because they can cause aircraft control problems. As more weight is applied to the ladder at the side or tail of the aircraft, the pilot has to counter the aircraft shift in center of gravity (CG) in the opposite direction. For this reason, aircraft have different rope ladder restrictions based on their capabilities. Ensure team members are fully briefed on exit procedures. Refer to specific MDS for additional data.

9.13.4. Climbing considerations prior to conducting rope ladder operations, personnel don a safety harness with a carabiner positioned for emergency fastening to the ladder. This may be required if the aircraft ascends too high, transitions to foreword flight, or personnel become too fatigued to continue climbing.

9.13.4.1. If aircraft begins to settle with personnel on attached to the rope ladder, remain on the rope ladder until lowered on the ground/ into the water release/detach from the rope ladder ensuring no entanglements, then move to pre-briefed clock position from beneath the aircraft. The pilot should attempt to fly the aircraft to avoid landing on personnel below .

9.13.4.2. If using the rope ladder as a team, designate one member to grasp the bottom rung to steady the rope ladder. There are various methods of climbing the rope ladder. One method is to climb up the sides of the rope ladder using the edges of the rungs for foot placement as opposed to the center of the rungs. While climbing, grasp the ladder rungs hand over hand from both the front and back-sides. Climbing rope ladder like climbing a standard rigid rope ladder will cause the rope ladder to twist. Personnel place feet in any manner that is comfortable. As in all climbing, personnel use their legs to climb the rope ladder. Personnel overusing their arms during climb can cause extreme fatigue and result in personnel falling from rope ladder.. Once you have reached the top, continue the transition from vertical climbing to horizontal climbing on the rope ladder.

WARNING: Do not climb off the rope ladder until you have a secure hand hold well inside the helicopter.

9.13.4.3. When patient/survivors cannot physically climb the rope ladder, and it is the only means into the aircraft, secure them to the rope ladder or instruct them to climb up a few rungs, sit down on a rung, and intertwine their body within the rungs. They should not try to climb up the rope ladder and into the helicopter. The aircraft can then lift the survivor and move to a LZ to complete the pick-up.

9.13.5. Water Operations.

9.13.5.1. In preparation for recovery, personnel will attach a carabiner to personal load bearing equipment or life preserver harness in the event securing personnel to rope ladder in an emergency situation. Don a facemask, (mandatory for training), to protect your eyes from the rotor wash. Deflate your buoyancy compensator to reduce the likelihood of it catching on the ladder rungs while climbing. Swim fins/equipment should be attached to an equipment belt or harness to free hands and feet for climbing. Avoid climbing with hands inserted through the heel straps of fins. This can cause wrist or arm injuries in the event of a fall.

9.14. Special Patrol Insertion/Extraction (SPIE) System . The SPIE system was developed to rapidly insert or extract team members from an area where landing is not possible. However, it is relatively slow and impractical compared to fast rope and rappelling techniques. SPIE has gained applicability for extracting personnel from water. Thus, a SPIE operation can either be a dry or wet operation. This system can pick up 1 to 10 personnel at a time. The rope and personnel are treated as an external load so airspeeds, altitudes, and oscillations must be closely monitored.

9.14.1. Required Equipment:

9.14.1.1. SPIES rope

9.14.1.2. SPIES harness (commercial/improvised) with safety sling

9.14.1.3. Two nine foot, Type 13 cargo suspension slings

9.14.1.4. Type IV links

9.14.1.5. Leather work gloves.

9.14.1.6. Eye protection.

9.14.1.7. Helmet (as required).

9.14.2. Planning. Although SPIE is an expedient method of extraction, the need for special equipment such as the SPIE harness necessitates deliberate planning. In preparing for an operation, planners must determine if the tactical situation suggests the possible need to extract personnel using SPIE.

9.14.3. Setup and Preparation. The SPIE system consists of the SPIE rope, a harness, and a safety line. The following is a description of these components:

9.14.3.1. The SPIE rope assembly (NSN: 1670-01-065-085 1) is approximately 120 feet in length and consists of a doubled tapered eye splice at each end. The top tapered eye is encapsulated in polyurethane to protect it from abrasions. The rope itself is one inch in diameter and is coated with a nylon solution protecting the core of the rope, D rings are located in pairs on opposite sides of each other, spaced one foot apart and seven feet from center of one set to center of the succeeding set. Four additional D rings can be added to the rope to provide a total carrying capacity of 14 personnel. The rope assembly has a tensile strength (dry) of 24,000 pounds and a recommended maximum load of 5,000 pounds.

9.14.3.2. The SPIE harness is a parachute type harness. A 20" looped strap is connected to the crossover portion of the back straps. This serves as the primary anchor device when secured to a SPIE rope D ring with a locking carabiner.

9.14.3.3. The safety line consists of a standard 12' to 15' sling rope. The safety line serves as the secondary anchor device and is worn underneath the harness.

9.14.4. Installation. Two 9 foot, type 13 nylon cargo suspension slings (NSN: 1670-00-856-0266) are routed through the top tapered eye of the rope assembly and secured to the four rappelling rings of the H bar with Type IV links (NSN: 1670-783-5988/MIL-L40085).

9.14.4.1. Pad the entire left edge of the cargo hook well with appropriate material (i.e. two thickness of one half inch felt pads, carpet, fire hose, etc) to prevent damaging the SPIE rope. If the cargo hook is installed, the rope assembly should be routed through the hook during deployment.

9.14.4.2. For night operations, attach chemlights to the SPIE rope assembly. Using three chemlights; tape two chemlights at the bottom of the rope and one chemlight 3' above the first set of D ring attachment points.

9.14.4.3. For water operations, tie three LPU bladders or any type of flotation device to the SPIE rope to provide buoyancy for the rope while in the water. Tie one flotation device at each end of the D-ring attachment point areas and one flotation device in the middle of the attachment point area, just above the middle two sets of D rings.

WARNING: The tensile strength of the SPIE rope is reduced when wet.

9.14.5. Land Operating Procedures. Once established over the LZ, the pilot will call "ROPES, ROPES, ROPES". At the ropes call the scanners will deploy the rope through the cargo hook bay or cargo doors and call "ropes deployed" (ensure rope is not entangled with personnel or equipment).

9.14.5.1. As soon as the ropes reach the ground, the team members hook into the D rings. When all members are secure and ready, the team leader will give the aircrew "thumbs up (at night, pre-arranged light signals may be used). If possible, the radio man will hookup close to the bottom of the rope and maintain radio contact with the helicopter in order to provide a verbal backup for the extract, the clearing of obstacles, and the descent into the LZ.

9.14.5.2. Upon receiving the thumbs up from the team, the scanners inform the pilot they are ready to lift. The aircraft should ascend once the SPIE rope is clear of all obstacles and slowly accelerate to 40-60 knots (do not exceed 70 knots or 50 knots in cold weather) proceeding to a secure area. Scanners inform the pilot when the last man is off the ground and once 100' clearance is reached, clear the pilot for forward flight. A minimum of 100' clearance should be maintained between the bottom of the SPIE assembly and ground obstacles, tactical situation permitting. During the flight, the scanners should advise the pilot of team status and check rigging frequently.

9.14.5.3. The pilot should approach the dismounting area at 250' or higher above the highest obstacle. Once the aircraft is positioned over the intended landing area, the scanners should clear the pilot to descend. Aircraft rate of descent should be less than 150' per minute. The scanners continue to advise the pilot of drift, distance from the ground, and when the team is on the ground and cleared from the ropes. At that point the rope may be retrieved.

WARNING: Personnel should be aware when using SPIES, that the pilot must use extreme care while making an approach to a high hover with a very slow rate of descent during the insertion to avoid the possibility of encountering power settling.

NOTE: A landing may be made with the SPIE rope attached to the helicopter. The team members, once unhooked, keep the rope taut by walking out to the 3 or 9 o'clock position as the aircraft slowly descends.

9.14.6. Water Operating Procedures. The SPIE is also suitable for the extraction of swimmers from the water. After the aircraft has established a stable hover over the swimmer's location, the aircrew should deploy the rope with flotation devices attached. When the team members have completed their hookup, the team leader will signal the aircrew with a "thumbs up" to commence the lift off.

9.14.6.1. The aircraft should initiate a vertical climb until all team members are clear of the water. After takeoff, flight speeds, altitudes, and insertion procedures are the same as for over land. (Exception: If the insertion is to a ship, the team members must take their landing orders from the personnel in charge of the landing platform. Two signals from the Landing Signalman Enlisted (LSE) are mandatory; hold and wave off.)

9.14.6.1.1. Contingency/Emergency Procedures.

9.14.6.1.1.1. If a team member develops an emergency during extraction, the team member should place both hands on top of his head to inform the crew. The pilot should lower the team to the ground or water as safely as possible.

NOTE: Injured personnel will not be re-lowered into the water.

9.14.6.1.1.2. Care must be taken during night operations due to limited visual cues between helicopter and team, proper altitude clearance must be maintained. During extraction the "thumbs up" signal may be substituted with chemlights or other signaling devices.

9.14.6.1.1.3. The aircraft lower strobe light should be off while conducting SPIE operations. Should the aircraft develop an emergency, the lower strobe should be turned on to notify the team of the emergency.

9.15. Stabilized Body Position (STABO) Environmental conditions and mission circumstances require a team to use the STABO extraction system for rapid extraction of one to four persons by helicopter. Helicopters extract the team and move them, suspended on lines beneath the helicopter, to an area where the aircraft can land and pick them up safely.

9.15.1. Planning. The limitations and capabilities of the helicopter are the primary factors in site selection for STABO operations. You must consider, the site altitude and temperature, as they determine air density and hover capability. There are no particular size criteria for STABO extraction sites as any small clearing is ideal.

WARNING: Forested areas can be dangerous when extracting more than one person because the safety ropes can become entangled in the foliage. If possible clear branches or trees that pose a threat to the operation.

NOTE: For training missions utilizing STABO, permission will be obtained to remove trees from and extraction site prior to training event.

9.15.2. Required Equipment.

9.15.2.1. STABO rope

9.15.2.2. STABO harness (commercial/improvised) with safety sling

9.15.2.3. Two nine foot, Type 13 cargo suspension slings

9.15.2.4. Type IV links

9.15.2.5. Leather work gloves.

9.15.2.6. Eye protection.

9.15.2.7. Helmet (as required).

9.15.3. Setup and Preparation. STABO consists of the following components:

9.15.3.1. The deployment bag is made of cotton canvas and is of the roll-type design. The bag, when packed, contains the suspension rope, bridle, and safety rope. The lower end of the bag contains a 10-pound weight that aids the deployment of the suspension rope from the helicopter.

9.15.3.2. The suspension rope is made of nylon and contains a spliced loop on each end. Attach a snaphook to each end loop. The design of the suspension rope allows connection to the D-ring in the end of the strap assembly of the anchoring device. Attach the opposite end to the D-ring of the bridle.

9.15.3.3. The personnel harness is made of nylon webbing stitched to a standard medium or large-size pistol belt, and comes in small, medium, and large sizes.

9.15.3.4. The bridle is a V-shaped device made of nylon webbing with a D-ring on the single end and a snaphook in each of the running ends.

9.15.3.5. The safety rope is 12' long and made of nylon. A spliced loop is on each end of the rope and each loop has a carabiner. Always use a safety rope when extracting two or more persons.

9.15.4. Planning/Preparation. The limitations and capabilities of the helicopter are the primary factors in site selection for STABO operations. Any small clearing can be used.

9.15.4.1. Land Operating Procedures . The scanners check all connections and deploy the rope at the "ROPES" call.

9.15.4.2. As soon as the ropes reach the ground, the team members hook into the D rings. When all members are secure and ready, the team leader will give the aircrew "thumbs up" (at night, pre-arranged light signals may be used). If possible, the radio man will hookup close to the bottom of the rope and maintain FM radio contact with the helicopter in order to provide a verbal backup for the extract, clearing of obstacles, and descent into the LZ.

9.15.4.3. The aircraft should ascend clear of all obstacles and slowly accelerate to 40-60 knots (do not exceed 70 knots or 50 knots in cold weather) proceeding to a secure area. A minimum of 100' clearance should be maintained between the bottom of the STABO assembly and any ground obstacles, tactical situation permitting. In emergencies, extended flights may be allowed at speeds less than 90 knots with turns less than 30 degrees.

9.15.4.4. The pilot should approach the dismounting target at 250' or higher above the highest obstacle. Once the aircraft is positioned over the intended landing area, the scanners should advise the pilot clear to descend. Aircraft rate of descent should be less than 150' per minute. The scanners continue to advise the pilot of drift, distance from the ground, and when the team is on the ground and cleared from the ropes. At that point the rope may be retrieved

9.15.5. Water Operating Procedures . The STABO is also suitable for the extraction of swimmers from the water. After the aircraft has established a stable hover over the swimmer's location, the aircrew should deploy the rope with flotation devices attached. When the team members have completed their hookup, the team leader will signal the aircrew with a "thumbs up" or appropriate signal.

9.15.5.1. The aircraft should initiate a vertical climb until all team members are clear of the water. After takeoff, flight speeds, altitudes, and insertion procedures are the same as for over land. (Exception: If the insertion is to a ship, the team members must take their landing orders from the personnel in charge of the landing platform. Two signals from the Landing Signalman Enlisted (LSE) are mandatory; hold and wave off.)

9.15.6. Contingency/Emergency Procedures.

9.15.6.1. If a team member develops an emergency during an extraction, the team member should place both hands on top of his head to inform the crew. The pilot should lower the team to the ground or water as safely as possible.

NOTE: Injured personnel will not be re-lowered into the water.

9.16. Rapid Equipment Delivery System and Equipment.

9.16.1. The insertion techniques discussed to this point have all dealt with insertions of personnel. Many missions require the additional support of equipment that would not be practical or possible to carry during personnel deployments. The Rapid Equipment Delivery System (REDS) technique was developed to provide insertion of mission essential equipment. REDS utilizes the traditional mountaineering skill of belaying in an untraditional environment. REDS can be implemented simultaneously AIE infiltration.

9.16.2. REDS Container/Contents Inspection/Storage Requirements: . Proper inspection, storage, and setup is critical to proper utilization. REDS kits and associated components are stored in the rescue equipment storage room. Ensure REDS kits and components have been inspected before and after each use, are controlled by hand receipts, and are returned in serviceable condition. Ensure any equipment maintenance/repair discrepancies are reported to the appropriate personnel in order to replace kit contents when necessary.

9.16.2.1. REDS Container Inspection:

9.16.2.1.1. REDS Container: The REDS container should be smooth on the outside to avoid getting hung-up during the deployment, and rigid to provide protection of its contents during deployment Inspect corners, bottom, and lid/lid attachments for any cracks, bending, or bowing.

9.16.2.1.2. Lowering Harness: Inspect for any tears or excessive wear and ensure all hardware is present and operational. If the harness looks as if it won't withstand another deployment, replace it.

9.16.2.1.3. Belay Rope/Equipment: Belay rope should be inspected prior to each use for serviceability. Units should establish a shelf-life for ropes used to belay REDS based on manufacturers specifications for rope strength/use. All belay/lowering hardware must be inspected for metal fatigue, cracks, unusual bends, and friction burns.

9.16.2.2. REDS Equipment Inspection/Storage Requirements:

9.16.2.2.1. Ryobi Saws: When saws are stored with blades installed, the saw blades must be protected with a rigid covering to prevent blade breakage. PVC pipe works well for this purpose. Include extra blades in the REDS maintenance kit. Ensure the tool kit for the Ryobi saw is included in the REDS kit. Ryobi saws need a mixture of gas and oil to operate properly. Include extra oil in the REDS maintenance kit for fuel mixture.

9.16.2.2.2. Hydraulic pump: May be stored with fluid in the tank. Fluid in connected hydraulic hoses should only be non-flammable hydraulic fluid or mineral oil. Ensure the generator hydraulic pressure switch is in the "tank" position to take the pressure off the system while not in use. If hoses are disconnected, any exposed hose fittings should be covered with dust caps to keep dirt out of the fittings. Keep extra fluid for the generator with the REDS maintenance kit. Ensure the throttle, hydraulic, and choke levers are working properly. Clean the spark plug to prevent plug failure.

9.16.2.2.3. Rescue combination tool (jaws): Must be kept clean and free of dirt and rust. The recommended procedure for storage is to close the tool fully, then open the tips approximately ½ inch. Next, release the pressure at the pump/tank and disconnect fittings as required. Hydraulic connections can remain connected while in storage, although it is not recommended for extended periods of time. Any disconnected coupler fittings on the jaws need to be kept covered with dust caps to keep those fittings free of dirt. Inspect jaw blades for warping. If any discrepancies are found with the tool, it should be replaced immediately.

9.16.2.2.4. Air bags: Should be stored to keep them relatively free of petroleum products. The recommended inspection procedure is to inflate each bag and keep inflated for no less than 3 hours.

9.16.2.2.5. REDS maintenance kit: Can be any suitable container that will accommodate the extra fluids and hardware needed for normal REDS maintenance. Maintenance kit need not deploy unless recurring use of the REDS is anticipated.

9.16.3. Packaging for Deployment:

9.16.3.1. The entire REDS deployment system consists of a belay system and the REDS kit in a lowering harness. Additional equipment, depending on the mission, may be added to the package with optional rigging configurations. For example, a stokes litter or med/SAR gear may be integrated and deployed with the kit.

NOTE: If a stokes litter is used, the foot –end is the attachment point to lower the stokes litter with REDS attached.

9.16.3.2. SKED litter may be attached as transport medium. It offers a hard plastic smooth surface (skid plate) on which to drag the REDS. The SKED may be full-sized, or modified to fit the REDS container. A pole-less litter wrapped around the container is another option to make ground transport easier. If the SKED is used, its straps should be modified with FASTEX fasteners for quick and easy disconnect. The SKED can be removed and used as an additional litter if required, after the REDS is in position.

9.16.3.3. Padding should be added inside and outside of the REDS container. Inside should be one inch rubberized foam pad on the floor of the container. Bubble wrap should be inserted as required into spaces between tools to keep them from banging together. Crushboard should be secured to the bottom of the kit between container and harness to cushion deployment impact.

9.16.3.4. The harness is designed to enclose the container and allow a connecting point for belay or air drop. It is made of 2" nylon webbing in a "cross" pattern. "V" rings are sewn into the straps to allow riser extensions to be attached. (See Attachment 2)

9.16.4. Belay System and Configuration: A sticht plate may be the device of choice if 9mm or 11mm rope is used. If smaller than 9mm rope is used, the belay device should be a Figure-8 with a double-wrap, allowing positive control of the REDS package. Whichever belay system is used, it is important to maintain an emergency quick-release capability from the helicopter and at the REDS kit connection.

9.16.4.1. Belay System Equipment:

9.16.4.1.1. Pelican hook 1ea

9.16.4.1.2. Tubular nylon sling extension, 2ft 1ea

9.16.4.1.3. Locking steel carabiners 2ea

9.16.4.1.4. Figure 8 or Sticht plate 1ea

9.16.4.1.5. 7-9mm rope, bird nested (Fig. 3) 125ft

9.16.4.1.6. Leather gloves 1pr

9.16.4.1.7. Rope bag 1ea

9.16.4.2. Belay system anchor points:

9.16.4.2.1. H-60s w/ internal tanks: Ceiling belay point forward of right door or FRIES bar.

9.16.4.2.2. H-60s w/o internal tanks: Ceiling belay point aft of right door or FRIES bar.

9.16.4.2.3. H-53s/47s: Floor tie-down ring or FRIES bar.

9.16.4.3. Pre-deployment preparation:

9.16.4.3.1. If a rope bag is used, the rope should be back-coiled in bag. If the bag is not used, the rope should be bird nested.

9.16.4.3.2. The equipment package should have a pelican hook, but a locking carabiner will work for a lowering point to ensure a quick release once on the surface. If a stokes litter is used, the lowering point for the pelican hook will be at the foot end of the litter.

9.16.4.3.3. Select a belay point on a ceiling tie down ring, floor ring (closest to exit) or the FRIES bar. Insure belay system does not interfere with fast rope operations. System can be connected on the same side as the fast rope. Monitor rope for contact with edge of door.

9.16.4.3.4. Clip locking steel carabiner with pelican hook and Sticht plate (or figure-8 device) to the belay point.

9.16.4.3.5. Route rope through figure 8 or Sticht plate and pelican hook to make a quick release system.

9.16.4.3.6. For safety of flight the REDS package will be secured using a trucker hitch and positioned away from the door. The equipment package will be secured to the floor with tie down straps and removed two minutes prior to deployment. Rope bag (or bird-nested rope) will be stored overhead in the cabin, or on top of package, whichever position allows the easiest access and use.

9.16.4.3.7. During night operations the kit should be marked with blue chemlites on top and two sides.

9.16.5. Deployment Sequence and Belay Duties: Belayer should position himself to monitor descent of REDS kit while maintaining full control of the belay. Belayer is last to exit the helo.

9.16.5.1. At the 1-minute call, position the REDS kit halfway out the helo door . Maintain enough control on the kit to ensure it can be retrieved in case of a go-around or mission abort.

9.16.5.2. On the command "ROPES", deploy the REDS. REDS and fast rope can be deployed simultaneously.

9.16.5.3. Belayer needs to maintain positive control while lowering the kit. The kit should reach the surface before the first fast rope.

9.16.5.4. When he determines the surface is clear, the belayer releases the pelican hook and deploys any excess line from the aircraft. Jettison may also be accomplished from the FRIES bar, if so equipped.

9.16.6. Surface Personnel Duties for REDS Deployment

9.16.6.1. Ensure all events are pre-briefed and personnel have rehearsed assigned duties as much as possible.

9.16.6.2. A team member should be assigned to disconnect the REDS belay system from the kit once the kit is on the surface. At least two team members also should be assigned to take the REDS to the choke point.

9.16.6.3. PJs are dispatched from the choke point to the downed aircraft to conduct initial casualty sweep, casualty marking, and scene assessment. Aid and Litter (A&L) teams may be dispatched to the downed aircraft to assist PJs in area sweep.

9.16.6.4. If extrication is indicated, A&L teams will transport the REDS kit to the site. PJ team members will orchestrate extrication and medical stabilization. Assisted extrication will always be a team effort.

Table 9.3. Heavy REDS Kit Contents.

HEAVY REDS KIT CONTENTS

(approximate weight 300lbs)

1 x REDS container

1 x O-cutters

1 x spreader

1 x hydraulic pump

1 x set of chains

1 x crash ax

2 x hack saws

4 x spare blades for hacksaws

1 x fire blanket

1 x reciprocating saw

6 x spare blades for saw

1 x air pump

1 x air lift bag, 12-ton

1 x air lift bag24-ton

1 x air lift bag, 36-ton

1 x Ram, small w/extensions

HEAVY REDS KIT CONTENTS
(approximate weight 300lbs)

1 x crosshead for ram tip

1 x flat base plate

1 x pulling heads

1 x extension pipe, 6in

1 x extension pipe, 13in

EMPLOYMENT METHODS:

Heavy REDS kit should be inserted with follow-on air/ground assets.. Due to the weight and associated problems with movement, the kit should be only be used at relatively secure (Explain "SECURE") incident sites. The heavier-duty tools are made primarily for extrication from larger structural components found in large aircraft, vehicles, and buildings.

STORAGE AND INSPECTION:

Ram: With the pump running and pressure to the Ram, close the bars fully. Extend the Ram arms out approximately ½ inch and release pressure at the pump. Disconnect the Ram from hoses and cover fittings with dust caps.

Table 9.4. Light REDS Kit Contents.

LIGHT REDS KIT CONTENTS
(approximate weight 225lbs)

1 x REDS container - see Note below

1 x lowering harness - 2" nylon webbing w/hardware and risers.

1 x generator (hydraulic pump)

1 x combo tool

2 x hose extension (for extraction tools)

2 x crash ax

2 x hack saw (double blades)

1 x tool kit for saw

1 x Ryobi saw with extra blades taped to saw

1 x 1-ton lift **bag** 1 x 7-ton lift bag 2 x 10-ton lift bag 1 x air pump

2 x one-way valve hose for lift bags

2 x fire blanket (2' x 3')

2 x chains (1 long/1 short)

LIGHT REDS KIT CONTENTS

(approximate weight 225lbs)

1 set tip pins

1 x REDS maintenance kit - oil for gas mixture, mineral oil for generator, saw tool kit, Ryobi saw blades, hacksaw blades, hose caps.

NOTE: Kit is maintained separately in another container.

NOTE: Container must be of sufficient size to hold all REDS components, offer protection when deployed (air-dropped or belayed from a hover). Example: NSN-listed standard green medical storage box #5, NSN 6545-00-914-3500, (30"L x 18"W, 16"D), or box #6, NSN 6545-00-914-3510, (30"L x 18"W x 20"D).

9.17. Tethered (T) Duck Operations . The "T" duck is the deployment method for a deflated and rolled Combat Rubber Raiding Craft (CRRC). The CRRC is a F-470 Zodiac weighing 280 pounds empty. T-Duck consists of deploying a deflated CRRC and personnel from the cabin of a helicopter.

9.17.1. Set Up and Preparation. The CRRC is prepared by the team. A harness holds the boat in its deflated and rolled configuration. This harness is equipped with a single point quick release, which also serves as the attaching point for the rope lowering the boat. The CRRC is loaded through the opposite door planned for deployment, usually loaded through the left door and pushed to the edge of the right door. CRRC is placed on the left side of the ramp on a 53 series aircraft. The motor should face the door and should be the first part to exit the aircraft. Normally, the CRRC is positioned at the right door of the H-60 with the engine protruding over the edge of the door. Coil fast rope and secure out of the way on fuel tank (60) or side-wall of aircraft. Activate one red chemlight at inflation handle (prior to takeoff in case the team cannot reach it during the, time warnings sequence). It is recommended before conducting operations, personnel unfamiliar with T-Duck operations see an actual CRRC installed on the aircraft.

9.17.1.1. Preparation of the aircraft cabin is accomplished by the team under the supervision of the cabin NCOIC. Ensure anchor points are capable of suspending the weights of personnel/equipment and do not interfere with deployment procedures. Normal equipment is a standard H-bar, two carabiners, chemlights (for night), brake device, and a rope. The rope should be compatible with the intended hover height, the weight of the load, and is stored in a deployment bag. One carabiner is attached to the left forward rappelling ring on the H-bar. If the load does not exceed 600 pounds, extend and use the H-bar. The second carabiner is attached to the 3500-pound top cargo tiedown ring on the left forward cabin wall and is the primary anchor. The running end of the rope is routed through the carabiner on the rappel ring or fast rope connection point, and fastens to the. A brake device is established at the anchor point or a friction knot is used on the anchor carabiner, and all slack is pulled in. The brake device or friction knot allows the designated belayman to control the boat's rate of descent.

NOTE: If the CRRC is placed in the right door, the fast rope can be recovered and coiled in the left door without affecting hoist/penetrator operations. However, the pilot cannot see the team deploy by fast rope. There are no requirements for location, coordinate with the aircrew and use Mission, Enemy, Terrain, Troops, - Time Available (METT-T).

9.17.2. Inspections.

   9.17.2.1. C02/Compressed Air Assembly:

      9.17.2.1.1. Inspect bottle.

      9.17.2.1.2. Teflon tape threads on all male connectors for high-pressure hoses.

      9.17.2.1.3. Check for proper washers for high-pressure hoses.

NOTE: All washers should be replaced every time the tank is changed.

   9.17.2.2. Harness:

      9.17.2.2.1. Check stitching for fraying and tearing. Check harness webbing to ensure serviceable.

      9.17.2.2.2. Check quick releases for smooth operation/actuation.

   9.17.2.3. Belay:

      9.17.2.3.1. Check rope for fraying and tearing (check sheath and inner core).

      9.17.2.3.2. Check belay device (rescue "W', longhorn, sky genie) for wear.

      9.17.2.3.3. Check carabiners for wear and locking mechanism works properly .

Table 9.5. "T" Duck Kit Contents.

F-470	Washers	40' fast rope
Harness	Long hose	Rubber bands
50' rope	Mars motor	Crescent wrench
Pulley	Quick releases	Longhorn
Short hose	Carabiners(4)	"T" fitting
Gloves	Safety strap	Teflon tape
Speed tape	Motor floats	Oars (modified)

   9.17.2.4. Packing Instructions:

      9.17.2.4.1. CRRC Preparation:

      9.17.2.4.2. Deflate boat completely.

      9.17.2.4.3. Set all valves to "inflation".

      9.17.2.4.4. Store foot pump and tools.

      9.17.2.4.5. Install C02/compressed air bottle.

      9.17.2.4.6. Attach two red chemlights to bottle valve handle.

      9.17.2.4.7. Check fuel connections to ensure compatibility with Mars engine.

      9.17.2.4.8. Connect fuel bladder A-3 bag to boat.

      9.17.2.4.9. Roll CRRC nose to tail.

9.17.2.4.10. Place a 4'x 3' piece of 1/4" plywood under the rolled boat for use as a skid plate (optional).

9.17.2.4.11. Attach H-harness to rolled CRRC.

9.17.2.4.12. Secure quick releases (around the CRRC and plywood) ensure "D" ring is on top of the rolled CRRC next to the engine cowling.

9.17.2.4.13. Tape extra strap webbing:

9.17.2.4.14. Attach a red chemlight to each quick release.

9.17.2.4.15. Secure paddles to CRRC with 550 cord.

9.17.2.4.16. Attach motor to transom and secure with cable and hook.

9.17.3. Aircraft Configuration.

9.17.3.1. Aircraft Inspection. 781 A and K - Check write-ups for doors, floors, FRIES bars, intercom systems, UHF radios, installation of special mission equipment (which might take up valuable cabin space), ramp controls, hoist controls, penetrator, and stokes litter.

9.17.3.2. CRRC Secured (In-Door/On Ramp):

9.17.3.3. Install Restraint Strap. Connect carabiner end to package and quick release end to floor.

9.17.3.4. Install Motor and A-3 Bag with fuel bladders, if not previously installed.

9.17.3.5. Attach belay device to the FRIES bar overhead cargo ring (T-Duck may bend the older H-bar. If the aircraft has the H-bar, attach the belay device to a red cargo ring).

9.17.3.6. Install belay rope and secure all locking carabiners.

9.17.3.7. Attach fast rope to Fries Bar (left door in 60 series, right side ramp in 53 series). Coil fast rope and secure out of the way on fuel tank (60) or side wall of aircraft (53).

9.17.3.8. Extend FRIES bars or arrange with crew to extend bars at the 5-minute warning.

9.17.3.9. Activate one red chemlight at inflation handle (prior to takeoff in case the team cannot reach it during the time warnings sequence). Ensure there is unrestricted access to the inflation handle.

9.17.4. Time Warnings.

9.17.4.1. Standard time warnings are used to ensure both the deploying team and the crew are ready. Standard time warnings of 20, 10, 5, and 1 minute are announced by the aircrew based upon their calculated arrival, TOT. The rope master may require more than the minimum time calls and should be on intercom until at least the 5-minute call. The 20 and 10 minute time warnings are designed to inform you of the approaching TOT; usually no actions are required other than mental preparation.

9.17.4.2. At the 5 minute call, don fast rope gloves, fins, and facemask, receive update on survivor/incident site data, activate chemlights, and inflate ends of CRRC tubes. Extend the fast rope bar and ready it for deployment prior to the 5-minute call.

9.17.4.3. At the 1 minute call, ensure belayman is in position, and release restraint straps from the CRRC. At this point, the AIE master may go off intercom.

9.17.5. Deployment Procedures

9.17.5.1. A standard fast rope is attached to the left side of the H-bar. Use standard fast rope and low and slow procedures for personnel deployment. The recommended minimum hover altitude is 30 feet AWL and airspeed less than five KIAS, hover preferable.

9.17.5.2. Boat and personnel deployment procedures should be thoroughly briefed with the personnel involved. During night deployments, chemlights are recommended for equipment identification. Chemlight colors and their specific use should be properly briefed to all deploying personnel to avoid confusion between types of equipment, emergency exits, and there corresponding colors.

9.17.5.3. When the aircraft is established in a hover over the intended deployment site , the pilot clears the cabin crew to begin the deployment. After ensuring the CRRC deployment rope is manned, and all slack is taken out of the rope (so as not to overload belay system), the personnel in the cabin slide the CRRC out the cabin door in a controlled manner (belayman and one team member deploy CRRC). The belayman lowers the CRRC to the water slowly. One or more persons then deploy from the opposite door and release the CRRC from the rope. The remaining personnel deploy while any additional equipment (rucks, spares, radios, etc.) is attached to the belay rope and lowered to the water. Aircraft departs as soon as team deploys and the fast rope is recovered.

WARNING: Ensure belay rope is slack prior to releasing from CRRC to avoid springing back up to the aircraft fuselage.

9.17.5.4. Personnel may low and slow if a sufficiently low hover is maintained, however, this is not the recommended method due to increased injury potential. Fast rope insertion is considered the insertion method of choice during "T" Duck operations.

9.17.6. Procedures in the Water.

9.17.6.1. First swimmer to the CRRC stabilizes the CRRC and places one hand on the inflation handle. Second swimmer to the CRRC stabilizes the CRRC, confirms someone has the inflation handle in hand-prepared to inflate, and once confirmed handle is in hand, releases the quick releases one at a time

NOTE: Ensure inflation valve is in hand prior to harness release. This must be a synchronized event.). Release one side of the harness, swimmer re-positions to release the second side of the harness, calls for inflation, and release the second side of the harness once the inflation begins.

NOTE: Do not release quick releases until inflation has begun. 9.17.6.2. Climb into CRRC, pull in all equipment, pull in and stow harness, connect fuel, dewater engine. Get underway (same as RAMZ procedures).

9.17.7. Emergency Procedures. Brief all personnel involved in the deployment concerning the actions required of them in case of an emergency. The AIE master should be on interphone during equipment deployment. Ropemaster must understand the pre-briefed hand signals and emergency procedures. A V-blade knife will be available in the cabin area during equipment deployments. The weight of the CRRC or any other load to be lowered from the fast rope bar must not exceed 600 pounds.

9.17.8. Considerations.

9.17.8.1. Belayman will maintain control of belay rope until the first swimmer has control of the CRRC.

9.17.8.2. In high seas, belayman should maintain control of the CRRC until de-rigging has begun.

9.17.8.3. Stokes litter/additional gear can be attached to package/rope, or deployed to the team upon completion of inflation sequence. Pre-planned procedures will be briefed with crew as part of pre-deployment briefing.

9.18. Kangaroo Duck (K-Duck) Operations. K-Duck operations are used when cargo space in the H-60 cannot support a T-Duck or the mission requires such speed and surprise that an already inflated CRRC is necessary. . The fully inflated CRRC is placed on a canvas harness and then the H-60 (with its lower main landing gear struts inflated to the Rapid Deployment Force (RDF) extension) hovers over the CRRC and lands on top of it. The CRRC is then cradled to the belly of the H-60 by attaching the harness to the 4000-pound rappelling rings on the H/FRIES-bar. The team is carried inside the H-60 cabin. The team's equipment, to include the motor for the CRRC, is securely stowed inside of the CRRC. These procedures are for delivering a fully inflated CRRC and a team (approximately eight people) during day or night operations. Once the H-60 is at 5 KIAS and 10 feet, the shear strap of the harness is cut, the CRRC is deployed and the team exits the helicopter.

9.18.1. Equipment Installation and Configuration. Normally the aircrew will provide and install the necessary equipment for conducting K-Duck operations. The PJ team is responsible for proper configuration of the CRRC.

9.18.2. CRRC Preparation.

9.18.2.1. Install the floor (also the wooden bow floor) and fully inflate the CRRC.

WARNING: Externally transporting the CRRC without the floor installed could cause the CRRC to fold up and possibly make contact with the rotors. Do not transport the CRRC without the floor installed. The optional floor extension is only necessary if it is desired to travel in excess of 130 KIAS.

9.18.2.2. Prepare and stow the motor with the motor arm down and strap the engine in place near the transom. Use suitable padding between the motor and floor, and pad the prop.

9.18.2.3. Ensure the paddles and gas tanks are placed in their positions and tied down.

9.18.2.4. Accompanying payload will be put into the CRRC as close to the center as possible. Do not store more than 50 lbs. in the bow, even with the wooden bow floor installed. All items must be in the CRRC completely so only the CRRC will touch the H-60. If payload items are large, i.e. rucks, water cans, etc., tie capsize line of 1" tubular nylon to the front towing ring. Run the line through each large item and tie off-the line on the last item making sure the free end of the line can reach the transom. All small items will be snap linked to the floor or tied to a larger item. Pad all items that need it.

9.18.3. Time Warnings.

9.18.3.1. Standard time warnings are used to ensure both the deploying team and the aircrew are ready. Standard time warnings of 20, 10, 5, and 1 minute are announced by the aircrew based upon their calculated arrival, TOT. The AIE master may require more than the minimum time calls and should be on intercom until at least the 5-minute call. The 20 and 10minute time warnings are designed to inform you of the approaching TOT; usually no actions are required other than mental preparation.

9.18.3.2. At the 5-minute call, don fast rope gloves, fins, and facemask, receive update on survivor/incident site data, and activate chemlights. Extend the fast rope bar and ready it for deployment prior to the 5-minute call.

9.18.3.3. At the 1-minute call, ensure AIE master is in position, and is prepared to cut the restraining strap. At this point, the AIE master may go off intercom.

9.18.4. Deployment Procedures.

9.18.4.1. Use standard low and slow procedures for personnel deployment. The recommended maximum deployment altitude is 10 feet AWL and airspeed less than 10 KIAS. CRRC and personnel deployment procedures should be thoroughly briefed with the personnel involved. During night deployments, chemlights are recommended for equipment identification. Chemlight colors and their specific use should be properly briefed to all deploying personnel to avoid confusion between types of equipment, emergency exits, and there corresponding colors.

9.18.4.2. When the aircraft is established in a hover over the intended deployment site , the pilot clears the cabin crew to begin the deployment. The helicopter is flown to the deployment site and a 10 feet and 10 knots approach is established. The pilot clears the team to deploy by calling "boats, boats, boats". The safetyman yells "boats" and points towards the exit. On the command "boats" the team leader cuts the shear strap and prepares for team deployment.

WARNING: Ensure all team member are clear of the harness straps prior to cutting the shear strap.

9.18.4.3. The team is cleared for deployment once the CRRC is released and team has visually checked prior to deployment to avoid inadvertent contact with the CRRC.

 NOTE: After the CRRC is released, there is a tendency for the helicopter to gain altitude above the desired deployment altitude due to the weight loss of the CRRC. The team leader may delay deployment of the team until a suitable deployment altitude is reached.

9.19. Helicopter Freefall Equipment Delivery. PJ teams are require to deploy with additional equipment to prosecute their mission that would be unsafe/unmanageable to deploy with directly. Equipment should be packaged in order to withstand the forces of being dropped. Utilizing the helicopter freefall equipment delivery method allows PJ teams to deploy safely with the required equipment. This subject area will deal mainly with raft deployment but will be expanded in future revisions of this AFI.

9.19.1. Seven or Twenty Man Life Raft. It is not recommended to use any aircraft emergency equipment intended to be used by the crew for the rescue of others except in emergencies. Mission planning should provide the information needed to elect carrying extra equipment for deployment to survivors.

9.19.1.1. Preparing the raft for drop. Remove the raft inflation D-ring from its pocket and leave the pocket unsnapped. Securely tie a 14-inch piece of web tape through the D-ring to form an approximate 5-inch loop. Secure the raft near the appropriate exit. Attach a 10-foot lanyard to the tiedown ring that is located by the forward most part of the side cargo door. Attach the other end to the 5-inch loop of web tape. Snap the carrying handles together beneath the raft. Attach chemlights to the raft at night prior to deployment.

9.19.1.2. Delivery Procedures.

9.19.1.2.1. The aircraft makes a shallow approach in order to establish level flight at 40 knots and 75 feet altitude on final. Two crewmembers should work together, one to control the raft and one to monitor the survivor and signal the other crewmember when to deploy the raft. After the crew drops the raft, call "raft away" and immediately recover the lanyard.

9.19.1.2.2. To aid the survivor, drop the raft upwind. This allows the wind/drift to push the raft towards the survivor. Use a smoke device on all life raft drops to assist in determining the exact wind direction and a drop reference. Use normal traffic pattern airspeeds and altitudes. Establish the final approach into the wind and delay the drop I second for every 5 knots of wind over 10 knots.

9.19.1.3. Safety Procedures. When conducting raft deployments, all personnel must wear the safety harnesses to preclude accidental exit from the helicopter. It may be necessary to use two crewmen to deploy the 20-man life raft. A "V" blade knife must be available to cut the raft if it should become entangled. Do not hold the 10 foot lanyard after the raft is deployed.

Chapter 10

CARGO AERIAL DELIVERY PROCEDURES

10.1. Purpose. The initial aerial supply or resupply of a deployed Pararescue (PJ) team will contribute to the success of the particular mission. No two missions require all of the same type of equipment to be aerial delivered. Pararescuemen (PJs) should be familiar with the packing and rigging of aerial delivery components. Additionally, each PJ must know the aerial delivery procedures used by the aircrew to deploy equipment to the team.

NOTE: Prior to loading hazardous cargo determine packing requirements for specific aircraft involved.

10.2. Types of Airdrops. PJ container loads are delivered by low-velocity airdrops and free drops.

10.2.1. Low-Velocity Airdrop. Low-velocity airdrop is delivered by cargo parachutes. The items can be rigged with an energy dissipater to ensure minimum shock upon ground impact. The majority of PJ supplies and equipment are deployed by low-velocity airdrop.

10.2.2. Free Drops. Free drop is any delivery without the use of parachutes or other retarding devices.

10.3. Cushioning Materials for Aerial Delivery Loads. Pieces of equipment packed within various containers may require padding or cushioning materials. Items can be separated with Styrofoam, cellulose wadding, felt sheets, or any material energy dissipating pads (honeycomb) suitable to protect them from breaking. Care must be exercised when packing components of assemblies to ensure all items necessary for operation of the assembly are packed in the same airdrop container.

10.4. Cargo Parachutes.

10.4.1. General. The inspection, repacking and maintenance of cargo parachute assemblies will be performed by base support. PJs only need be familiar with the time criteria for inspections and the routine inspection requirements. Refer to the appropriate T.O. for complete inspection, packing instructions, and storage.

10.4.2. Routine Inspection.

10.4.2.1. Check the external condition of the parachute packs, risers and static lines for visible defects, weak spots, broken threads, cuts, frays or other damage.

10.4.2.2. Check all hardware for rust, corrosion and smoothness of operation.

10.4.2.3. Inspect pack closing and static line break cords for defects in material, incorrect cord, improper routing, or improperly tied knot.

10.4.2.4. Inspect condition of parachute pack and ensure parachute canopy material is not showing.

10.4.2.5. Check parachute pack for tears, loose stitches, stains caused by oil or grease and weakened areas.

10.4.2.6. If the routine inspection reveals conditions indicating a need for repairs or a more thorough inspection, the parachute will be turned over to the parachute repacking facility, regardless of the date of last repack.

10.4.2.7. The following is a list of aerial delivery parachutes by type, diameter, capacity and weight:

10.4.2.7.1. G-8/M390, 8 Ft, 100 lbs, 11 lbs.

10.4.2.7.2. T-7A, 28 Ft, 100-500 lbs, 16 lbs.

10.4.2.7.3. G-13, 241/4 Ft, 200-500 lbs, 45 lbs.

10.4.2.7.4. G-14, 34 Ft, 200-500 lbs, 37 lbs.

10.4.2.7.5. T-10C, 35 Ft, 90-350 lbs, 20 lbs.

10.4.2.7.6. G-12, 64 Ft, 501-2200 lbs, 128 lbs.

10.4.3. Parachutes will not be stored in a cramped or damp condition.

10.5. Aerial Delivery Containers.

10.5.1. Types and sizes of containers are not specified, with the exception of fuel containers. Regardless of content or container, the personnel using the equipment should be familiar with the content, placement of equipment and peculiarities necessary for the operation of the equipment, i.e., catalytic heater.

10.5.2. The following is a list of aerial delivery containers by type, style, capacity and weight:

10.5.2.1. A-7A, Sling, 500 lbs, 6.0 lbs.

10.5.2.2. A-10, Net, 300 lbs, 7.0 lbs.

10.5.2.3. A-13, Rigid, 100 lbs, 7.0 lbs.

10.5.2.4. A-16, Rigid, 200 lbs, 45 lbs.

10.5.2.5. A-21, Bag, 500 lbs, 31 lbs.

10.5.2.6. A-22, Bag, 625-2200 lbs, 58 lbs.

10.5.2.7. AKIO SCOW, Sled, 200 lbs, 38 lbs.

10.6. Aerial Delivery Procedures.

10.6.1. General. The ability to deliver PJ support supplies and equipment to an incident site is of the utmost importance and mission success may be dependent upon support airdrops.

10.6.1.1. The cargo airdrop patterns are similar to the PJ deployment pattern. The minimum altitude for day paradrop is 300 feet and day freefall equipment drops is 150 feet.

10.6.1.2. Items dropped to personnel in the water are normally dropped with retrieval lines attached. For drops to surface vessels, the MA-1/2 kit may be used as a delivery vehicle and the equipment to be delivered substituted for the number 2, 3, or 4 bundles. If the life rafts are not needed, a delivery kit can be constructed by replacing the life rafts with MK 6 Mod 3 flare/ smokes. When a parabundle is dropped using the above procedure, a parachute must be attached to the MK 6 Mod 3.

10.6.1.3. Equipment delivered at night will have a cargo marker light attached. Attach the light by securing a double length of 5 foot nylon 550 cord to the marker light, then attach the other end to the equipment. Stabilize the light to the equipment with type Number 5 cord. Pass the parachute static line under the type Number 5 cord to ensure light break-away when deployed. The SDU-5/E strobe light or chemlite may be used in lieu of the cargo marking lights.

10.6.1.4. To facilitate crew coordination, the impact point of spotter chutes/streamers and bundles will be identified using clock positions relative to the final approach flown; e.g., "the spotter chute landed at 12 o'clock, 45 meters", when relaying a drop report to the aircraft overhead.

10.6.2. Surface Directed Equipment Delivery. This provides for a method of aerial delivery to a PJ team when visual contact cannot be established due to cloud formation, fog, trees, etc. The following procedures are recommended:

10.6.2.1. The ground controller using radio communications, flare signaling or smoke devices will assist the aircrew in positioning the aircraft directly overhead. It may be necessary for the ground controller to suggest a compass heading or a term such as "turn left 10 degrees now." It may also be necessary to state "You are directly overhead now." The situations are too varied to provide specific guidance, however, these procedures have proven successful in the past.

10.6.2.2. Once the position directly overhead has been established, the pilot using navigational aids/visual reference points should establish a pattern to return the aircraft to that spot each time.

10.6.2.3. The actual release point will have to be estimated by both aircrew and the ground controller. An into the wind drop heading is suggested, however, conditions may dictate otherwise. The release point will have to be calculated based on ballistic data altitude, type of parachute, surface wind and aircraft heading.

10.6.2.4. To be effective, this procedure will require close coordination between all parties concerned. The pilot should keep the ground controller aware of his intentions, position in the pattern and countdown to drop.

10.7. Fuel. Units operating in or subject to operate in cold climate areas must have special fuel (Coleman/white gas, butane/propane) readily available to deploy with PJ forces. Lanterns, stoves, and heaters carried, stored, or deployed from aircraft will be empty and void of fuel or fumes. When this equipment is required as part of the alert load, fuel must accompany it. Fuel carried aboard aircraft will be in standard metal fuel containers and be padded to prevent accidental rupture. The following examples are the preferred methods of carrying fuel on aircraft:

10.7.1. Place one to three one gallon cans of Coleman fuel, which are factory sealed, into a metal 1500 round ammunition component box. An absorbent, non-flammable packing material such as vermiculite will be placed around fuel cans to prevent shifting and contact with other cans. Prior to placing the lid on the ammunition box, ensure rubber gasket is intact to provide seal.

10.7.2. Aluminum fuel bottles (pint or quart, no pour spout) must have an unvented screw on cap and gasket. They can be carried as stated above, or in a field pack. When carried in a field pack, it will be centrally located where it is protected on all sides and not in contact with hard objects, or in the center of a rolled sleeping bag.

NOTE: Recommend fuel bottles be filled at temperatures of 75 to 80 degrees Fahrenheit.

10.7.3. Butane/propane cylinders should be carried in a container provided by the manufacturer or carried in metal ammunition component boxes with sufficient packing material to prevent shifting and contact with other cylinders.

10.7.4. When fuel containers are carried on aircraft with floor heating systems, containers will be insulated from the floor. Ammunition component boxes or other similar containers used as storage/delivery containers will have the word "FLAMMABLE" stenciled in one-inch letters on two sides. Under the word "flammable", in one-inch letters, will be the type fuel contained within. Different type fuels such as white gas and butane will not be stored in the same container. Field packs containing fuel will have tags affixed in a conspicuous location. Tags will be stenciled in one-inch letters as stated above. If fuel containers are required to be airlifted on AMC aircraft, they must meet packing requirements for hazardous cargo due to the higher altitudes at which these aircraft operate.

10.7.5. Storage of fuel at PJ sections must be coordinated and approved by base civil engineering and the base fire department.

Chapter 11

DIVE OPERATIONS

11.1. General. All pararescue diving operations will be conducted by qualified divers and equipment will be maintained IAW manufactures data and unit standard operations procedures (SOPs). Suggested equipment source includes "Authorized for Navy Use" (ANU).

11.1.1. Commercial or civilian divers will not participate in PJ diving operations or use military diving equipment unless approved by the unit commander.

11.1.2. The basic guidance for dive operations is contained in United States (US) Diving Manual , Revision 4 . While the Navy has primary responsibility for developing dive procedures and equipment that are of common interest to the DoD, it does not include specific procedures unique to Pararescue and the rescue and recovery mission. Deviations to the US Diving Manual are contained in this AFI and MAJCOM approved guidance.

11.1.3. Refer to AFI 11-202V3 for flying after diving policy.

11.1.4. Establish unit diving Operating Instruction (OI) to govern local diving operations. Ensure risk management and risk assessments are briefed for all diving evolutions.

11.2. Dive Medic. The diving medic will be qualified PJ and if possible certified as a Diving Medical Technician (DMT). Units should utilize Dive Medical Officers (DMOs) on all dives if available in addition to having a certified DMT. All Dive Medics will:

11.2.1. Be present on all open and closed circuit dives..

11.2.2. Provide routine/emergency medical treatment to diving personnel.

11.2.3. Ensure required medical equipment is available at the dive site.

11.2.4. Coordinate with the dive supervisor on the medical evacuation plan.

11.2.5. Ensure dive re-compression chamber has been notified and is on stand-by during dive operations.

11.2.6. Ensure helicopter emergency evacuation is on-call, available radio frequencies/alternate communications established/briefed, and is briefed on location of dive site.

11.3. Diving Supervisor. The Diving Supervisor will be a qualified PJ and certified in OJT records as a Diving Supervisor (DS) All Diving Supervisors will:

11.3.1. Be familiar with the equipment, conditions, safety precautions, and hazards inherent to diving operations.

11.3.2. Be in charge of the diving operation. No diving will be conducted during the diving supervisor's absence. Remain topside and on-scene while divers are in the water. In the event of a diving accident, the diving supervisor will remain on-scene until all divers have safely exited the water and the accident has been resolved

11.3.3. Coordinate and plan all aspects of the diving operation and ensure divers have been properly briefed/follow diving plan.

11.3.4. Ensure equipment is operational and able to perform the intended function to complete the mission.

11.3.5. Be responsible on all matters pertaining to the planning, execution, safety of the dive, and ensure dive tables limits are not exceeded.

11.3.6. Ensure dive plans include the location and operational status of the nearest re-compression chamber. Ensure arrangements have been made for expeditious transportation of any diving casualties and for contacting a DMO if not-on-scene..

NOTE: Information pertaining to decompression chambers and transportation can be found in NAVSEA 0910-LP-708-8000/FM 20-11-1, Directory of World Wide Shore Based Hyperbaric Chambers, Vol. I and II. The above action and coordination will be accomplished before the mission with follow-up coordination and confirmation on the day of the mission.

11.3.7. The dive supervisor or his representative will contact the appropriate weather agencies and obtain appropriate information for the area of operation.

11.3.8. Document all training.

11.4. Stand-By Diver. The stand-by diver is a fully qualified diver, assigned for back-up or to provide emergency assistance, and is ready to enter the water at a moments notice. PJs will be proficient and current for the type of scuba used during the dive. The stand-by diver's function is to provide emergency assistance to divers and can also be the dive medic. All stand-by diver's will:

11.4.1. Attend the entire dive operation briefing.

11.4.2. Be briefed and knowledgeable of the rescue procedures for the scuba equipment being used by the divers.

11.4.3. Monitor the progress of the dive and be ready to respond if called upon.

11.4.4. A stand-by diver with tender is required for all diving operations. The stand-by diver need not be equipped with the same equipment as the primary divers, but shall have equivalent depth and operational dive capabilities. A stand-by diver shall don all SCUBA equipment and be checked by the Diving Supervisor. The stand-by diver may then remove his mask and fins and have them ready to don immediately for quick deployment. At the discretion of the Dive Supervisor, the stand-by diver may remove the SCUBA tanks for safety and fatigue reasons. When the stand-by diver is rigged for SCUBA, he must be equipped with a working octopus regulator.

11.5. Safety.

11.5.1. Every dive will be preceded by a dive brief, dive risk assessment, and attended by all personnel involved in the dive. If key support personnel are unavailable to attend the dive brief, the diving supervisor will ensure personnel are briefed separately.

11.5.2. When more than one diving platform is required because of the nature of the operation, e.g., launch and recovery from different locations or a large number of divers, one or more assistant diving supervisors will be assigned and will perform diving supervisor duties.

11.5.3. A method of diver recall is required for all dives.

11.5.4. A marking buoy should be used whenever possible to mark the location of divers in the water. At the discretion of the diving supervisor, a light source may be attached for easier location during night dives.

11.5.5. All scuba cylinders used by the safety diver during diving operations will be charged to at least 75 percent of the working pressure. NOTE: Navy requires the safety divers tanks to be jammed to a minimum of 75% of the working pressure as it is unrealistic to jam the tanks to 100%. During the charging process of the tanks, the tank heat up. Once the tanks cools down it can lose up to 20% of its pressure. The requirement for 75% of the working pressure allows for changes in the bottle pressure caused by heating and cooling during jamming and transport.

11.5.6. For diving operations conducted between sunset and sunrise, flashlights or diving lights are mandatory for the diving supervisor, standby diver/medic, Chemlites or dive lights are mandatory for each diver.

11.5.7. Any time a divers air supply reaches 500 psi and below or diver activates his reserve, the diver must immediately notify his buddy/others divers and indicate he is returning to the surface. The dive buddy should surface with diver and/or comply with dive supervisors briefed dive plan instructions.

11.6. Lost Diver/Equipment Procedures.

11.6.1. Initiate diver recall immediately upon determining a diver/equipment is lost.

11.6.2. Mark the last known location of the diver with a buoy.

11.6.3. Contact parent unit ASAP. At no time will the name of any lost diver be passed over the radio.

11.6.4. Organize divers on hand and decide if there is adequate bottom time to conduct a search. If so, commence a search of the immediate area using the buoy as the center of the search area. Do not move the buoy if no bottom time is available with divers on hand or it is suggested that available bottom time is inadequate for the task at hand. Conduct a surface swim search and contact command for additional resources.

 NOTE: These procedures apply to all RAMZ training deployments in the event parachuting equipment is lost and or boat support becomes swamped and sinks.

11.7. Safety Boats.

11.7.1. A safety boat is a motorized boat used for picking up divers in the event of a diving emergency. A safety boat is mandatory for any dive conducted in open water (open water is considered beyond the distance in which a safety swimmer can effectively be used from the shore). The safety boat must be highly maneuverable and be ready to rapidly respond to a diver needing assistance.

11.7.2. Safety boats will display the proper flags, pennants, or lights.

11.7.3. The appropriate number of safety boats will be available to support dive personnel and the operation.

11.8. Diving with Foreign Units. When PJs are participating in diving operations with foreign military units, the safety of US personnel will remain the responsibility of the senior PJ representative present. In most cases it will be the PJ team leader (TL), regardless of the seniority of other senior US or foreign officers present. In the conduct of these operations, it is highly probable that foreign diving safety and

operational procedures will differ from those set forth in this instruction and its references. The senior PJ present will exercise discretion and mature judgment to ensure the foreign procedures remain consistent with safe and sound diving principles and practices.

11.9. SCUBA

11.9.1. Personnel Requirements. Minimum personnel required for SCUBA operations are:

11.9.1.1. Two divers.

11.9.1.2. One dive supervisor.

11.9.1.3. One stand-by diver.

11.9.1.4. One DMT (can be the same individual as dive supervisor or stand-by diver)

11.9.2. Compass Swim Procedures. MAJCOM/unit SOPs will dictate requirements , however the following procedures are recommended:

11.9.2.1. In order to maintain team integrity and communication during tactical dives or surface swims the use of swimmer lines may be warranted. Along the swimmers line a variety of formations can be assembled. The most common formations for team compass dives/swims are on-line, column (in line), column (offset), left or right echelon, or the wedge. The appropriate use and techniques of these formations can be outlined in the units SOPs.

11.9.2.2. Buddy Lines. A buddy line, 6 to 10 feet long, is used to connect the buddy divers at night or in conditions of poor visibility. The buddy line will either be S-folded in the respective divers hand or attached with a single pull quick release, so communications can be maintained, but quickly released in the event of entanglement. Any line used in scuba operations should be strong and have neutral or slightly positive buoyancy. Nylon, dacron, and manila are all suitable materials.

11.9.2.3. The compass man sets heading on compass and informs all divers of heading before entering the water.

11.9.2.4. The team enters water, gives the "OK" signal to the boat party, and connects buddy lines to each other.

11.9.2.5. The team leader initiates thumbs down descent signal.

11.9.2.6. The team descends and neutralizes at a pre-briefed depth. Each member checks his own compass in order to orient himself to the general direction of forward movement.

11.9.2.7. The TL checks to see if the compass man is ready and gives two tugs/squeezes for the move out signal.

11.9.2.8. The team moves out in the briefed formation and swims to shore or for a pre-briefed time period. Signal halts, i.e., 1 tug/squeeze is given.

11.9.2.9. The TL sends the compass man to the surface on a safety line/lanyard.

11.9.2.10. The compass man signals (pre-briefed line tugs/signals) the TL if the team is able to surface safely.

11.9.2.11. When cleared to surface, the TL initiates ascend signal.

11.9.2.12. The team will surface using a slow, controlled ascent.

11.9.2.13. The TL conducts a head count of personnel and continues with the mission.

11.10. Environmental Considerations.

11.10.1. Water temperature is directly proportional to the duration a diver/swimmer can effectively operate before becoming fatigued and hypothermic.

11.10.2. Salt water versus fresh water. This should be considered when selecting weights.

11.10.3. Tides and currents must be calculated in advance in order to determine optimum launch and recovery times as well as avenues of approach.

11.10.4. Beach types determine the type of landing to be made when utilizing a CRRC.

11.10.5. In-land salt seas (i.e. Great Salt Lake) are heavily brined and may contain bacteria (cyano-bacteria) which can affect divers during any type of dive operation. Full-face masks should be considered for dive ops in in-land salt seas. Divers may require additional dive weights in order to stay submerged due to the high salt content.

11.11. Search Patterns . The search pattern is the heart of most underwater rescue and recovery operations. A dive team's skill in conducting search patterns is directly proportionate to mission success. To successfully search an underwater area, a team must understand the intent and proper execution of search techniques.

11.11.1. For a search pattern to be effective it must have the following attributes:

11.11.1.1. Starts at a known point, covers a known area, and ends at a known point. This results in either the object being found or eliminates the area from further search.

11.11.1.2. Allows clear communication between the diver and surface personnel through line signals or communication system

11.11.1.3. Is adaptable to various environments.

11.11.1.4. Does not require specialized equipment.

11.11.1.5. Provides ability to mark location of found objects.

11.11.1.6. Can be adapted based on size of search object.

11.11.1.7. Is simple enough that the dynamics of the pattern can be explained to a helpful bystander during an emergency situation.

11.11.1.8. Does not require inordinate amounts of manpower and uses available divers effectively.

11.11.1.9. Can be run from shore or boat.

11.11.1.10. Allows for buddy team diving or a single diver with topside tender.

11.11.2. Equipment.

11.11.2.1. Marker Buoys. There are two types of marker buoys: submersible and surface. Submersible buoys are neutrally buoyant until deployed and are used for marking the objects location. Surface buoys are used to mark boundaries, searched area, and last seen point. The risk/benefit factor determines whether buoys are worth the risk of entanglement and confusion added by an additional line or the time spent placing them.

11.11.2.2. Search/Tender Lines. Search/tender lines are characteristically of marine type, flexible, and neutrally buoyant.

11.11.2.3. Search Pattern Weight. When searching deep water or outside the limits of a shore based pattern, use a boat based search pattern. The search pattern weight allows for adjustment of the search line. The search line runs parallel to the anchor line, through a carabiner or pulley attached to a weight on the bottom and outward to the diver. This allows the diver to search an area in the same manner as from shore except the pivot point is now directly off the weight.

11.11.3. Rescue/Recovery Mode and the Risk/Benefit Factor. Dive team operations should be planned and executed around three terms: Rescue Mode, Recovery Mode, and Risk/Benefit.

11.11.3.1. Rescue Mode is when there is a chance to save a life. The PJ TL must make quick decisions and initiate the start of the search ASAP. The PJ TL pursues only enough information from witnesses to begin the operation.

11.11.3.2. Recovery Mode does not involve saving human life. As the term implies, recovery mode is executed at a slower, more deliberate pace to ensure all human remains/equipment are recovered.

11.11.3.3. Risk/Benefit Factor is a subjective evaluation of the merits of the operation. Does the payoff merit the risk to the team?

11.11.4. Scene Sketch. The PJ TL should compile and document as much information as possible. A scene sketch provides general information concerning the site and allows the TL to document the search area covered. An accurate sketch enables the TL to quickly brief the team members on areas of responsibility, search areas covered, and during concurrent operations provides the overall scene leader with his sector information.

11.11.5. Conditions Determining the Search Pattern Used.

11.11.5.1. Underwater visibility is one of the major considerations when formulating an operational plan. The diver's visibility may affect the amount of overlap in a search pattern. In zero visibility, the diver often must conduct the entire search by feeling around with his free hand. In shallow areas, divers and other rescue personnel should avoid wading or treading water as stirring up sediment will greatly reduce visibility.

11.11.5.2. Depth is another factor determining the type of search pattern best for an operation. Depth can limit or cancel an operation completely, depending upon the divers' experience and the Risk/Benefit Factor assigned the operation. Searching deep waters can require an excessive amount of line and create an awkward angle inhibiting the diver's progress. These situations often require the pattern be run off a search pattern weight as detailed earlier in boat-based patterns, or one of the versions detailed for shore-based patterns for deep water. Depth will also reduce, sometimes drastically, the divers bottom time while running the pattern.

11.11.5.3. Bottom contour plays an important role in the search process, a diver's task is easier when the bottom is smooth. When littered with debris, large rocks, or other obstructions, the line tender may need to be elevated. This increases the angle of the line allowing it to pass over the obstacle. Another method of bypassing obstructions is to use buoys at a point between the tender and the diver.

11.11.5.4. In some cases a large obstruction might serve as a search pattern boundary. Some obstructions on the bottom may required a line tender in scuba gear standing on the bottom himself to create the pivot point in the search pattern line and to relay signals from the surface tender.

11.11.5.5. In Rescue Mode, the dive team leader may want every diver in the water searching different areas with individual line tenders. However, there must be an option of calling a divers to the surface so he may be redirected to the aid of another diver. In Recovery Mode, where the pace is slower, a backup diver should always be standing by to respond to a help signal.

Figure 11.1. SideView of Shore Based Sweep Pattern Using Vehicle to Elevate Line Tender.

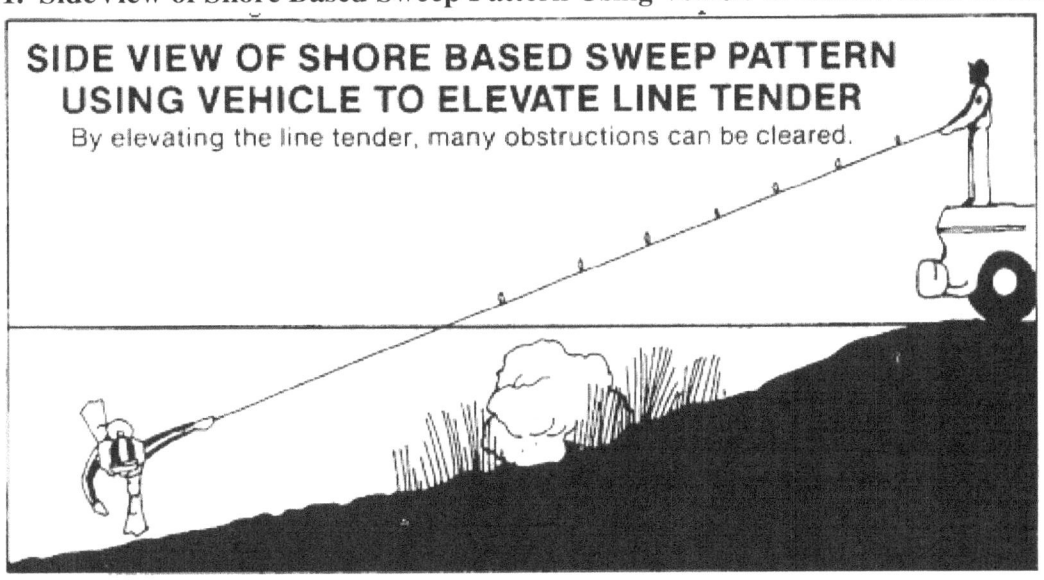

Figure 11.2. Side View of Shore Based Sweep Pattern Using Float to Lift Line Over Obstructions.

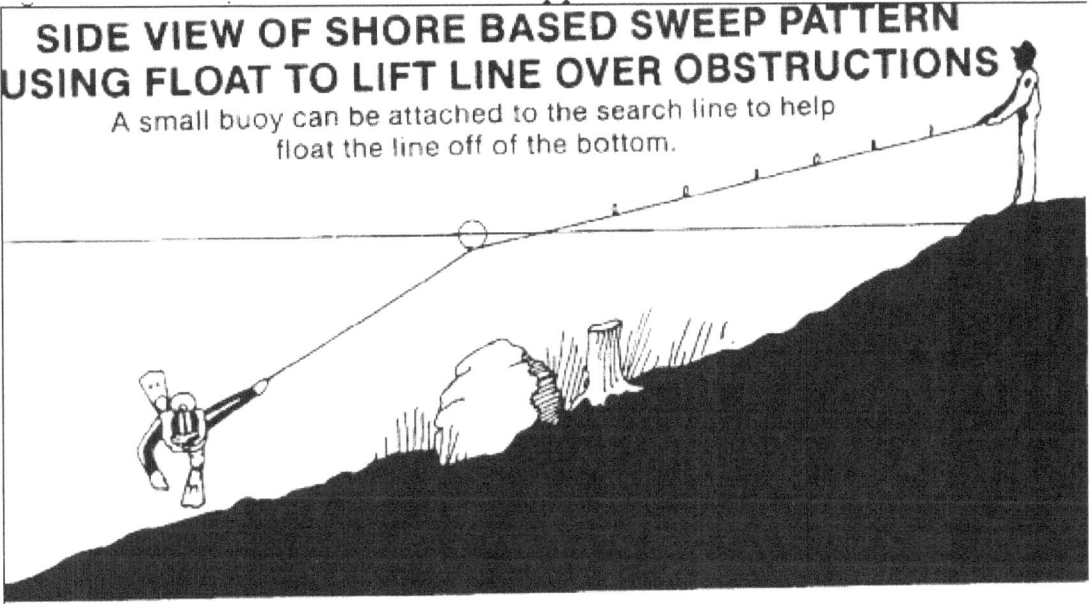

Figure 11.3. Side View of the Shore Sweep Pattern With Float and Second Diver to Clear Obstructions.

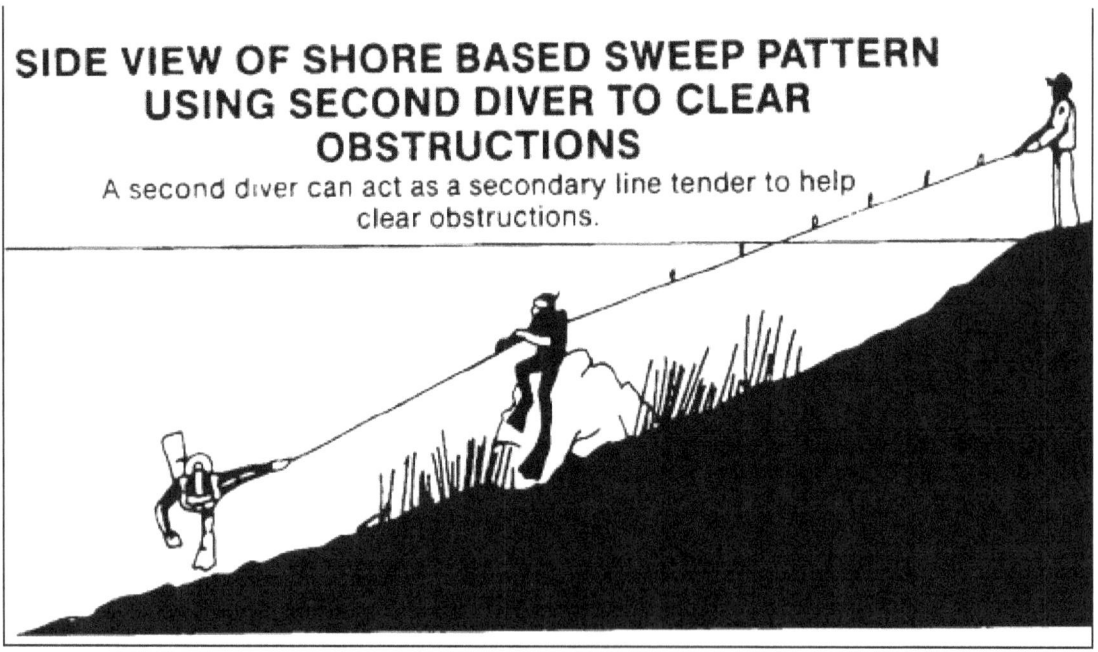

11.11.6. Line Tender. The line tender is generally the dive supervisor, during this phase of the operation, the tender makes sure the diver is properly dressed and equipped while at the same time a pre-dive checklist is reviewed.

11.11.6.1. Pre-dive Checklist Includes:

11.11.6.1.1. Determine whether the operation is in the rescue mode or recovery mode

11.11.6.1.2. Record divers starting psi.

11.11.6.1.3. Establish the minimum psi the diver is required to surface or end the dive.

11.11.6.1.4. Determine the maximum depth in which the pattern will run and maximum bottom time referenced to decompression tables.

11.11.6.1.5. Review all line signals.

11.11.6.1.6. Review procedures for a diver in distress.

11.11.6.1.7. Review procedures for a found object.

11.11.6.2. During the actual execution of the search pattern, it is the line tender who serves as the controlling factor of the operation. There are search patterns where the line tender is another diver underwater, but usually it is best that the tender be topside. In this way, the entire operation can be viewed clearly in relation to the last-seen-point, topside landmarks or compass headings.

11.11.6.3. The actions of the line tender are similar to that of a fisherman. The line tender keeps controlling tension on the line, is the sole communicator with the diver, and directs the divers efforts through a series of line signals.

11.11.6.4. It is important for the line tender to remain in a fixed position while the diver is running the pattern. The tender may opt to drive a stake in the ground next to their feet to ensure stability. This fixed position will be much harder to maintain while based in a boat. However, in all types of situations the line tender should be aware that a movement as seemingly as insignificant as changing an arm position could make a big difference to the diver underwater, sometimes to the point of disorienting the diver.

11.11.6.5. In the rescue mode, the line tender may receive information that indicates a better search area while the diver is running a pattern. In such cases, the skilled line tender can change the location of the diver increasing the area the search pattern covers, without resurfacing the diver. To do this, the tender walks toward the new location as the diver is swimming that direction. Such skills and techniques have made possible rescuing drowning victims within minutes of the dive teams arrival.

11.11.7. Overlap. The two major factors in determining the amount of overlap used in a pattern are visibility and the size of the object of the search. The line tender regulates the degree of overlap in the search pattern. In zero visibility, the search pattern will have to be tight with a good degree of overlap. In clearer conditions, less overlap may be needed. However, some degree of overlap is usually necessary to ensure a thorough search. While looking for a small object, the line tender may have the diver double back over the area covered on each sweep.

11.11.8. Knot Tying. When a diver enters the water, the line tender ties a small loop in the line to mark where the pattern began. As each pass is completed, the line tender ties a figure-8 knot in the line, marking the distance that the diver is covering. The diver holds the line by the figure-8 tied at his end of the line. It is important the diver be able to release the line at any time in the event the line becomes entangled.

11.11.9. Search Patterns. Simplicity is usually the best approach when selecting a search pattern. Do not put a diver in the water just for the sake of onlookers. A single diver is usually more efficient than two divers while running most search patterns. Again, the Risk/Benefit Factor is the major consideration whether operating in either Rescue Mode or Recovery Mode.

11.11.9.1. Line signals. All personnel involved in control of the search should be thoroughly familiar in the use of line signals. Listed below are the most common signals:

11.11.9.2.

11.11.9.2.1. Line tender to diver

11.11.9.2.1.1. Two tugs - stop, change direction, and take out line

11.11.9.2.1.2. Three tugs – come to surface

11.11.9.2.2. Diver to tender

11.11.9.2.2.1. Two tugs – need more line

11.11.9.2.2.2. Three tugs – found object of search

11.11.9.2.2.3. Four or more tugs – need help

NOTE: Do not use one tug as a signal as it is easily misinterpreted.

11.11.9.3. Shore Based Patterns

11.11.9.3.1. The Sweep. This pattern is used in the majority of dive team operations. Normally the sweep is run from shore, a bridge, a dam, or a pier, but can be applied to a boat under the right conditions. In ideal conditions a pattern can be run up to 200 feet from the line tender.

Figure 11.4. Side View of Shore Based Sweep Pattern.

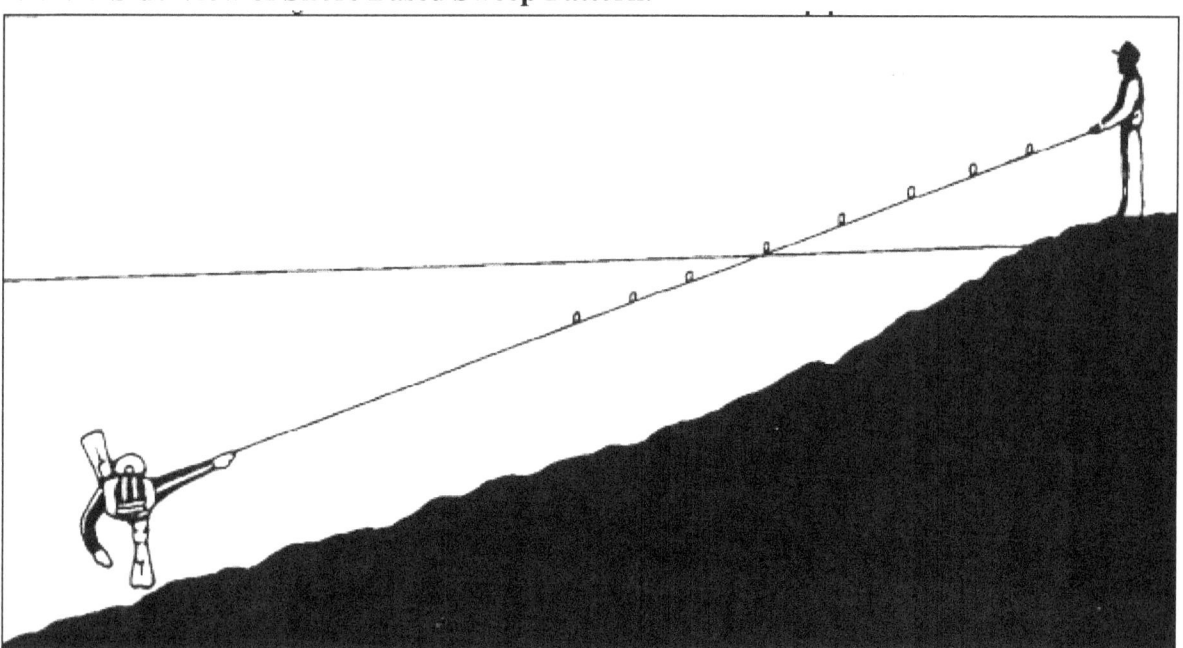

Figure 11.5. Top View of Shore Based Sweep Pattern.

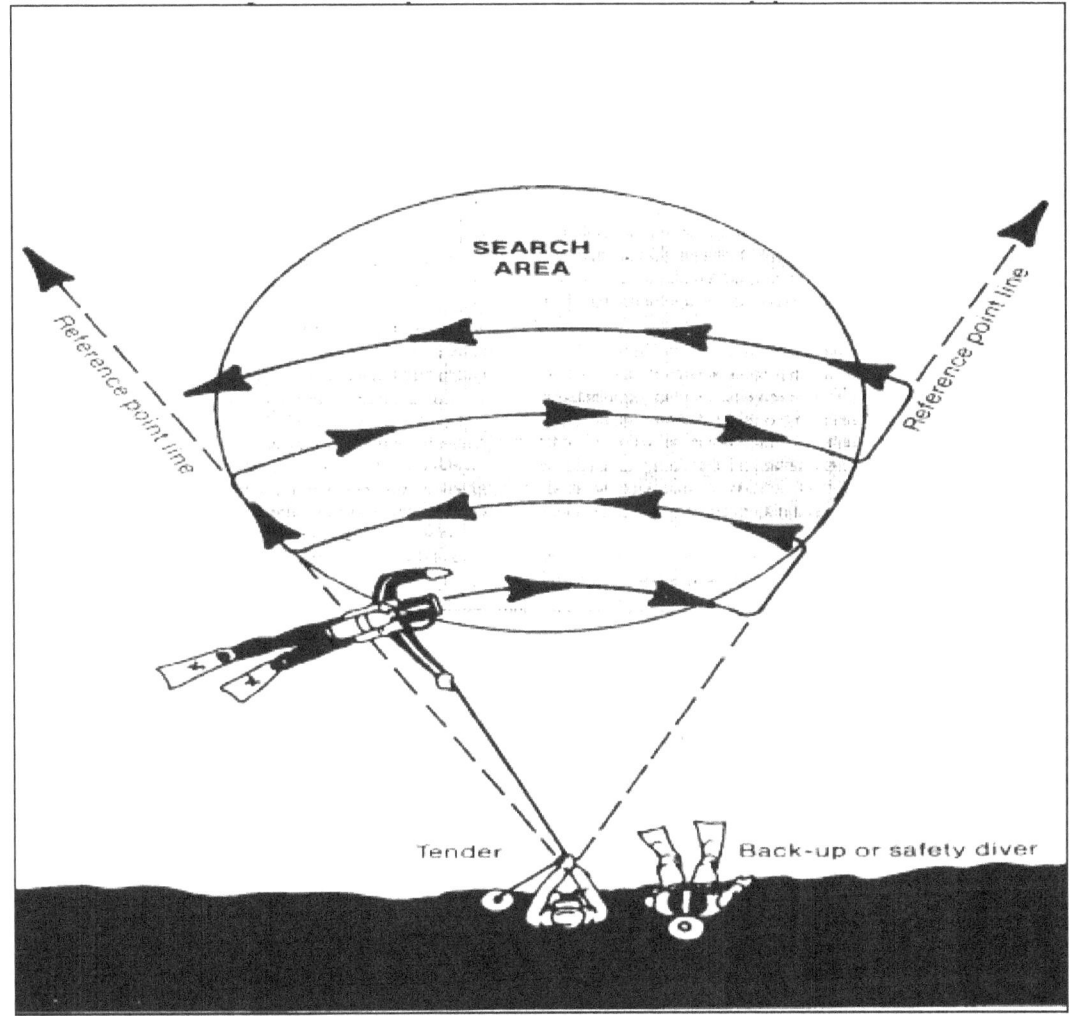

11.11.9.3.1.1. When executing, the diver swims back and forth in arcs controlled by the tender. Ensure tension is maintained between the tender and the diver so line signals may be passed.

11.11.9.3.1.2. The divers start point depends on the last seen location. For example, in a standard shore based pattern the diver works his way out from the location. It is important to note most witnesses over estimate the distance thus the search should begin closer towards the shore. The farther out the greater the chance of witness miscalculation. A good rule of thumb is to start half the distance from the last seen point.

11.11.9.3.1.3. As the diver works his way out, the tender needs to pay out more line allowing the diver to make wider arcs. The tender should align the ends of the arc with a landmark. If no landmarks are present the tender may need to take compass bearing to determine the end.

11.11.9.3.1.4. On searches where the bottom contour tapers sharply to the shoreline the tender avoids running the diver all the way up to shore to prevent persistent sinus and ear equalization. When a deep drop off is searched, the divers should search the deepest portion first conserving energy and bottom time for shallower areas.

11.11.9.3.1.5. If a large obstruction is encountered, the pattern can be run to the obstacle and a separate/simultaneous search run on the opposite side.

11.11.9.3.1.6. When a drop off or cliff is encountered preventing a consistent sweep the team has several options: The tender can be elevated, floats attached to the line, or the tender may be moved to a boat.

11.11.9.3.2. The Parallel Pattern. When searching large areas free of obstructions, the parallel pattern may be used. This parallel search is especially advantageous when the search object is suspected to be close to shore, but the last seen point is unclear.

11.11.9.3.2.1. The line tender and diver execute the pattern by moving parallel to each other moving from one point to another. At the completion of each pass, the tender feeds the diver more line and both reverse course proceeding in the opposite direction.

Figure 11.6. Shore Based Parallel Pattern.

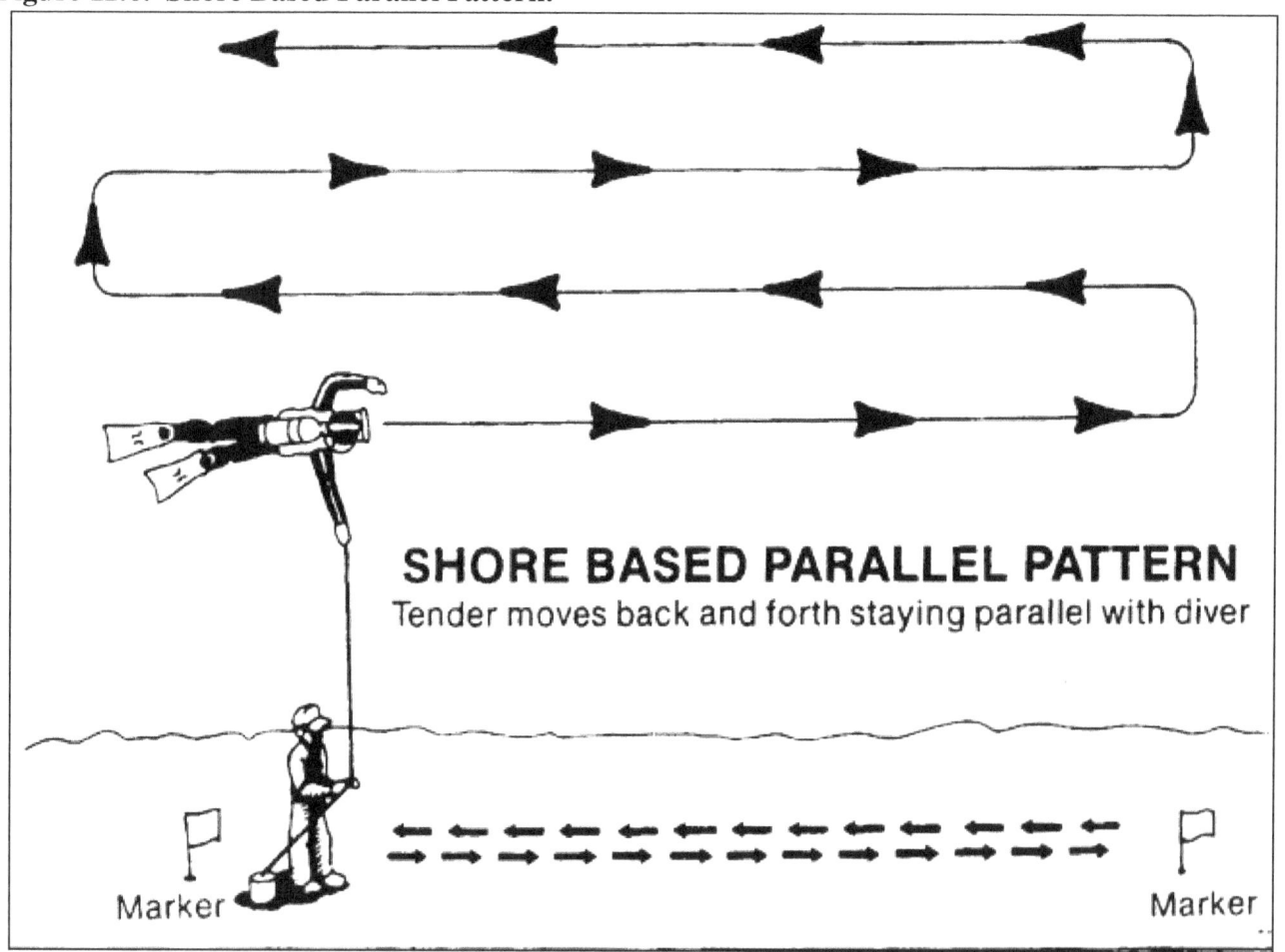

11.11.9.3.3. Snag Method. The snag method may be employed using either a sweep or a parallel pattern. When a large object (i.e., an aircraft) is being sought, and a large area is being searched, a substantial distance can be covered with each pass. The line tender allows the diver more slack than he would during a standard search (where the diver personally covers every inch of the search area). When an object is snagged by the line, the diver then swims to it.

Figure 11.7. Snag Method.

11.11.9.3.4. Circle pattern. The circle pattern is used for searching large areas of water with poor visibility, no noticeable currents, and ice diving. It consists of one or more divers swimming in the same direction, beginning at an anchor point and searching in gradually increasing circles. The number of circles necessary will depend upon the clarity of the water and the size of the object being searched for.

11.11.9.3.4.1. Set the initial anchor point, attach the search line and lay a 50 foot reference line along the bottom from the anchor point to the outside circumference of the circle. Space the divers along the search line and begin the search.

NOTE: Search lines greater than 50 feet in length may increase slack in the line causing an erratic pattern, unnecessary diver exertion, and fatigue.

11.11.9.3.4.2. The divers start from the anchor point. Based on visibility, the diver lets out an appropriate amount of line to effectively search the intended area.

11.11.9.3.4.3. The divers continue expanding the circle until the end of the reference line is reached at which time a new reference point is established and the process repeated.

11.11.9.3.5. Straight line pattern. The straight line pattern is used to search small inlets or channels where the distance covered is commensurate with the length of the search line. For effective use of the pattern, there can be no noticeable current or the line must be laid to run according to the current run. The procedures are the same except that the lines are angled slightly to take advantage of slight current. There are two ways to work the pattern.

11.11.9.3.5.1. Attach an anchor point on either shore, keeping the line taut. Using one diver on each side of the line, they search the width of the channel. Move the shoreline anchor points down the number of feet commensurate with visibility and repeat the process.

11.11.9.3.5.2. Attach the search line at the shore on one end and the other end at the bottom, allowing it to run with the current if necessary, and work the pattern as above. In order to keep the pattern intact, it is sometimes necessary to place weights along the search line, especially if you are working with an irregular bottom. Mark the search area upon completion of each pattern.

Figure 11.8. Straight Search.

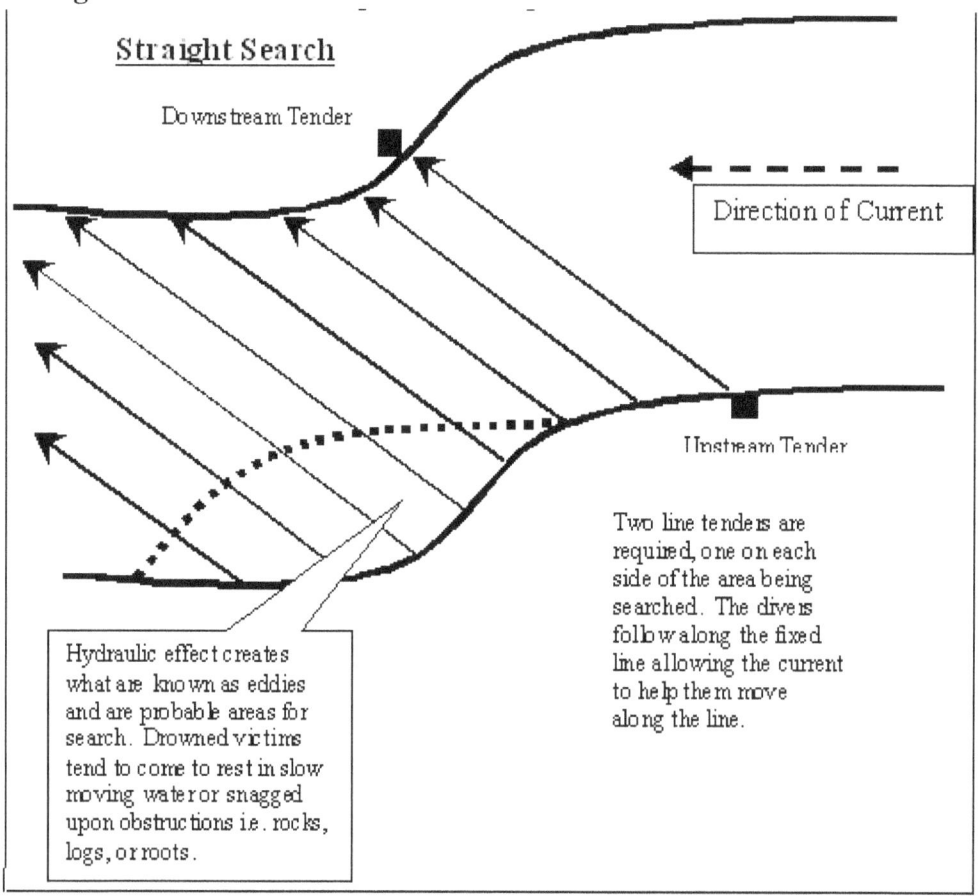

11.11.9.3.6. Grid pattern. The grid pattern is used to search for very small objects or to document location of items (i.e., crash site pieces). Although a grid can be laid underwater, it is easier to assemble the grid on the shore by tying the lines together and then lowering it as a whole to the bottom where it can be stretched and anchored. The pattern is seldom used because of the difficulty in setting it up and execution. If there is any significant current it may not be feasible. Each corner of the grid is anchored at the bottom and the divers then carefully search/ document each square.

Figure 11.9. Combination Pattern.

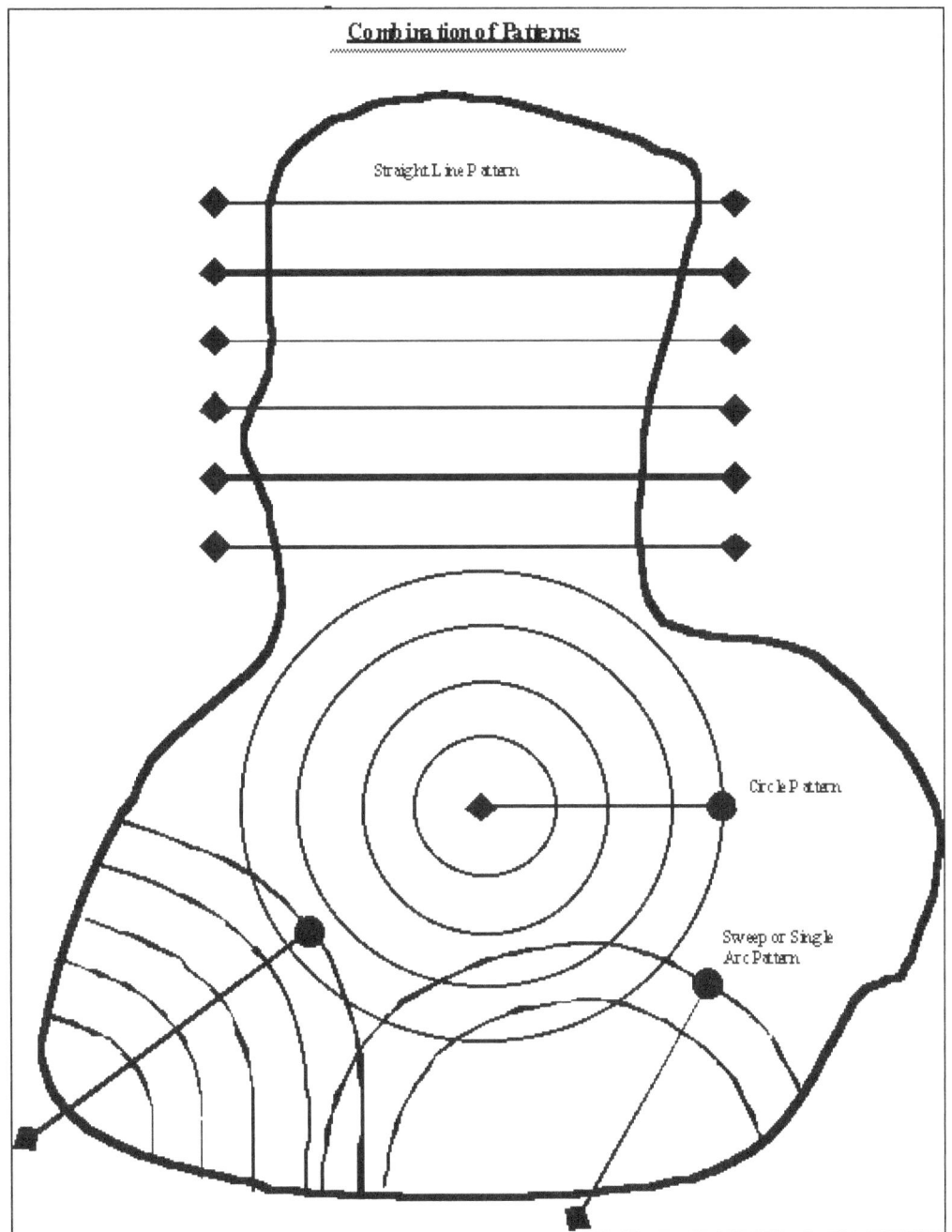

11.11.9.3.7. Boat-Based Search Patterns. Many times a water accident occurs farther from shore than a shore-based search pattern can reach. During boat-based search patterns in shallow water, the line tender in the boat controls the diver's actions while watching his bubbles.

11.11.9.3.7.1. In deep water, the boat-based pattern may require the search line to be fed through a carabiner attached to a heavy anchor, which serves as a search pattern weight (see illustration). When using this method, the tender lets the diver complete a 360-degree pass, stops him, and reverses his direction. This reversal of direction avoids wrapping the search line around the anchor line, and gives the diver a better sense of progress than swimming in concentric circles. When turning the diver, tender uses either a reference point on shore, or a compass heading.

11.11.9.3.7.2. In the event the search is being made in shallow water (15 feet or less), it may be more efficient to run a sweep pattern from a boat anchored at least 30 to 40 feet from the last-seen-point.

11.11.9.3.8. Diver tow. The diver tow is used to cover large areas with good visibility. It is accomplished by towing divers using a tow bar or individually at speeds less than five miles per hour.

11.11.9.3.8.1. The towline must be at least three times the water depth in order to achieve a proper search angle. For diver safety, there must be an effective diver/boat communication method. This is accomplished by attaching a separate line that is slightly longer than the towline for the purpose of passing signals. When accomplished using more than one tow bar, the line tender monitors the signal line of each diver.

WARNING: Establish a quick release at the boat end. Divers must not be physically anchored to the tow bar.

NOTE: For increased maneuverability, use individual lines. The divers must constantly monitor each other to prevent entanglement.

NOTE: When depth must be increased/decreased during the dive use a dive plan or sled.

11.11.9.3.8.2. Set the marker buoys to establish the search area and boat pattern.

11.11.9.3.8.3. Once divers are in the water, the boat driver slowly accelerates using the marker buoys for reference. When the search object is found, one or more divers drop off the tow bar. One diver should remain with the object and one surfaces to indicate position. The diver(s) remaining on the tow bar signal the boat to stop. Alternatively, a marker buoy is dropped to indicate position.

11.11.9.3.8.4. When water is too rough for the tender to observe the diver's bubbles from topside, it may be possible to put another diver in the water to act as the line tender on the bottom at the search pattern weight (anchor). If another diver is not available, the diver running the pattern may use a weighted line laid out in the search area. When the diver comes to the line he then reverses direction.

Figure 11.10. Boat Based Circular Pattern.

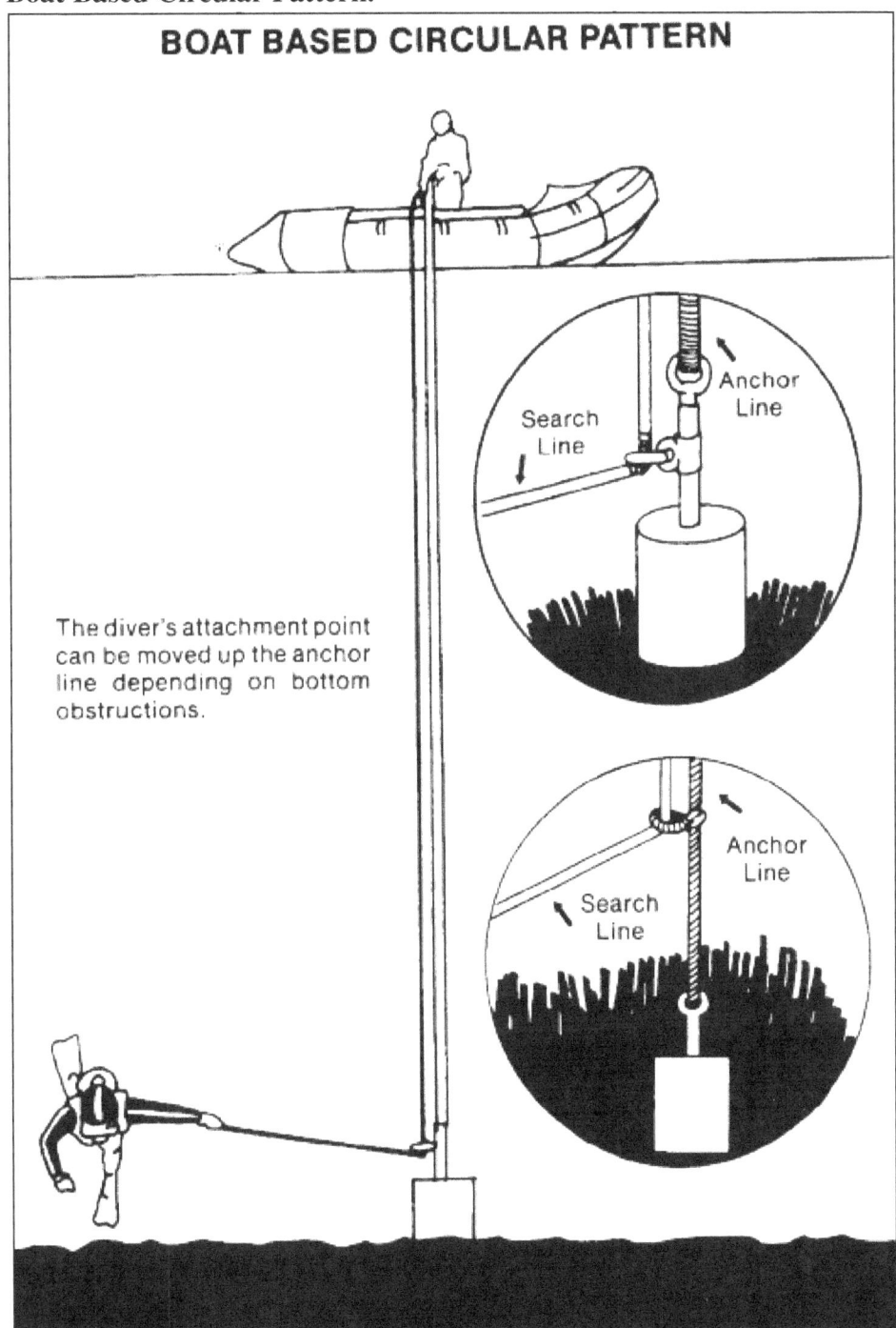

Chapter 12

LAND NAVIGATION

12.1. Purpose. A PJ team on the ground must be thoroughly familiar with all day/night navigation procedures, maps of the mission area, and navigation instruments such as the lensatic/silva compass and GPS receivers. This knowledge can be used effectively to locate survivors and travel to their location, to pin-point positions for evacuation, for route selection, or to select air evacuation sites. Most techniques and procedures for navigation will be found in Army FM 21-26

12.2. Silva Compass. The Silva compass is used in a similar fashion to the Lensatic compass. However, the Silva compass has a unique feature that precludes the user from having to orient the map to North on the ground. Instructions for use are provided by the manufacturer. The numerical graduations on the compass dial are not luminous as in the Lensatic compass. There are luminous points on the compass which allow a heading to be followed after being set. A local modification may be made in which a luminous dot is made on the direction of travel line directly next to the compass housing. This will allow a better alignment between the 0 degree mark and the line of travel arrow to dial in a heading under total darkness.

12.3. Altimeter Used as a Compass Aid . The barometric altimeter is useful for weather forecasting and as a navigation aid. The altimeter is used as a navigational aid to determine elevation above sea level. The altimeter reading is the result of the atmospheric pressure acting on the pressure plate within the altimeter. For navigational purposes, the altimeter is always used in conjunction with the map and compass. The user of the altimeter must understand why it must be set to local conditions and the most common field applications.

12.3.1. Setting the Altimeter. The altimeter's operation is totally dependent on the barometric pressure of the area in which it is used. The user must know present position and altitude to calibrate the altimeter to local barometric pressure conditions. This is done by rotating the outer ring of the altimeter until the altimeter needle reading corresponds to the known elevation. To maintain the accuracy of the altimeter, periodic checks and the necessary adjustment must be made from a known altitude at known locations. This is required due to altimeter needle changes with dropping or rising barometric pressure. When the weather conditions have changed, the altimeter will also have changed. Reset the altimeter from known locations with quickly changing weather and always at the start of each day's activity. Without the periodic adjustment of the altimeter, the accuracy will be unreliable and result in faulty readings that could be potentially dangerous. A fall or rise in barometric pressure of .10 millimeters of mercury will place the setting 100 feet low or high.

12.3.2. Field Applications. The most common and frequent use of the altimeter is to maintain a given elevation or confirming a location with comparison to map and compass navigational calculations.

12.3.2.1. Maintaining Elevation. The most basic use of the altimeter is to maintain a given height while traversing a mountain. Continued travel up and down hill is, for the most part, unnecessarily tiring for a team enroute to a victim. Maintaining a constant elevation, as much as the topography of the terrain will prevents the expenditure of energy that may be required once on scene or during the evacuation of a victim.

12.3.2.2. Confirming Location. In conjunction with the map and compass, the altimeter may be used to confirm the present position of the user. This is particularly important in adverse weather conditions such as a snow storm, fog or low clouds which may prevent the usual comparison between a suspected position and the surrounding terrain. A team may believe their location to be on a summit, for example, when in reality the true location is on a false summit. If the weather was clear, higher ground could be easily seen. In limited visibility a comparison may be made of the height given on the map for the summit and the altimeter reading. This comparison will confirm you have not reached the summit and aid in determining your exact position. The altimeter can be compared with a like contour reference on the map to determine the exact location. A more serious use of the altimeter is to assist in position location when descending a ridge line with many connecting ridges at various heights. If a change of direction is indicated which requires leaving the presently traveled ridgeline for another ridge, accomplish the following procedures:

12.3.2.2.1. Determine the altitude of the connecting ridge to be traveled from contour lines on the map.

12.3.2.2.2. Proceed on a compass bearing to the ridge.

12.3.2.2.3. Stop when on the ridge line and compare the altimeter with the contour line elevation on the map.

12.3.2.2.4. Check the surrounding contour to compare the rise and fall of the terrain with the map contours as a back up check.

12.4. Global Positions System (GPS). GPS is a man-portable system, powered by batteries, and uses satellites to determine present location/position.

12.4.1. GPS is extremely accurate and highly portable. All PJs will be trained to use GPS and training documented in members OJT record.12.4.2. GPS should be used to reconfirm your suspected location. Due to the limited battery life, do not use the GPS as a constant navigational aid while traveling. ,

NOTE: GPSs are mechanical systems and may break. Although highly beneficial for determining your exact location, all PJs should be proficient in land navigation using map and compass and terrain following procedures.

12.5. Transmitting Coordinates. Many inaccuracies may exist when comparing an actual site location with its identified map location. These inaccuracies come from plotting/pulling errors, datum transformation errors, symbol displacement errors, and incorrect specifications. These errors can be compounded if datums are mixed when reporting positional information. When passing or transmitting coordinates it is important the complete source of the coordinates be given. In order to avoid confusion the source will include the map or chart producer, series, sheet number, edition, date and datum.

Chapter 13

INDIVIDUAL COMBAT TACTICS

13.1. Purpose . Pararescue (PJ) personnel need to be prepared to deploy at short notice in support of component and joint Combat Search and Rescue (CSAR) requirements. To effectively accomplish this requirement they must be able to transition from peacetime to combat operations in minimum time and be inter-operable with other CSAR forces.

13.1.1. Pararescue missions are characteristically not pre-planned. Missions of opportunity must be taken into consideration prior to the fact. Training must be broad enough to meet major CSAR considerations and flexible enough to meet an individual scenario.

13.1.2. PJ personnel must prepare themselves for combat by acquiring the vital knowledge and skills needed to ensure success. This base of knowledge provides the foundation for team employment, Survival Evasion Resistance and Escape (SERE), and contingency planning.

13.2. Tasking.

13.2.1. Mission taskings are normally established by the component or Joint Force Commander (JFC). Most rescue taskings are filtered through the Joint Rescue and Recovery Center (JRRC). The JRRC determines whether to commit resources base on threat, time, distance, and medical condition (if applicable). Other factors, such as availability of aircraft to support the operation and logistical support, play important roles in their determination to commit resources. Notification of tasking is initiated upon approval of the tasking authority.

13.2.2. The mission planners are usually the first to receive information concerning tasking. They are the first direct link to the PJ team and provide the necessary information for the team to begin initial planning. They also act as the point of contact in requests for information outside the immediate chain of command.

13.3. Planning.

13.3.1. Security during planning should be a paramount concern of all team members. All team planning and preparation should be accomplished in a secured area.

13.3.2. Knowledge of the team's execution plan must be restricted to "need-to-know" basis.

13.3.3. The execution plan consists of four parts: Mission Preparation, Deployment, Employment, and Redeployment.

13.4. Tactical Equipment and Clothing.

13.4.1. To fully use the protection afforded by clothing and equipment, it is necessary to understand the principles involved and the correct function of each item.

13.4.2. Clothing Information.

13.4.2.1. The basic uniform and clothing must meet the requirements of the Area of Operation (AO). Considerations should include the insulating properties, the camouflage patterns and the scope of the scenario. Clothing should be soft and well fitting to prevent excessive noise and snagging.

13.4.2.2. Clothing for tactical operations should never be starched as this breaks down the fibers, increases heat retention and IR detectability. Trouser legs should be tucked into the boots to prevent migration of insects. Whenever possible, the soft cap is worn. It provides a less distinctive outline and makes less noise. Footwear should fit comfortably and be waterproofed. Clothing should be worn in layers to avoid over-heating. Care should be taken to ensure the clothing is functional in a field environment and it can be worn for extended periods of time. Nylon, Dacron, or other synthetic clothing should be flame retardant and not "pill" (small balling of the fabric). Clothing should be as light as possible without degrading its intended purpose.

13.4.3. Equipment Information.

13.4.3.1. Equipment should be chosen for durability as wells as function. Items should be camouflaged for tactical operations and not cause excessive noise. Like clothes, equipment should be scrutinized for need versus weight and function.

13.4.3.2. Fighting Load. The typical fighting load consists of essential items of individual clothing, equipment, weapons, and ammunition. Some items are "as required" based on the operational tasking. Arrangement of these items for wear can be determined by team leader (TL) discretion or individual preference.

13.4.3.3. Load Bearing Equipment (LBE)/ Vest. The tactical LBE/vest is used to hold the basic equipment and munitions necessary for the mission. Items carried by the LBE/vest must be readily accessible for immediate use. Individuals carrying munitions must be versed in their use and practice loading, reloading, or deployment of munitions.

13.4.3.4. Rucksack. Next to the LBE/vest, the rucksack is one of the most important pieces of equipment. Proper fitting of the ruck is essential for comfort and safety. Prior to the mission ensure the ruck is properly adjusted. It is imperative a quick release is operable in case the ruck must be jettisoned and the ruck in no way interferes with weapon firing. Frequently used items should be easily accessible and the ruck contents should not rattle. For winter operations, the rucksack should be as large as possible (8500 C.I.) while maintaining freedom of movement.

13.4.3.5. Munitions. The amount and type of munitions will vary based on the combat situation. Normally, munitions are selected based on the degree of threat, Rules of Engagement (ROE), time and distance to be traveled, and total equipment load.

13.4.3.6. Sleeping Gear. Items used for sleep are usually the most bulky of equipment items. Sleeping bags should be chosen on average temperature and climate of the AO. Like clothing, sleeping gear should be layered for maximum effectiveness, (i.e. sleeping pad, bivi sack. outerbag, innerbag, vapor barrier bag). Compression sacks help reduce size and keep items together for rapid access or storage.

13.4.3.7. Environmental Protections. Tents, ponchos, ground mats, stoves, etc. are examples of equipment which provide environmental protection. Selection is based on terrain, temperature, and climate. When conducting operations, consider the survivor, as well as team.

13.4.3.8. Food and Water. Food should be nutritionally balanced for the individual and environment. Water requirements and the degree of purification is based on military and biological threat. Purification systems, which do not require heat and remove the greatest amount of bacteria, should be chosen.

13.4.3.9. Night Vision Equipment. Night vision equipment should be closely monitored and cared for. The two types currently in service are active (infrared) and passive (image intensification) in nature.

13.4.3.10. Active (Infrared) devices provide a capability for night viewing regardless of the level of ambient light. Filtered white light from flashlights and searchlights can provide the required infrared light.

13.4.3.11. Passive (Image Intensification) devices intensify ambient light levels to provide visible images. Starlight and moonlight ordinarily provide sufficient light to employ these devices. Artificial illumination at low intensity increases their effectiveness during particularly dark periods. Direct or bright artificial illumination renders these devices temporarily ineffective. Image intensification devices generally provide a surveillance capability at greater ranges than infrared equipment. Night vision devices increase the effective range of the eye at night.

13.4.3.12. Advantages of night vision equipment:

13.4.3.12.1. The unaided eye cannot detect infrared light used to illuminate a target area normally.

13.4.3.12.2. Night vision devices can be used to detect the enemy's use of infrared source.

13.4.3.12.3. Image intensifier night vision devices do not require an artificial light source. Therefore, these devices cannot be detected.

13.4.3.12.4. On moonless nights when illumination from the night sky is not adequate, image intensification devices may be used effectively by providing small amounts of artificial illumination.

13.4.3.13. Limitations. By improper use, employment of some night vision devices can be detected. Operators of these devices must be thoroughly familiar with the appropriate technical manual for equipment limitations. Such detection by the enemy may disclose friendly positions. Some of the major limitations are:

13.4.3.13.1. Infrared light can be detected and the source located. Infrared light is subject to countermeasures by physical means (e.g., IR vector aided fire) by chemical smokes or by counter illumination.

13.4.3.13.2. Night vision devices are line of sight instruments. Dead spaces in surveillance, experienced during the day, are generally the same at night. Some night vision devices are adversely affected by bright light.

13.4.3.13.3. All night vision devices are adversely affected by bad weather conditions. If the objective lens gets fogged or wet, the image will be distorted.

13.4.3.13.4. For best operations, image intensifier devices require clear moonlight and night sky conditions. Infrared devices require clear, dark conditions for best operations.

13.4.4. Many factors influence the decision as to what items of clothing and equipment the team should wear or carry. These include the weather, mission at hand, actual duties to be performed, overall physical condition of individuals and their degree of proficiency. If a movement is involved, consider the distance to be traveled and the method of travel. If movement is on foot, under normal conditions, the maximum weight an individual can wear and carry and still be effective is 65 to 70 pounds.

13.4.5. The weight of individual clothing and equipment is very important. Give particular attention to additional equipment required for a given operation. Since the individual combat load required for rescue operations exceeds that of other tactical operations by more than 40 pounds, the weight of such items (such as binoculars, radios and batteries, special tools, weapons, etc.), become major considerations and is included at all levels of planning.

13.4.6. In addition to the individual combat load, other clothing and equipment is required for the protection and comfort of each individual under conditions of extreme cold.

13.4.7. Take positive action to ensure a balance exists between what is worn and what is being carried in the way of equipment. Dress as lightly as possible, consistent with the weather in order to reduce the danger of excessive perspiring and subsequent chilling. The complete uniform must be readily available to meet environmental conditions. A large proportion of extreme weather casualties results from too few clothes being available when a severe change in the weather occurs.

13.4.8. Individual equipment and clothing can be broken down into three categories; first, second, and third line. Each line is based on the level of threat and can be likened to shedding layers of security (i.e. Enemy contact, movement from the site, shed third line, continuing contact, shed second line, capture or survival retain first line).

13.4.8.1. First line equipment and clothing is the basic necessities required for personal defense, survival, evasion or escape. It is the minimum equipment, when combined with your knowledge, to gain safety from a tactical scenario that has been compromised to the point the mission can no longer be accomplished. Examples include, mission uniform worn, fire materials, navigation tools, food and water gathering materials, and signaling/recovery devices. These items are lightweight and carried on the person.

13.4.8.2. Second line equipment and clothing consists of the combat load. The combat load includes the equipment absolutely essential to perform the tasked operation. Weapons and munitions, communication/signaling devices, first aid/medical kits, limited rations, Protective Mask (gas), and combat knives are examples. These items are normally carried in the load bearing vest/harness. The individual tactical vest/LBE should balance when open for ventilation. The combat load must fit properly, and be appropriately camouflaged. All equipment should be secured to the harness. Ammunition must be readily accessible. The knife should be secure in an area where it will not injure the individual. A final check should be made to ensure no equipment on the harness/vest rattles.

13.4.8.3. Third line equipment and clothing supplement the combat load and represents added protection as well as extended operational capability. Rations, additional uniforms, batteries, sleeping gear, munitions, medical equipment, stoves and special use equipment are examples. The load is designed to provide the minimum necessities for living in the field and is normally carried in the rucksack. Only those items essential to mission accomplishment are carried. Excess weight induces fatigue and subsequent decreased combat efficiency.

13.4.9. It is essential that prior to any operation the TL scrutinize the mission requirements to ensure each person is adequately equipped. The TL will acquire information from Essential Elements of Information (EEIs) to determine type camouflage and basic clothing needs. TLs should always plan on the worst case scenario.

13.5. Camouflage. Camouflage is perhaps the most important defense a PJ has against an enemy. It consists of the measures taken to conceal an individual from enemy observation. The proper use of camouflage increases mission success through the use of natural and artificial materials. Remember these rules:

13.5.1. Take advantage of all available natural concealment.

13.5.2. Alter the form, shadow, texture, and color of objects.

13.5.3. Camouflage against ground and air observation.

13.5.4. Camouflage each bivouac position.

13.5.5. Study the terrain and vegetation in the area. Arrange grass, leaves, brush, and other natural materials to conform to the area. For example, do not expect tree branches stuck into the ground in an open field to provide effective camouflage.

13.5.6. Use only as much material as needed. Excessive use of material (natural or artificial) can reveal a position.

13.5.7. Obtain natural material over a wide area. Do not strip an adjacent area of all foliage because such bared areas attract enemy attention.

13.5.8. Dispose of excess soil by covering it with leaves and grass or by dumping it under brushes, into streams, or into ravines. Piles of fresh dirt indicate an area is occupied and reduces effectiveness of camouflage.

13.5.9. After camouflage is completed, inspect it from the enemy's viewpoint. Check often to ensure it remains natural looking and actually conceals a position. If it does not look natural, rearrange or replace it.

13.5.10. Practice camouflage discipline. The best camouflage fails to provide concealment if tracks lead to the position or if trash is scattered about. Everyone in an element must share this responsibility. The TL must enforce camouflage discipline.

13.5.11. Exposed skin reflects light and attracts the enemy's attention. Even very dark skin will reflect light because of its natural oil.

13.5.12. Paint the shiny areas (forehead, cheekbones, nose and chin) with a dark color. Paint the shadow areas (around the eyes, under the nose, and under the chin) with a light color. Paint the exposed skin on the back of the neck and hands. Wear flight gloves if practical instead of painting hands.

13.5.13. When applying camouflage, use the buddy system, work with another man and check each other.

13.6. Cover and Concealment.

13.6.1. Cover is protection from the fire of enemy weapons. It may be natural or artificial. Natural cover (ravines, hollows, reverse slopes) and artificial cover (foxholes, trenches, walls) will protect individuals from grazing fires and partially protect from plunging fires. The habit of locating and taking advantage of every bit of cover the terrain offers combined with the proper use of movement techniques will ensure effective protection from enemy fire. Concealment is protection from enemy observation. It, too, may be natural or artificial. It must be remembered that concealment is not protection from enemy fire. Individuals must not make the mistake of believing they are protected from enemy fire merely because they are concealed from enemy eyes.

13.6.2. Natural concealment is frequently provided by the surroundings and needs no alteration to be used. Examples are: bushes, grass, and shadows. Artificial concealment is made from materials such as burlap or nets. Natural materials such as bushes, leaves, and grass, which are moved from their original location, can also be arranged to form artificial concealment. Care must be taken to consider the effects of seasons on the concealment provided by both natural and artificial materials.

13.6.3. Individual Concealment Techniques:

13.6.3.1. Avoid Unnecessary Movement. Remain still as much as possible, movement attracts attention. An individual may be concealed when still, yet easily detected when moving. Movement against a stationary background causes an individual to stand out clearly. When changing positions, move carefully over a concealed route to the new position.

13.6.3.2. Use All Available Concealment.

13.6.3.3. Background is important. Blend with it to prevent enemy detection of individual positions. Trees, bushes, grass, earth, and manmade structures forming the background vary in color and appearance. It is possible to blend with them. Move to trees or bushes, which blend with the uniform and absorb the outline of the human figure.

13.6.3.4. Shadows help concealment. An individual in the open stands out clearly. Shadows are found under most conditions of day and night.

13.6.3.5. Stay Low to Observe. Observe from a crouch, squat, or the prone position. Present a low silhouette, making it difficult for the enemy to see.

13.6.3.6. Expose Nothing That Shines. Reflection of light on a shiny surface instantly attracts attention and can be seen for great distances.

13.6.3.7. Keep Off the Skyline. Human figures on the skyline can be seen from a great distance, even at night, because a dark outline stands out against the lighter sky. The silhouette formed by the human body makes a good target.

13.6.3.8. Alter Familiar Outlines. Military equipment and the human body are familiar outlines to all soldiers. Alter or disguise these revealing shapes.

13.6.3.9. Keep Quiet. Noise, such as talking or rattling, can be picked up easily by enemy patrols or listening posts.

13.7. Fundamentals of Movement.

13.7.1. As with all types of tactical movement, your personal attitude is the most important aspect. Accepted among many is the "stop light" method of increasing your perception of a given situation. "Green" condition is reserved for when there is likely to be no enemy contact. "Yellow" condition is reserved when enemy contact is likely to occur and senses are extended, nothing is taken for granted and an increased perception is required. "Red" condition is reserved for the enemy. In red condition all senses are excited and you project yourself to see red (the color psychologically causes violent reaction). When in red condition, your most aggressive attitude is displayed. Follow these general rules to move without being seen or heard by the enemy:

13.7.2. Prepare yourself and your equipment.

13.7.3. Tape identification tags together and to the chain so they cannot slide or rattle.

13.7.4. Tape or pad any parts of the weapon or equipment that rattle or are so loose that they may snag. Be sure the tape or padding does not interfere with operation of the weapon or equipment.

13.7.5. Use the ankle ties when you do not blouse the field trousers. Do not tie them too tightly. No other tie-down should be used at any time. They may interfere with circulation in the legs and feet. In cold weather, poor circulation may lead to frostbite or other cold injury.

13.7.6. Wear a soft cap, with its less distinctive outline.

13.7.7. Do not carry unnecessary equipment. One cannot move rapidly when weighted down.

13.7.8. Do not wear sunglasses or glasses unless they are of the non-glare variety. Otherwise they may reflect sunlight and attract attention.

13.7.9. Move by bounds; that is, short distances at a time. Halt, listen, and observe. Then move again.

13.7.10. Look for the next spot to stop before leaving the concealment of one position. Observe that area carefully for enemy activity. Select the best available covered and concealed route to the new location; take advantage of darkness, fog, smoke, or haze to assist in concealing movement.

13.7.11. Change direction slightly from time to time when moving through tall grass. Moving in a straight line causes the grass to wave with an unnatural motion, which may attract attention. The best time to move is when the wind is blowing the grass.

13.7.12. If birds or animals are alarmed, remain in position and observe briefly. Their flight or movement may attract the enemy's attention or provided a clue to the whereabouts of the enemy.

13.7.13. Take advantage of the distraction provided by noises.

13.7.14. Cross roads and trails. Look for a large culvert, a low spot, or a curve. Cross quickly and quietly.

13.7.15. Follow the furrows as much as possible when crawling over a plowed field.

13.7.16. Avoid steep slopes and areas with loose stones.

13.7.17. Avoid cleared areas to prevent being silhouetted.

13.7.18. The Rush. The "rush" is the fastest way to move from one position to another while under fire.

13.7.18.1. Short rushes from one covered position to another may be used when enemy fire allows brief exposure. Maneuver teams, buddy teams, or individuals may advance by short rushes to avoid accurate enemy fire.

13.7.18.2. Try not to stay up any longer than 3 to 5 seconds. Do not give the enemy time to track with automatic fire. The rule is: rush from cover to cover. If cover and concealment are not available, follow the principle of "I'm up, he sees me, I'm down, roll" (no more than three seconds), this ensures that the time of exposure to enemy forces is negligible.

13.7.18.3. Scout the area ahead. Get up and move in the lowest profile possible to the next site. Keep weapon pointed and ready in the most likely spot the enemy may fire against you. As soon as you hit the ground, come up ready to fire.

13.7.18.4. Do not rush from a position shortly after firing. Shift right/left or crawl before springing to the feet.

13.7.18.5. After completing a rush to a position providing concealment but no cover, roll or crawl to a new position before firing.

13.7.18.6. This type of movement is very difficult with a ruck, and may cause loss of equipment. If carrying a large load and cannot roll, shift to one side.

13.7.18.7. If the enemy sees you he will fire at the last point he saw you at. Vary the direction you roll or shift.

13.7.19. There are times when one must move with the body close to the ground to avoid being seen. There are two ways to do this, the low crawl and the high crawl. Use the method best suited to the conditions of visibility, cover and concealment available and speed required.

13.7.20. The high crawl is used when cover is more prevalent and speed is essential to the outcome. The body is kept off the ground and your weight is rested upon the elbows, forearms, and knees. If carrying a rifle, it is either carried across the body slung in the crotch of the elbows, or across the back. Movement is made by alternately pulling with each arm and pushing with one leg (if profile is to remain low) or both legs if in adequate cover. Maintain a profile consistent with cover and speed consistent with silence.

13.7.21. The low crawl is used when cover and concealment are inadequate and when an enemy response is expected. Normally this movement is used to bypass enemy positions or barriers. The low crawl is extremely slow, so speed cannot be essential to the outcome.

13.7.21.1. Lie as flat to the ground as possible, legs together and ankles placed flat. Hands are outstretched in front and flat in position to seek out obstacles such as mines, trip wires, etc. The head is placed flat with eyes in a position to scout for obstacle. Heels and buttocks must not rise above the ground. The purpose is to hug the ground as close as possible.

13.7.21.2. Prior to movement use the hands to clear an area large enough for the body to follow. Do not transition out of the cleared area.

13.7.21.3. To move forward extend arms fully to the front and draw one leg far enough to push and maintain a low profile. Pull with forearms and push with leg. Repeat procedure as needed. All movement must be slow and deliberate.

13.7.21.4. When transitioning barriers to the front, move by the most direct route possible commensurate with the area cleared.

13.7.21.5. If crossing a large area, the low crawler on point may be relieved, as it is extremely dangerous, tiring, and nerve wracking. The point will move to a position which allows the man behind to cross over the top. The man behind will act as if the point is an extension of the ground.

13.7.21.6. Orders may be passed from team members as to direction by pressing on the foot of the person in front. The member passing the instructions holds on to the foot in which direction he wishes to go until the desired direction is achieved. Holding both feet signals for movement to stop.

13.7.22. Stealth Walking. There are two general types of stealth walking, the toe first and the heel first. Walking in a stealthy manner can be very tiring as well as time consuming and is used when silence is absolutely paramount. Usually this type of walking is for contact procedures and sentry neutralization, but may be used whenever stealth is needed.

13.7.22.1. When used during sentry removal, consider removing any equipment that isn't needed. Follow procedures for sentry removal for additional information.

13.7.22.2. Body position. The body must remain relaxed with just enough tension to impart your movement with force if necessary. The upper body is straight and at an angle sufficient to block a frontal attack. The arms are up and in a position to block blows. If weapon is at hand, you hold the weapon with intent and consider it to be used as a bludgeon if need be. Legs are bent and shaped as a horseshoe, shoulder width apart, ready to transfer weight and maintain balance. Maintain 360 degree awareness and do not stare at the objective (staring may cause the "sixth sense" to be activated). Be prepared to attack in any direction.

13.7.22.3. Toe First Method. Pick a point about one half normal stride, preferably free of dry leaves and other obstacles. Slowly lift the forward foot and move it forward clearing obstacles with the toes. Use the outside of the foot to place it lightly down placing pressure as needed to maintain silence. Rotate the foot into position until the ball of the foot is placed and lower the heel. Very slowly, shift the body weight forward until the weight is on the forward foot. Repeat the process with the other foot, (ensuring you do not cross the legs), moving towards the forward foot and place approximately shoulder width apart. Terrain and situation will determine speed and silence.

13.7.22.4. Heel First Method. Pick a point about one half normal stride, preferably free of dry leaves and other obstacles. Slowly lift the forward foot and move it forward clearing obstacles with the toes. Use the outside of the foot to place it lightly down placing pressure as needed to maintain silence. Rotate the foot into position until the heel of the foot is placed and lower the toes. Very slowly, shift the body weight forward until the weight is on the forward foot. Repeat the process with the other foot, (ensuring you do not cross the legs), moving towards the forward foot and place approximately shoulder width apart. Terrain and situation will determine speed and silence.

13.8. Man Tracking.

13.8.1. A knowledge of man-tracking techniques provides information needed to evade enemy trackers and locate evading friendly personnel. Man tracking techniques may have to be employed in the final stages of locating the evader. In difficult threat situations, the evader's fear of being captured may cause him to be reluctant to identify where he is hiding, requiring a more extensive search to make contact.

13.8.2. Qualities of a Tracker. Tracking can be effectively employed using basic techniques, common sense and some degree of experience. There are traits and qualities one must develop and refine to qualify as a combat worthy tracker. A tracker must have patience. He must be able to proceed slowly, quietly, yet steadily while observing available indicators and interpreting them. He must avoid using reckless speed that may cause him to overlook important signs, lose the trail completely, or blunder into an enemy force. A good tracker must be persistent. He must have the ability and desire to continue his mission even though indicators are scarce or conditions of weather or terrain are difficult. If he loses a trail, he must have the determination and persistence to find it again. He must develop an acute sense of observation. He must be able to see things not obvious at a glance. He must have the ability to use his senses of smell and hearing to supplement his observation. A good tracker must also develop a sixth sense. He may often be led to inspect an area simply because it "does not look right." This ability often enables a tracker to regain a lost trail or discover new or additional indicators. An effective tracker must also know the evader or element he is tracking. He cannot properly interpret clues he has found unless he has some knowledge of the individual(s), their habits, equipment, or level of training. A good tracker must also have an understanding of nature, a good memory, intelligence, and he must be physically fit enough to accomplish the mission.

13.8.3. Concepts of Tracking. As a tracker moves along the ground, following a trail, he begins to build a picture in his mind of the objective he is tracking. To accomplish this, he constantly asks himself questions such as: How many people am I following? How are they equipped? Do they know they are being followed? By comparing indicators, the tracker begins to answer the questions he constantly asks himself. For example, if he finds a footprint and a scuff on a tree about waist high, it may indicate an armed individual passed this particular spot. There are six concepts that apply to tracking: displacement, staining, weathering, littering, deception, and interpretation/immediate use of intelligence data.

13.8.3.1. One or more of the first five concepts can define any indicator the tracker discovers. By putting to use the sixth concept, the tracker combines the first five concepts and uses all indicators he has discovered to form a composite picture of the evader being followed. To accomplish this, he must interpret what he has seen. Once an interpretation has been made, applicable intelligence data should be made available for the trackers immediate use on the spot. For example, indicators may point out contact is imminent. If intelligence data indicates extreme stealth and caution may be required, the tracker must be appraised of this fact at the earliest possible moment. By examining each concept individually, one can see several concepts can apply to one indicator at the same time. It is hard to visualize any indicator could not be defined by at least one of the concepts of tracking.

13.8.3.2. Displacement. Displacement takes place when anything is moved from its original position. Displacement is probably best demonstrated by a well-defined footprint in soft, moist ground. The shoe or foot of the individual that left the print displaced the soil by compression, thus leaving the indentation in the ground.

13.8.3.2.1. Analyzing Footprints. Footprints may indicate direction and rate of movement, number of persons in the moving element, whether or not heavy loads are being carried, sex of members of the element, and whether the members of the element realize that they are being followed. If footprints are deep and the pace is long, rapid movement is apparent. Extremely long strides, deep prints with the toe prints deeper than heel prints, indicate running. Prints can be counted to determine the number of people in the element. If the prints are deep, short, and widely spaced, with indications of scuffing or shuffling, the person who left the print is carrying a heavy load. The sex of a member of the element being following can be determined by studying the size and position of the footprints. Women tend to be pigeon-toed, while men walk with their feet straight-ahead or pointed slightly to the outside. Prints left by women are usually smaller and the stride is shorter than that taken by men. If the element realizes that they are being followed, an attempt to hide their tracks may be made. Persons walking backwards have short, irregular stride. The prints have an unnaturally deep toe. Soil will be kicked in the direction of movement.

13.8.3.2.2. Footprints are only one example of displacement. Anything moved from its original position by a moving person is an example of displacement. Foliage, moss, vines, sticks, or rocks scuffed or snagged from their original place form valuable indicators. Vines can be dragged, dew droplets can be displaced from leaves, or stones and sticks may be turned over to indicate a difference of color underneath. Grass or other vegetation may be bent or broken in the direction of movement. Other Signs of Displacement:

13.8.3.2.3. Bits of clothing, threads, or dirt from boots can be displaced from a person's uniform and deposited on thorns, snags, or the ground. Thorns should be inspected for bits of clothing or other matter ripped from the uniform of the person being tracked.

13.8.3.2.4. Wild animals and birds flushed from their natural habitat by the person being tracked are examples of displacement. Cries of birds excited by unnatural movement are an indicator. Tops of tall grass or brush moving on a windless day is an indication someone is moving the vegetation from its original position. Displacement can result from clearing a trail by either breaking or cutting ones way through heavy vegetation with a machete. These trails are obvious to the most inexperienced tracker. A man sleeping will also flatten the vegetation.

13.8.3.2.5. In almost any area, there will be insects and spiders. The observation of any changes in the normal life of these insects may be an indication someone has recently passed. Bees that are stirred up, ants that have had their holes covered by someone moving over them, or spiders that have had their webs torn down are valuable clues. Spiders often spin webs across open areas, trail, or roads to trap flying insects. If someone is careless and does not move under these webs, he is leaving an indicator to an observant tracker.

13.8.3.2.6. If the party being followed attempts to use a stream to cover their trial, the trackers may still be able to follow successfully, algae and other water plants may be displaced by slippery footing or by someone who walks carelessly. Rocks may be displaced from their original position, or turned over to indicate a lighter or darker color on the opposite side. The party entering or exiting the stream may create slide marks, footprints or scuff marks. It must be considered that normally a person or animal will seek the path of least resistance. Therefore, when searching the stream for indications of departures, open areas along the banks may often yield results.

13.8.3.3. Staining. Staining occurs when any substance from one organism or article is smeared or deposited on something else.

13.8.3.3.1. The best example of staining is blood from a profusely bleeding wound. Blood signs often will be in the form of spatters of drops left by the wounded person being followed. Bloodstains are not always on the ground. Blood can be smeared on leaves or twigs from a man's height to the ground.

13.8.3.3.2. Water collecting in footprints in swampy ground can be muddy if the tracks are recent. With time, however, the mud will settle and the water will clear. This can be used by the tracker to indicate time. Normally, the mud will clear in approximately one hour. This, of course, will vary with the terrain.

13.8.3.4. Weathering. Weather may either aid or hinder the tracker. It affects indicators in certain ways so that the tracker may determine their relative ages. Wind, snow, rain, or sunlight may, however, obliterate indicators entirely, thus hindering the tracker. By studying the effects of weather on indicators, the tracker can make a determination as to the age of the sign. For example, when bloodstains are fresh, they are bright red. Air and sunlight change blood first to a deep ruby red color, then to a dark brown crust when the moisture evaporates. Scuff marks on trees or brushes darken with time, sap oozes, then hardens when it makes contact with the air.

13.8.3.4.1. Footprints are greatly affected by weather. When a person's foot displaces soft moist soil to form a print, initially, the moisture holds the edges of the print intact. As sunlight and air-dry the edges of the print, small particles that were held in place by moisture fall by their own weight into the print. Careful study of this process by the tracker can lead him to a determination of approximate age of the print. If particles are just beginning to fall into the print, the tracker should become a stalker. If the edges of the print are dried and crusty, the prints are probably at least an hour old. This will vary with terrain and should be taken as a general guide.

13.8.3.4.2. How Weather Effects Tracking. A light rain may round out the edges of the print. The tracker must remember when the last rain occurred in order to place these prints into a proper time frame. A heavy rain may erase all signs. Wind also affects tracks. Besides drying out the print, litter, sticks, or leaves may be blown into the print. By remembering wind activity, the tracker may guess the age of the tracks. Trails exiting streams may appear to have been weathered by rain because of water running from clothing or equipment into the tracks. This is particularly true if the party exits the stream in a file. This will permit each person to deposit water into the tracks. The existence of a wet, apparently watered, trail slowly fading into a dry trail indicates the trail is fresh.

13.8.3.4.3. The effect of wind on sounds and odors is one aspect of the effect weather has on tracking. If the wind is blowing from the direction of the trail the tracker is following, sounds and odors may be carried to him. If the wind is blowing in the same direction as the trail being followed, the tracker must be extremely cautious since the wind will carry his sounds towards the enemy. Wind direction can be determined by dropping a handful of dry dust or grass from shoulder height. By facing in the same direction the wind is blowing, sounds can be localized by cupping the hands behind the ears and slowly turning. When the sounds are loudest, the tracker is facing the origin of the sound. In calm weather, when no wind is blowing, the air currents that carry sounds to the tracker may be too light to feel. The tracker must remember that the air cools in the evening and moves downhill to the valleys. If a tracker is moving uphill in the day or at night, air currents will probably be moving toward him, provided no other wind is blowing. As the sun warms the air in the valleys in the morning, it moves uphill. These factors should be considered when plotting routes for operations. If a tracker can keep the wind in his face, sounds and odors will be carried to him from his objective or the party being tracked.

13.8.3.4.4. A tracker should also consider the sun. It is difficult to shoot directly into the sun. If the tracker can arrange to have the sun at his back and the wind in his face, he has a slight advantage. This is a minor point; however, it is worth mentioning that the tracker should use every trick, advantage, and skill available to him. If he uses his senses, experience, and knowledge, he will be better equipped to accomplish his mission and it is likely that he will continue to learn more about his skill as he practices it.

13.8.3.5. Littering. As a poorly trained or poorly disciplined evader or element moves over a piece of terrain, it is likely a clear trail of litter will mark its path. Gum or candy wrappers, ration cans, cigarette butts, remains of fires, or even piles of human feces are unmistakable signs of recent movement. Weathering must be taken into consideration when estimating the age of litter. Rain flattens or washes litter away and turns paper into pulp. Ration cans, exposed to weather, will rust first at the exposed edge when it is opened. Rust then moves in toward the center. Again the tracker must use his memory to properly determine the age of litter. The last rain or strong wind can be the basis for a time frame.

13.8.3.6. Deception Techniques. Deception by diversion and camouflage applies to tracking when the element being followed employs techniques to confuse the tracker or slow him down. Walking backwards to leave confusing prints, brushing out trails, moving over rocky ground or through streams are examples of technique employed to confuse the tracker. Least used routes are taken in an attempt to confuse the tracker by avoiding all manmade trails or roads. The tracker can, however, by using the proper concepts, follow the party if he is experienced and persistent. The evader or element being followed may use several methods to attempt to minimize trail signs. Rags wrapped around footwear, or soft-soled tennis shoes may make footprints more rounded on the edges and less distinct. An element may exit a stream in a column formation or a scattered, line abreast formation. This reduces the chances of leaving a well-defined exit. A careful, observant tracker can determine by a study of the signs if an attempt is being made to confuse him. If the individual being followed attempts to throw the tracker off by walking backwards, the footprints will be deepened at the toe and soil will be scuffed or dragged in the direction of movement. By following carefully, the tracker can normally find a turnaround point. A trail can be brushed out. The experienced tracker could easily recognize this technique. If the trail leads across rocky or hard ground, the tracker should attempt to circumnavigate the area to pick up the exit trail. This process works in streams as well. On rock ground, even the most careful evader could displace moss or lichen growing on the stones. An experienced tracker can trace these signs. If these methods fail, the tracker should return to the last visible indicators and then head in the direction of movement in ever-widening circles until he again falls upon visible signs. Remember that an evader that attempts to hide his trail moves at a reduced speed. Therefore, an experienced tracker, who is not fooled by these attempts, gains time on the individual being followed.

13.9. Tactical River and Stream Crossing. The following additional information is provided in addition to referring to Army FMs.

 NOTE: Water temperatures must be determined and planned for when conducting river/stream crossings, especially in the tactical environment.

13.9.1. Fording. If a wide, shallow (less than 1.5 meters deep) stream is encountered, a secluded shallow spot for fording should be selected. A security element should cross first after a suitable observation period of the opposite bank. It should move rapidly across in a column, the lead man probing ahead with a fathoming stick. If the water is flowing rapidly, a safety rope should be secured on both banks to prevent falling and being carried downstream.

13.9.2. Swimming. If a stream is too deep to ford, swim across it. A UDT life vest makes this a fairly easy task. Put the vest on, inflate the vest until adequate buoyancy is achieved and breast stroke across. Clear any weapons immediately upon reaching the opposite bank. If the possibility of crossing streams/rivers exists, the UDT vest should be taken on the operation. Without a UDT vest, river crossing can become extremely hazardous.

13.9.3. Rope bridges. Rope bridges provide temporary means for crossing rivers where the span is not great (less than 20 meters) and where there would be savings in time over other methods. The technique for installing rope bridges is covered in FM 31-72.

13.9.4. Inflatable raft. If numerous rivers will have to be crossed, a one-man raft may be a practical method of getting gear and personnel across. The gear is placed in the raft and the personnel swim along side holding on to the raft. This method becomes especially valuable when moving injured personnel or survivors who cannot swim.

13.9.5. Improvised rafts. Rafts can be constructed from natural material in the area or from ponchos or other gear carried. Care in construction is necessary to avoid having the raft come apart during the crossing of the river.

13.9.6. Boats. Individuals may have an occasion to use an opportune boat found on the bank of the river that requires crossing. When this method is used, always consider that someone is going to look for the boat and report it to the authorities. After using the boat, do not pull it up on the opposite bank and leave. It will give away a critical position. After crossing the river, get out of the boat where the water is about knee deep, and push it into the current. Let it drift away.

Chapter 14

SMALL TEAM TACTICS

14.1. Purpose. Pararescue (PJ) operations evolved through the use of teams to effect the rescue or recovery of personnel and equipment. By working in teams, Pararescuemen (PJs) attain better efficiency and survivability in a hostile environment.

14.2. Team Size and Composition.

14.2.1. The team size will consist of two or more PJs. Careful consideration must be given to manpower availability, the nature and complexity of the mission and the constraints of time, distance, terrain, and condition of evaders or survivors when determining the size and composition of the PJ team to be employed.

14.2.2. Each team will be lead by a Team Leader (TL). The TL will be identified from among the most highly qualified members of the PJ section. The TL will be responsible for all aspects of team employment. The TL will serve as the military authority within the team.

14.3. Emergency Plan of Action (EPA).

14.3.1. Teams must plan for the unlikely event they cannot complete the mission or individual elements/personnel become separated from the main body during ingress or employment. EPAs should be left with the mission authority when possible. Each team member (TM) must be able to brief the EPA at any time.

14.3.2. An example of an (but not all inclusive) EPA: If more than 50 percent of the team becomes casualties, remaining personnel will move to nearest emergency recovery point, one person will remain behind to treat wounded (usually those wounded that may use a weapon will be first candidates). Medical supplies beneficial to remaining personnel will be left as well as ammunition /supplies that may effect recovery at a later time. In extreme weather, or failure of resupply, the team will move to the nearest emergency recovery point. If temporary or actual abandonment occur, the team will move to appropriate save area for evasion (SAFE) for linkup with recovery network or if possible return to friendly area by most direct route as possible. Radio contact will be kept to a minimum for conservation of batteries. If the team is shot down during ingress/egress the team will follow the aircrew EPA.

14.4. Resupply.

14.4.1. Resupplying a team either by air, water, or land may expose the team to enemy detection. If possible, the team should avoid the exposure inherent in resupply operations by carrying enough supplies and equipment to accomplish its mission. The TL must decide whether he will take all the required supplies and equipment or plan a resupply operation during the mission. The TL decides what supplies and equipment are required to accomplish the mission. He considers:

14.4.1.1. The requirements of the mission.

14.4.1.2. The method of infiltration.

14.4.1.3. Enemy capabilities.

14.4.1.4. Duration of the mission.

14.4.2. Contingency Resupply Plans. Even when a TL plans to complete his mission and return using only accompanying supplies, he coordinates for resupply. Contingency resupply plans are necessary because of the uncertainties of combat search and rescue (SAR) missions. The mission may change; the team may receive additional tasking; or it could receive an order to delay exfiltration due to shifting priorities or enemy action.

14.4.3. Cache for Resupply. Caching is concealing operational equipment in the field. Caches can be constructed underwater, in hollow trees, and most commonly, underground. Stores must be waterproof, rust- proofed, booby-trapped, and preserved as necessary. Site selection is critical, choose an isolated area away from human activity or possible future activity, (i.e. roads, buildings). Natural references are more likely to remain than man-made landmarks. Minimize alteration of surrounding vegetation. Building and camouflage material must be obtained from another location, but camouflage must not be "out of place." Preserve all topsoil and vegetation. It must be removed carefully so it can be replaced to look natural. Subsoil is usually a different color and would stand out. Once complete, the cache must be immaculately camouflaged so it is impossible to detect from the air or ground. Consider planting small live plants common to the area if topsoil was disturbed. Consider areas that will not be changed by weather. Avoid using draws near rivers that will uncover the cache in floodwaters.

14.5. Reentry of Friendly Lines.

14.5.1. Planned Authentication/Reentry of Friendly Lines. If the mission dictates crossing into or working near friendly areas the PJ TL must plan prior to conducting operations. Radio contact may be established to indicate the teams arrival or plans must be strictly adhered to. To preclude the possibility of being duped by an enemy force the TL should halt the main element a safe distance from the entry site and observe the area. Upon positive results, the TL will ensure the proper procedures are understood by the point man (PT) (the fastest and most accurate of TMs) and the PT should be sent to make contact. Upon authentication of the PT the TL will direct the team to move to the friendly area. The PT will vouch for the team or will indicate to the team the sentry commanders prescribed method of entry. Upon movement through the entry point do not give indications as to the sentries position. The key is successful implementation of pre-planned procedures.

14.5.2. Unplanned Authentication/Reentry of Friendly Lines. In the event a friendly patrol is inadvertently contacted the PT must keep his head and not escalate the situation into a conflict. The PT will freeze the team and at a suitable time appraise the TL of the situation. If contact is not desired the TL may direct the team to remain unobserved. Team actions should be those they would use against an enemy force in the event a physical confrontation takes place. If the TL directs contact or contact cannot be helped, the TL will respond to the friendly teams inquiries. The team element will follow only the TL directions.

14.5.3. The Challenge and Response for Reentry of Friendly Lines. The use of challenge and response is necessary in the event inadvertent contact is made with friendly patrols or an individual must reenter friendly lines. The enemy may approach friendly lines from any direction; therefore, friendly outposts, observation posts, or sentries will halt and identify personnel before they are close enough to be a danger to them.

14.5.3.1. In most cases, identity is established by proper use of the challenge and response. When the sentry sees or hears someone approaching, and does not recognize him as friendly and authorized to pass, he will call, "Halt!" He will speak clearly and just loudly enough to be distinctly heard. He will keep the individual covered and will not expose himself. Upon halting, he will ask in a low, clear voice, "Who is there?" Always reply in a low, clear voice, giving the answer which best identifies the individual. For example, "Sgt. Doe, PJ." He will then say, "Advance and be recognized," and continue to cover the individual without exposing himself. He will halt the individual two or three meters from his position. In a low, clear voice he will give the individual the challenge; for example, "Bull". Always answer with the correct response; for example, "Dog." The challenge may be a combination of numbers. For example if the number is nine, the challenge may be "I saw three dear in the clearing". The response could be "I saw only six". If he is not completely satisfied, he will require the individual to produce identification or question the individual further. He will ask questions only a friendly person would be likely to know.

14.5.3.2. When a group approaches and is halted, the leader should answer for the group. For example, "PJ team." The sentry will then say, "Advance one man to be recognized." When the challenge and response have been given and identity is established, the other members of the group must also be identified. This can be done in two ways. The PJ TL can vouch for the others and pass them to the sentry's flank to reduce movement and noise at that position and help prevent revealing the sentry's location to the enemy. The PJ TL or his representative can identify each man as he passes, notifying the sentry when the last man has passed. The sentry's commander will have prescribed the manner to be used.

14.5.3.3. If the challenge and response are not known, as the case would be if separated from the team or aircraft and isolated in the enemy area, each individual must produce satisfactory identification or otherwise be detained.

14.5.3.4. The challenge and response are normally changed every 24 hours (see Intel for exact changeover times). If at all possible, know the current ones.

14.6. Aerial Movement Responsibilities (Infiltration) .

14.6.1. Actual configuration of aircraft for infiltration is normally the responsibility of the rotary-wing flight engineer (FE) or the fixed-wing loadmaster (LM) assigned to the mission. To facilitate planning and duty performance, the TL should provide the FE/LM with the following information at the earliest opportunity:

14.6.1.1. Team composition and desired TM location in the aircraft.

14.6.1.2. Desired placement of equipment not worn/carried by TMs.

14.6.1.3. Weight and cube of all team equipment.

14.6.1.4. Number, type and location of personnel restraint devices and emergency parachutes to be used.

14.6.1.5. Signals to be used between the TL and FE/LM in event of intercom failure.

14.6.1.6. Aircraft load-out/jump procedures and sequences, and recall signals in event of team recall.

14.6.1.7. During rotary-wing operations, personnel other than PJs should operate aircraft weapons.

14.6.2. The TL is directly responsible for knowing the general location of the aircraft throughout the ingress phase. In this regard, the TL will:

14.6.2.1. Flight follow, on a map/chart identical to that used by the aircrew or use in flight navigational aids inherent to the aircraft (i.e. KG 10-21), to follow the progress of the aircraft toward the Landing Zone (LZ)/Drop Zone (DZ). Keep TMs appraised of aircraft position relative to LZ/DZ.

14.6.2.2. All maps, prepared for aircraft navigation and which have no specific application to the tactical ground situation will be left with the aircraft when the team off-loads/deploys. Suppressive fire will only be applied at the direction of the aircraft commander (AC) or as an immediate offensive response to enemy ground fire and will be applied in accordance with the Rules of Engagement (ROE) in force at the time. Suppressive fire will initially be applied with aircraft weapons.

14.6.3. Authentication of the LZ/DZ is the mutual responsibility of the AC and TL. The TL will not commit his team to an LZ/DZ he cannot recognize or has not specifically authenticated.

14.7. Insertion Procedures.

14.7.1. After authentication of the LZ/DZ, the off-load/deployment will be accomplished on the pre-planned visual signal from the FE/safetyman or aircraft jump lights. No TM will exit the aircraft until the deployment signal has been given.

14.7.2. TMs will charge and safe their weapons before clearing a hovering or landed aircraft or prior to aircraft load.

14.7.3. For parachuting operations, the rifle and handgun will be loaded with a round chambered. Safeties will be on. For training, a live round, or blank round, will not be loaded in the chamber.

14.8. Initial LZ/DZ Assembly Actions.

14.8.1. TMs will attempt to maintain visual contact with each other off-loading. During the planning phase, the TL will designate a predetermined initial rally point (IRP) close to the LZ/DZ insertion/impact point. The team will assemble at this point and conceal equipment, i.e., parachutes and associated gear, and re-check/update insertion point navigational aids. The others keep watch for enemy activity/movement. If necessary these duties may be rotated to ensure adequate security of the team. The TL can account for all personnel, and TMs can adapt their night vision, adjust to night-noises, and listen for sounds of the enemy.

14.8.2. When a reception party is on hand, a single TM will make contact while the remainder of the team maintains cover and security. Any contact with a reception party must be predetermined and is executed IAW established contact plans and mission requirements. Route implementation will be as determined during the initial planning phase.

14.8.3. Light and noise discipline will be strictly observed during all LZ/DZ assembly actions. TMs will move from the LZ/DZ as rapidly as possible, sterilizing the area.

14.9. Surface Movement.

14.9.1. Surface Movement. There are basic fundamentals of team movement. The TL plans and executes every part of the mission using principles to avoid detection by the enemy. All TMs will be briefed on routes and contingencies prior to deployment and will be updated periodically as the situation permits. Rallying points will be selected during the movement. All danger areas will be checked out prior to crossing.

14.9.2. Day Movement. The team is dispersed to the maximum consistent with control, visibility, and other factors. Areas of security responsibility are assigned to all members of the team while on the move and at halts. Movement along high ground must be made cautiously to avoid silhouetting the team against the sky. Open areas are avoided. An even pace is maintained. Sudden movements attract attention. Suspected enemy locations and key terrain features are avoided.

14.9.3. Reduced Visibility Operations. The basic fundamentals of movement for daylight are generally the same for periods of limited visibility. Operational techniques must be modified to take advantage of the concealment of darkness when planning and conducting operations. Missions conducted during periods of reduced visibility are less likely to be detected by the enemy. By combining the favorable influences of daylight and night operations a significant advantage can be gained over the enemy.

14.9.4. Night movement. The techniques of movement at night are generally the same as day movement except control of the team is more difficult and movement is slower. The team is dispersed less than in the day. Quiet movement is more essential. Sounds carry farther than in the day because of less background noise at night and a change in air density. Movement is slower to reduce danger of men becoming separated from the team. Through the use of night vision devices, surveillance along the route of travel and in the objective area (OA) can be made under near daylight conditions regardless of ambient light levels.

14.9.5. Preparation. The individual TM's preparation for a tactical operation will include camouflage of his equipment and exposed body surfaces; a serviceability check of his equipment; and padding or taping of this equipment to prevent rattling. At night, a sufficient time must be provided prior to departure for TMs to adapt their eyes to darkness. If flying to the area of operations, night adaptation goggles should be used in the event the aircrew turns on the white lights.

14.9.6. Making a Terrain Analysis. To pick a route, the terrain must be analyzed in the area in which the team will operate. Another way is to make an aerial reconnaissance. If the tactical situation prevents aerial reconnaissance, the TL must make his analysis from a map and aerial photograph study. Analyze the terrain in terms of its tactical aspects - OCOKA: Observation and fields of fire, Cover and concealment, Obstacles, Key terrain, and Avenues of approach. Look for terrain features that will help navigation, and identify danger areas.

14.9.7. Route Selection. In planning the operation, primary and alternate routes must be selected based upon a detailed map and aerial photo study. Selecting primary and alternate routes and dividing each route into legs will help the team remain undetected by having planned changes in the direction of movement. All aspects of terrain have to be considered. At night, as in day, routes should avoid obstacles and enemy positions. When the team crosses obstacles or ridgelines, care must be taken not to become silhouetted against the skyline. Routes will be planned to accomplish the mission while taking advantage of existing terrain features for navigation, security and ease of movement. Team movement along the top of ridges or through open terrain or populated areas should be avoided.

14.9.8. Route Selection in Different Types of Terrain.

14.9.8.1. Mountains. In selecting a route over mountainous terrain, weigh the added security of steep ridges and cliffs against the disadvantage of tiring the team. Natural lines of drift such as ridges, draws, and streams are characteristic of mountainous terrain, and are difficult to avoid.

14.9.8.2. Desert. In the desert, routes must exploit all concealment offered by any vegetation, shadows, or ravines. Plan routes for use at night that will bring the team to a concealed position before daylight. Make water replenishment a major factor in route planning.

14.9.8.3. Jungle. In a jungle, the topsoil is loose and soft. Slopes are slippery, and walking on them leaves an obvious trail. Routes should follow ridgelines or low ground where movement is faster, less tiring, and less likely to leave a trail. As the few roads, trails, and rivers in a jungle are in heavy use by civilians and the enemy, avoid them when possible and cross them only when visibility is reduced.

14.9.8.4. Snow/Ice. In areas with an abundance of snow and ice, care must be taken not to leave obvious tracks. Move near vegetation or dark areas. Walk on hard, bare earth when possible. Care must be exercised in selecting areas free from avalanche hazard yet afford good security for the team.

14.9.9. Navigational Considerations. Navigation procedures are provided in AFM 36-2216. The following additional considerations are provided:

14.9.9.1. Select prominent terrain features along the route and memorize their locations. Use these features as checkpoints and to help divide the route into legs.

14.9.9.2. Legs should be manageable; not too short, nor too long. Terrain is a major consideration for length.

14.9.10. Planned rallying points are pre-designated points along any intended line of movement where the team can regroup if it is forced to disperse. These rallying points, near DZs/LZs, objectives, extraction sites, and along intended movement, should be established during planning phase. The team should depart or pass the planned rallying points at specific times in order to ensure the team is on schedule and can complete the mission.

14.9.11. Security. Security measures are designed to protect the team by providing sufficient warning and permit reaction time to counter enemy threats. The team must provide security against enemy air and ground actions. The degree of security a TL deems necessary depends on the probable need, degree of threat, and proximity of enemy troops. Certain security techniques discussed throughout this manual are particularly applicable to night operations. The file and column formations will provide more flank security than other formations. If it becomes necessary to put out flank security, control will be more difficult and speed of movement will be reduced. Point and rear security elements are fundamental security measures essential to team organization. Darkness reduces detection. Use these hints to gain greater security.

14.9.11.1. Use near/far visual recognition signals to identify TMs (i.e., IR light, reflective tape, etc.).

14.9.11.2. Use the buddy system; work closely with your teammate.

14.9.11.3. Rotate watch and rest periods with teammates.

14.9.11.4. Keep all light concealed. If light is necessary, use a flashlight with a red filter under a poncho.

14.9.11.5. When moving, watch and feel for trip wires.

14.9.11.6. Use flash and sound suppressers on your weapons. This will make it much more difficult for the enemy to pin point your location if you are forced into a fight.

14.9.11.7. Keep quiet. Do not reveal your location by talking and making unnecessary sounds.

14.9.12. Halts. Any member of the team, as the tactical situation permits, may call halts. Halts are called for security or rest purposes. Security during a halt will be maintained as on the move. The team should be halted occasionally to observe and listen for enemy activity. This is called a "security halt." When the TL signals halt, all men will stop in place, go down to one knee, maintain quiet, and look and listen. It is permissible to move a few feet to take advantage of cover/concealment when the halt signal is given. Halts will be given upon reaching a danger area and periodically during movement enroute. If the team halt is for more than a brief duration (i.e., to eat, sleep, clean weapons, etc.) a bivouac site will be established.

14.9.13. Avoiding Ambush. Proper security and visual observation of the route are the best means to avoid ambush. The team must be alert and suspicious of all areas. Certain areas will be more susceptible to an ambush. These areas: roads/trails, narrow gullies, riverbanks, and open areas must be approached with extreme caution.

14.9.14. Movement tips. Move 20 minutes and halt and listen for 10 minutes. This is not a hard formula, but the team should have periodic halts. Move and halt at irregular periods if possible. Stay alert at all times. The team is never 100 per cent safe until it is back home. Continuously check on the PT to ensure he is on course. Do not run long compass legs during movement. Change direction regularly. When practical, use the navigation technique of dead reckoning. Avoid over-confidence, it leads to carelessness. Maintain strict noise discipline. Camouflage to avoid detection. Each man on the team must continuously observe the man in front of him and the man behind him to ensure the team stays together.

14.10. Formations. Formations will allow a team to move in an orderly manner with maximum control. The team must practice noise discipline during movement and be alert at all times. However tired a team may be, they must never be allowed to plod along, with eyes on the ground.

14.10.1. Point man (PT). The PT is the first man in the formation. His alertness determines the team's safety. The PT provides early warning of danger areas, front security, route finding while guiding off the compass man, setting the pace, and moves as far head of the team as visibility and terrain permit. In addition, he must have a thorough knowledge of the route. The PT walks ahead of the patrol, usually twice the distance of normal team spacing, and is responsible for frontal security when using the file formation (180 degrees). When operating in the line formation he will keep normal spacing and is responsible for 270-degree coverage to the side and rear. When operating in the Wedge formation he is responsible for 180 degrees frontal coverage at normal spacing. At the direction of the PJ TL the PT will set the pace determined by terrain, climactic and team conditions. In addition the PT must rely upon his knowledge of navigational procedures and path finding capabilities to ensure the team is efficient during movement in regards to noise and light discipline. The PT is directed by the navigator to ensure the general heading of the team is adhered to. He must be suspicious in nature of anything that may affect the security of the team such as ambushes or likely observation. When contacting the enemy he is responsible for initiating the appropriate immediate action drill (IAD). Also, the PJ TL may direct him to be responsible for enroute rally points and reconnaissance of danger areas and rally points. When securing a resting site the PT may be directed to recon the area ahead for signs or observation of enemy activity and to provide an Observation Post (OP)/Listening Post (LP). The PT must ensure he receives all hand signals delivered by the PJ TL. When a particular situation results in which direct contact with the TL is needed, the PT will find a suitable place to halt the team and make his way back to the PJ TL ensuring the navigator assumes his responsibilities during the halt. It is essential the appropriate weapon for point be selected based on Intel and the area of operations. The PT must have a thorough understanding of all team procedures and be an accurate shot. Replacement of the point is suggested either when the PT becomes so fatigued that security of the team is diminished, usually this is around 30 minutes. Next to the assistant team leader (ATL) he must be the most knowledgeable/experienced in small unit tactics.

14.10.2. Compass-man/Pace-man/Navigator (NAV). He is the navigator (NAV). He ensures the team is on the proper route selected during mission planning. If necessary, he guides the PT to keep him on course. Teams should designate a backup NAV and all TMs should familiar with the route. The NAV, when in the file formation, will normally remain twice the distance from the PT as the rest of the team. When deployed in the line formation the NAV remains an equal distance to the PT as from the team and is responsible for frontal coverage. When in the wedge formation the NAV sets up to the right and behind and is responsible for right side security. The NAV's duties include keeping the PT on the proper course. Overall responsibility for guiding the team to the survivors location and to the extraction site rest upon him. He must be proficient with map and compass, GPS navigational techniques, as well as terrain navigation in all types of conditions. The NAV recommends course or alternate routes to the PJ TL for consideration and is responsible for map Intel information. When directed by the PT the NAV may assume his duties. The NAV may receive hand and arm signals directly from the TL or the PT. The NAV may assume additional duties other than normal. Next to the radio operator (RO) he must be the most knowledgeable in small unit tactics.

14.10.3. Team Leader (TL). The PJ TL is a TM who has been designated in command of the PJ team. The PJ TL is responsible for all criteria of the mission to include planning and execution. When patrolling he is responsible for the command and control of the PJ element and overall conduct. He will conduct PJ operations based on guidance provided and will adhere to all policies required for the mission. The PJ TL's duties are to numerous to mention other than to give the above statement. The TL is responsible for ensuring hand and arm signals are observed by the entire element. He normally receives and sends out his hand signals directly to/from the NAV and RO. He should also be highly proficient in all the duties of the team. He needs to know the location of the team at all times and is the ultimate authority for the teams' movement. Although he will receive input/information from the other TMs his decisions are to be followed implicitly by the other members of the team, regardless of whether or not they agree with those decisions. The PJ TL is responsible for security to the left in the file formation, to the front in the Line formation and to the rear when in the Wedge formation.

14.10.4. Assistant Team Leader (ATL). Takes command if the PJ TL becomes unable to continue in command. He is usually backup NAV and pace-man. When in the File Formation the ATL is equal distance from the rear security (RS) and RO and is responsible for left side security. When in the Line Formation he is equal distance and is responsible for frontal security. When in the Wedge Formation the ATL is to the right and rear and is responsible for rear and right side security. The assistant TL will assist the PJ TL throughout all phases of the teams' employment. He will normally be directed to carry out tasks that require the same knowledge the TL possesses. The ATL must be capable of assuming command in the event the TL is incapable or when the team is required to split up in order to carry out the mission objective. The ATL normally is responsible for the survivor. The File Formation is recommended when moving with a survivor. The ATL receives hand and arm signals directly from the TL, RO or the RS. The ATL is responsible for security to the right of the File Formation. The ATL usually is the second pace man. The pace mans responsibilities include keeping track of distance the team has covered and to back up the NAV on his estimate of distance. When halted for the purpose of determining route selection and to ensure correct location the Pace man and NAV confer to determine distance. Additional duties, if so directed by the TL, may include keeping direction and heading. The ATL is the logical choice, as he may have to assume the TL duties or separate from the team, in which case he is already aware of the team location. He also needs to keep the rear portion of the team informed on location.

14.10.5. Radio Operator (RO). On a four-man or smaller team, the PJ TL carries the radio. On a larger team, an RO is designated. The RO usually also acts as a secondary pace-man. When in the File formation the RO is equal distance from the TL and the ATL and is responsible for right side security. When deployed in the Wedge Formation the RO is responsible for left side security behind and to the left of the PT. When in the Line Formation the RO remains an equal distance and is responsible for frontal security. RO duties includes carrying, maintenance, and operation of communication equipment, either electronic/visual. He will be knowledgeable of the required communication schedules and the procedures for receiving/transmitting information. When possible the RO should remain as close to the PJ TL as possible to provide ready access of equipment or to relay information. The RO recommends the type of equipment and selection of reception/transmission sites, to be used based on the area of operations and the comm. requirements established by the operating agency. The RO must be capable of individual operation under adverse conditions in the event he must separate from the main element in order to carry out the comm. aspect of the mission. The RO receives hand and arm signals directly from the TL or the ATL. Next to the point he must be the most knowledgeable in small unit tactics.

14.10.6. Rear Security (RS). He is the last man in the formation and is responsible for security to the rear during movement, halts, danger areas, and rallying points. He polices up dropped objects, assures as little track is left as possible, and that the team is not being followed. He passes up the count every time movement is resumed (only necessary when the front of the formation is not in visual contact with the rear). When in the File Formation the RS usually travels at the tail end of the patrol element and is responsible for rear security (180 degrees). When deployed in the Line Formation he is an equal distance from the ATL and is responsible for side and rear security. When deployed in the Wedge Formation he is responsible for left and rear security. He is responsible for sanitization of the team ensuring a noticeable trail is not left. Upon enemy contact the RS will initiate IAD procedures. When securing a resting site the RS may be directed to recon the area aft for signs or observation of enemy activity and to provide an OP/LP. The RS is responsible for providing the count to the PJ TL after all halts and after crossing danger areas. The RS receives hand and arms signals either directly from the PJ TL or the ATL. When directed by the PJ TL the RS may assume the PT mans duties. The RS is usually the least experienced member of the team.

14.10.7. Control of Formations. An important factor in successful team movement is the control the TL can exercise over the formation. He must be able to maneuver his men as the situation requires; to start, shift, or stop their movement as needed.

14.10.7.1. Control by voice and other audible means. Oral orders are a good means of control. Orders are spoken just loudly enough to be heard. A good technique is to exhale all air from the lungs and then whisper into the ear or microphone. They are shouted only in an emergency where noise discipline is not required. Inter-team radios are an excellent means of control provided they are suitable for the intended purpose (size, weight, power output, etc.) and good radio discipline is maintained. However, always assume the enemy has the capability to intercept and locate the team with direction finding equipment.

14.10.7.2. Silent control measures. Arm and hand signals can be used when appropriate. All members must know the signals and be alert to receive and pass them to other members. Infrared equipment may be used for sending and receiving signals and for maintaining control at night. All members assist in maintaining control by staying alert and passing signals and orders to other members. A signal to halt is be given by any member of the team, but the signal to resume movement is only given by the TL.

14.10.7.3. Accounting for personnel. An important aspect of control is the accounting for personnel. The TL will account for his men after crossing danger areas, after enemy contact, after crossing an obstacle, after halts, and periodically while moving. The count is sent forward when the TL turns to the man behind him and says "send up the count." This is passed back to the last man who begins the count by tapping the man in front of him and stating "one" in a low voice or whisper. The second man then relays the count forward using the same procedure and stating "two." This continues until the count reaches the TL. The last man in the formation automatically "sends up the count" after halts, danger areas and enemy contact. This system may be modified to use only hand/arm signals to replace audible counts. Another modification is to eliminate tapping when "sending up the count." It is not necessary to "send up the count" if the entire team is within sight of the TL.

14.10.8. Types of Formations. There are three major types of formations: the File, Line, and the Wedge. All other formations are derived from these three basic forms.

Figure 14.1. Figure of File Formation.

DIRECTION OF TRAVEL is: ⇐

POINT NAV TL RO/PACE ATL/NAV RS

X   X   X   X   X   X

14.10.8.1. The "File" formation (Figure 14.1.) is the most commonly used formation for tactical movement. It can be used in dense terrain, trails, poor visibility, when teams are small or speed and ease of movement is desired.

NOTE: Personnel in "file" formation are not necessarily in a direct line behind each other, they may be slightly offset.

14.10.8.1.1. Control of the file formation is maintained by passing communications back and forth through the entire team. Attention must be on the man in front and behind. Check the man behind frequently to ensure he has not stopped or is trying to pass up a signal. Each TM cues on the PT's actions: stop, drop, etc. Each person must be aware of zones of scanning and security. Distances between individuals: will vary according to visibility, terrain and need to maintain control.

14.10.8.1.2. The general order of movement is PT, NAV, TL, RO, ATL, and RS. The limit of the fastest pace set is from the rear. For example if a team was to be separated between the RO and the ATL the fault would lie with the RO for not stopping to allow the rear to maintain contact.

Figure 14.2. Figure of Line Formation.

DIRECTION OF TRAVEL is: ⇑
POINT NAV TL RO/PACE ATL/NAV RS
  X   X   X   X   X   X

14.10.8.2. The "Line" (Figure 14.2.) formation is used when crossing linear danger areas, in an area search, or in a near ambush IAD. It provides maximum firepower forward, but should not be used as a traveling formation.

Figure 14.3. Figure of Wedge Formation.

DIRECTION OF TRAVEL is: ⇑

            O

                  O

      O   TL

                  O

  O

14.10.8.3. The "Wedge" formation (Figure 14.3.) is a "V" formation with the apex of the V facing the direction of travel. The wedge is a good formation to use if forced to cross open ground. A single wedge using all TMs is used to break out of encirclement. It directs maximum firepower to the front and flanks. In a single wedge, the TL is in the center. He also acts as NAV. When the signal is given to form a wedge, odd numbered men form at the left side, even numbered men the right side.

14.10.9. Movement of Formations. PJ formations can move using the techniques of traveling, traveling overwatch, and bounding overwatch. These techniques are not fixed formations. Distances between TMs may vary based on the terrain or visibility. As the terrain becomes more rugged, the vegetation becomes dense, or if the visibility is reduced, the distance between TMs must be reduced. Visual contact must be maintained between TMs.

Figure 14.4. Overwatch Threat Guideline.

TECHNIQUE OF MOVEMENT	LIKELIHOOD OF CONTACT
Traveling	Not likely
Traveling overwatch	Possible
Bounding overwatch	Expected

14.10.9.1. Traveling. Use the traveling technique when speed is necessary and contact with the enemy is not likely. One element follows the other, keeping about 20 meters apart depending on the terrain. When traveling, the best location for the TL normally is with the lead element to aid navigation, movement, and control. (See Figure 14.4.)

14.10.9.2. Traveling Overwatch. Use the traveling overwatch technique when chance of enemy contact is possible, but not expected. Caution is justified but speed is desirable. The trailing element drops behind the lead element about 50 meters and is prepared to support the lead. If the lead element receives fire, the trailing element is far enough to the rear so the same enemy fire will not hit it, yet close enough to fire/maneuver in support of the lead element. When using traveling overwatch, the TL goes where he can best control his team in the event of contact. Normally, this is with the trailing element, keeping any key weapons (i.e., grenade launcher, M-60) near himself and under his direct control.

14.10.9.3. Bounding Overwatch. Use the bounding overwatch technique when contact is "EXPECTED". One element advances while the other element is in a good position ready to fire. The key to this movement is the proper use of terrain. All men in the team must exploit all cover and concealment. The chance of exposure to enemy observation must be avoided. A bound is normally not more than 100 to 150 meters forward of the overwatch element. It must be closely tied to terrain, the range of the overwatch fire element's weapons, and the ability of the TL to control elements of his team. Bounding overwatch can also be used in reverse order to withdraw under fire.

14.10.9.4. Considerations. The enemy situation determines which of the three movement techniques will be used. In open terrain, keep men widely dispersed. When enemy contact is possible, have one element forward and overwatch with the other element. Elements maintain visual contact, but the distance between them is such that the entire team does not become engaged if contact is made. Vary movement techniques to meet the changing situation. TLs move within the formation where they can best control the situation and do their job.

14.11. Security Measures.

14.11.1. Security during halts.

14.11.1.1. Likely enemy contact. When required to halt the TL indicates by hand and arm signal and the team assumes the security posture of going down on one knee and covering their specified area. The TL will determine the amount of time for rest. Upon hand and arm signal by the TL the team will once again resume movement.

14.11.1.2. Possible enemy contact. Upon finding a suitable rest site the team will pass the site. When required to halt the TL indicates by hand and arm signal and the team assumes the security posture of going down on one knee and covering their specified area. The TL will indicate either verbal or visually that an extended period of rest is required and direct the team to move once again. The PT and RS will post a suitable distance (usually within visual range) from the rest site and provide and OP/LP for the team. The rest of the element will backtrack between the PT and RS where they will recover off the line of march. Upon decision to move again the TL will indicate to the OP/LP and the team will resume movement.

NOTE If an extended period of rest is required the TL may replace the OP/LP personnel on a rotational basis.

14.11.1.3. Unlikely enemy contact. When the TL is relatively sure no enemy contact will be made he may call for a FLOP. The flop is just what it sounds like; the team rests in place in a somewhat relaxed posture.

14.11.2. Security during meals, rest, or comm. contact.

14.11.2.1. Pre-planned. On extended operations requiring long periods in the field or when operations are extended in the field due to error or direction, the TL may require meal/sleep or comm. contact. If so, the PJ TL should halt the team at a suitable site and conduct a map study to determine a suitable location both primary and alternate. When planned in advance the TL will conduct the map study prior to execution. Each site should afford cover and concealment, as well as, coverage of routes of approach and several escape routes if needed. Suitable areas for an extended stay require the same amount of attention as similar to an objective rallying point (ORP). Upon direction from the PJ TL the NAV will direct the PT towards the site. A short distance from the site (determined by map study) the NAV would halt the team (if so directed by the TL). The TL will direct the PT to make a reconnaissance of the area and report his findings. Upon completion of an acceptable report the TL will direct the team to the site. Upon reaching the site the TL will direct the first watch to take up the security watch and indicate their watch period. Generally, the PT, RS, and ATL will form a triangle within visual contact (comm. may be directed or indicated) and secure their sectors of fire. Each security position will have their weapons at the ready and continue observation until relieved. Unusual findings must be reported immediately to the TL. The additional members of the team may now be directed to sleep, eat, or make comm. contact. At the end of a given watch period the ATL will ensure his replacement (TL) before the others are permitted to secure theirs. After the ATL comes the PT, NAV and then the RS/RO. Upon completion of the stay the TL will indicate the team is going to move and sanitization of the site will commence. The team will now continue with the mission.

14.11.2.2. Unplanned (rest only). Upon finding a suitable site the team will pass the site. When required to halt the TL indicates by hand and arm signal and the team assumes the security posture of going down on one knee and covering their specified area. The TL will indicate either verbal or visually that an extended period of rest is required and direct the team to move once again. The PT and RS will post a suitable distance (usually within visual range) from the rest site and provide and OP/LP for the team. The PJ TL will indicate the posting period by the command "Post, 15, comm., barriers", or a similar instruction, indicating post to position/15 minutes/communication/ erect security measures, for recall (if recall is not made after 15 minutes has elapsed the PT/RS will recover to the site). The rest of the element will backtrack between the PT and RS where they will recover off the line of march. After a suitable period of time the PT and RS will join the team indicated by the TL. It is advisable that prior to rejoining, the PT and RS secure the route of march with some form of barriers (such as claymores, Booby traps, etc.) The team will situate themselves in wagon wheel fashion with each TM forming a spoke with head towards the middle; each TM should be able to touch one another. No member will leave the team unless each person is aware of the movement and barriers have been secured (i.e. control of the detonating device is under supervision). Weapons will be readily accessible and a minimum of equipment will be used. Team equipment will be placed in the middle. This provides rapid exfiltration of the area if needed. The TL will decide whether a security watch is required (fatigue of the team, relative security of the area, etc.). Upon completion of rest, the team will sanitize the area and the PT and RS will recover the barrier devices. The TL will direct movement from the area.

14.12. Reconnaissance and Surveillance. Reconnaissance and surveillance provide the team with timely, accurate information of the enemy and the terrain he controls as well as provides first hand intelligence (probably the most likely result of a ground mission). This information may be vital to working tactical decisions. The PJ TL and TMs should constantly be aware of the tactical benefit of good intelligence and how it may effect the outcome of their mission and mission to come.

14.12.1. Recon/Surveillance must be conducted in these situations:

14.12.1.1. Danger areas

14.12.1.2. ORP

14.12.1.3. Extraction LZ

14.12.1.4. RPs

14.12.1.5. Whenever the situation dictates

14.12.2. When the PJ TL determines that a recon patrol is necessary, the teams are briefed on the mission and will briefback as required. The TL usually determines a base of operations from which to conduct the reconnaissance or surveillance. TMs will carry enough equipment to conduct the mission. Generally rucks and non-essential equipment are left at the base of operations. Teams that are chosen for a mission of this type must have extreme patience and be able to remain static for long periods of time. Teams must be prepared to memorize everything of intelligence value in the event they are not able to electronically relay in formation or keep records. It is important to make sure all info is disseminated throughout the team.

14.12.3. Sample Briefing to Recon team:

14.12.3.1. What to do in the event of enemy contact.

14.12.3.1.1. Rally points

14.12.3.1.1.1. Procedures for activation

14.12.3.1.1.2. Extraction

14.12.3.2. Returning to base of operations.

 NOTE: Carefully consider the implication of a recon team "leading" the enemy back to the base of operations.

14.12.3.3. Review of capture procedures

14.12.3.3.1. Emergency signal

14.12.3.3.2. Code of conduct

14.12.3.4. Wounded/killed procedures

14.12.3.5. Reporting procedures.

14.12.3.5.1. Electronic

14.12.3.5.1.1. Call signs

14.12.3.5.1.2. Authentication

14.12.3.5.2. Visual

14.12.3.5.3. Comm.-out

14.12.3.6. Equipment to take. "See equipment"

14.12.3.7. Physical recon/surveillance

14.12.4. SALUTE. The "SALUTE" format is a simple field expedient way of covering the important aspects of field intelligence.

14.12.4.1. "S" - Size

14.12.4.2. "A" - Activity

14.12.4.3. "L" - Location

14.12.4.4. "U" - Unit

14.12.4.5. "T" - Time

14.12.4.6. "E" - Equipment

14.12.5. Types of Reconnaissance.

14.12.5.1. Area. The TL may require information of an extended area, or may desire information of several locations within the area. An area recon patrol secures this information by reconning the area, or by making the coordinated point recon of designated locations within the area. The minimum size of a recon team is two.

14.12.5.2. Point. The TL may require information of a specific location or small specific area. Recon patrols secure this information by reconnoitering or surveillance.

14.12.6. Equipment.

14.12.6.1. Weapons. Weapons are generally limited to personal defense, such as individual weapon and grenades. At least one TM will carry an automatic weapon in the event enemy contact is unavoidable. The TL must ensure it is understood contact is not to be made if at all possible.

14.12.6.2. Minimum equipment in addition to personal: pencil and note book for notes and sketches (waterproof), two compasses, binoculars, maps of area covered, flashlights (penlight preferred), comm. equipment used for reporting.

NOTE: In addition to personal maps, consideration should be given setting aside a set of maps specific to the purpose of marking Intel.

14.13. Rally Points. Rallying points are points along any intended line of movement where the PJ team can regroup if it is forced to disperse. Rallying points are also used for planned rendezvous such as extraction. They are determined both during mission planning and while executing the missions. Their locations are memorized by all TMs.

14.13.1. Types of Rallying Points. There are six types of rally points the team must be familiar with. The six types are defined as follows:

14.13.1.1. Initial Rallying Point (IRP). A point where the team can reassemble after insertion to a LZ/DZ.

14.13.1.2. Pre-Planned Enroute Rallying Points (ERP). These are points between the IRP and the extraction rallying point that are selected during mission planning using maps and aerial photography. Pre-planned enroute rallying points use prominent terrain features for reference to easily identify and locate the point (i.e., meet at a point which is 300 meters on a 275 degree magnetic heading from the fork in the river; don't meet at the fork).

14.13.1.3. Selected Enroute Rallying Points. These are intermediate points along the route that were not pre-planned. This includes near and far side of danger areas. They are chosen by the TL and designated by him using the hand-and-arm signal for "rallying point" here. The signal is passed to all TMs, who will momentarily stop to turn and observe it from its backside, which is the way it will look if returning.

14.13.1.4. Objective Rallying Point (ORP). The ORP is a point near the objective (i.e., evader/survivors last known location) where a PJ team will make its final preparations prior to actions at the objective. It may be located short of, to the left or right flank, or beyond the objective.

14.13.1.5. Extraction Rallying Point (EXRP). This rallying point is in the vicinity of the extraction LZ, not at it. The extraction LZ is kept under surveillance from the EXRP.

14.13.1.6. Alternate Rallying Points (ARP). All pre-planned rallying points need a planned alternate in case the primary is compromised or unsuitable.

14.13.2. Selection of Rallying Points. A rallying point should be near an easy to identify landmark or terrain feature. The TL or PT will designate or confirm rallying points. All TMs must know the current rallying point. Rallying points should provide cover and concealment. They should be defensible and away from natural lines of drift. A rallying point should be out of sight, sound, and small arms range from the enemy. The rallying points should not be a key terrain features that might draw the enemies' attention (i.e., an abandoned village). When the desired location for the ORP has been determined, the TL will select an element (one or two men) that will be responsible for reconning the ORP prior to its occupation. This recon ensures it is suitable for an ORP. Once the ORP is occupied and established, the team will set up all-around security by securing it in the shape of a circle or a triangle. The TL may establish a bivouac site as required.

14.13.3. Use of Rallying Points. If the team is dispersed on the LZ, DZ, or in the friendly area, the team rallies at the initial rallying point if unable to implement a recall. If dispersed after departing the IRP, but before reaching the first enroute rallying point, the team rallies at the initial rallying point or at the first enroute rallying point. The TL determines the course of action, and he must keep the team appraised as to which is the in-use rallying point. If dispersed between the enroute rallying points, the team rallies at the last rallying point or at the next pre-planned rallying point. The TL, who also keeps the team aware of what the in-use rallying point is, determines the course of action. As practical, the TL should designate the next rallying point on the route of march as the in-use rallying point. Retracing the route just passed could lead to an ambush and wastes precious time.

14.13.4. Actions at Rallying Points: Actions to be taken at rallying points must be planned in detail. Plans for actions at an initial rallying point and an enroute rallying point must provide for the continuation of the mission as long as there is a reasonable chance to accomplish the mission. The first man to reach the rallying point after breaking contact rechecks to ensure he is in the right location. Timing is started from his arrival, for a pre-planned amount of time (i.e., one hour). If no one comes in an hour, he leaves for the next rallying point or the extraction point. The clock is restarted with each arriving individual until finally all are accounted for, or follow-on actions are initiated. After one hour, actions would be as stated above. As TMs arrive, recognition signals or challenge and response password must authenticate them. Security must be posted. Ammunition and team gear redistributed. Treat any wounded.

14.13.5. Team Rally Points.

14.13.5.1. Time Frames.

14.13.5.1.1. Initial. Waiting Time limited to __XX__ min./hrs. after completion of required actions, if team does not regroup in this time frame, next enroute rally point will be used for linkup.

14.13.5.1.2. Objective. Waiting Time limited to the time frame needed to accomplish the mission with remaining personnel, if mission cannot be completed with current personnel the team will wait XX hrs, if team still does not have sufficient personnel then it will move to the extraction site.

14.13.5.1.3. Enroute. Waiting Time limited to XX min/hr after the first man arrives then depending on location, team will move to next logical rally point and repeat procedures.

14.13.5.2. Authentication for rallying. Action/Counteraction.

14.13.5.2.1. Visual. Prior to reaching the rally point the individual(s) will stop a short distance form the area and observe (observation time depends upon time allowance). After a suitable observation period the person(s) will move into the area at a XX degree angle to the right/left of the largest identified terrain feature. The person(s) will further indicate he is a TM. Upon reaching the rally point the individual(s) will recon the area for other members. If the individual(s) is not challenged they must assume they are the first to arrive at the scene and will take cover/concealment. If additional members arrive, upon visual authentication they will challenge and move them to the secure site. If the time period elapses, all individuals should move to the next rally point and repeat the procedures.

14.13.5.2.2. Radio. Follow the above guidelines for visual with the exception that radio contact is made prior to entering the area and you follow the directions given by the appropriate party.

14.13.5.2.3. Beacon. Follow the procedures for visual with the exception that you use the beacon to home in on the team.

14.13.5.3. Authentication for rallying. Password/Reply can be as simple as the sum of numbers totaling a predetermined number: i.e. sum is nine. The challenge is called out "five" the reply is "four".

14.14. Bivouac Sites.

14.14.1. A bivouac site is a position established when the team halts for an extended period of time. It is not intended to be a fortress to stand and fight from. It is a place defensible for the time necessary to break contact, has escape routes to a pre-designated rallying point, provides good concealment, and allows the team early warning of approaching enemy personnel. There must be a thorough understanding of bivouac location, avenues of escape, rally points, critical times, a password authentication system for identifying TMs, and immediate actions in the event of ambush or detection. All personnel items and team equipment will remain packed unless actually in use during periods of bivouac. The bivouac site will be thoroughly sterilized prior to departure.

14.14.2. When a team must halt for a long time in a place not protected by friendly troops, it must take active and passive security measures. It is best to occupy an area, which, by its location, provides passive security. Use such an area for a bivouac site.

14.14.3. Establishing a bivouac may be a part of the team's overall plan or it maybe an on-the-spot decision. In either case, it should be occupied only for the minimum time necessary to accomplish the purpose for which it is established. Except in emergencies, 24 hours is the longest time a bivouac is occupied. The same bivouac should not be reused at a later date. A bivouac site is established when there is a need to: sleep, prepare food, hide the team during a detailed reconnaissance of an OA or recovery zone, clean weapons and equipment or formulate plans/issue orders.

14.14.4. Selecting a Bivouac Site. Plan for a bivouac site before occupying it. Reconnoiter and secure it at all times. Choose terrain which: has little tactical value, has dense vegetation that provides good cover and concealment and impedes foot movement, is remote from human habitation, relatively near a source of water, and has escape routes to a rally point. Avoid locations near known or suspected enemy positions, built-up areas, ridgelines and crests, except as necessary to allow communication or roads, trails, and natural lines of drift.

14.14.5. A tentative location for a bivouac site is usually picked by map reconnaissance during mission planning. Selection may also be made by aerial reconnaissance or be based on prior knowledge of a suitable location. However, the suitability of a particular place must always be confirmed on the ground. Plans to establish a bivouac site must include the selection of an alternate bivouac site and a rallying point. The alternate bivouac site location is used if the initial site proves unsuitable or if the team must prematurely evacuate the initial base. The rallying point is for use in case the team evacuates the bivouac site in the event of an emergency.

14.14.6. Pre-Occupation Activities.

14.14.6.1. Halt the team 200-400 meters from the tentative bivouac site. The team establishes a security halt, ensuring front, rear, and flank security. The TL and NAV will recon the tentative site, while the ATL remains behind in charge of the remaining team. The ATL receives a contingency plan (i.e., emergency rallying points, communication schedule) from the TL in case of enemy contact.

14.14.6.2. The tentative bivouac site must be reconned to determine its suitability. The recon element will use a buttonhook to get to the site. If found satisfactory, the TL or NAV will return to the main body of the team, back tracking the buttonhook. The remaining individual (with the radio) will set up an OP and keep the site under surveillance.

14.14.7. Occupation. The team moves to the bivouac site using the same path the recon element took. Ensure the buttonhook is used and enter the bivouac site from the same spot. Rear security camouflages the trail from the point where the halt was conducted to the site itself. The TL designates where each individual goes as they file past him, possibly using terrain features such as a rock, a tree, etc. The OP is moved into position within the buttonhook to watch for enemy along the route the team took. The ATL makes the preliminary check of each TM's position, and makes minor adjustments as required. The TL makes the final adjustment. The TL ensures there are good fields of fire, cover and concealment, interlocking fire zones, etc.

14.14.8. Defensive Positions. Static defensive positions will not normally be used. However, some basic principles apply when bivouacking. When resting always be in a position of maximum cover and concealment. A good area provides a 360-degree field of view to observe any enemy approach. Three withdrawal routes should be planned from any position. These routes should offer cover, concealment, terrain, and vegetation to aid in the loss of any pursuit force. It is essential to maintain vigilance in any static area. For a long-term static position, i.e., 30 minutes or longer, OP(s) should be established for the most critical avenues of approach. The TL determines the number of OPs. The decision is based on numbers of available personnel and a threat assessment of the area.

14.14.9. Only one point of entry and routine exit. This point is camouflaged and guarded at all times by the OP. Restrict movement both inside and outside the bivouac site.

14.14.10. Enforcement of camouflage, noise, and light discipline. Fires are built only when absolutely necessary and, as a rule, only in daylight. They are kept as small as possible. Where terrain permits, build fires in pits to reduce the danger of visual detection and to facilitate extinguishing the fires and camouflaging their sites. Use the driest and hardest wood available (dead limbs still on trees) to avoid smoke. In most areas, the best time to build fires is when the air is thin and smoke dissipates quickly (usually around noon). Early morning may be appropriate, but in areas where there is ground fog, consider the risk of detection because of lingering odor. Perform noisy tasks, such as breaking branches, only at designated times but never at night or during the quiet periods of early morning and late evening. When possible, perform noisy tasks when other sounds will cover them, such as the sounds of aircraft, artillery, or distant battle sounds.

14.14.11. A one-hour stand-to morning and evening should be observed 30 minutes before and 30 minutes after light in the morning, and 30 minutes before and 30 minutes after dark in the evening. Every man is awake, accustomed to changing light conditions, aware of his equipment layout, armed, and ready for action. All equipment will be packed. Each TM must know the position of men and weapons to his flanks, front, and rear and the times and routes of any expected movement within, into, and out of the bivouac site.

14.14.12. The TL develops and implements a plan to ensure necessary men are awake.

14.14.13. The TL develops and implements a withdrawal plan, if required. The plan should include multiple withdrawal routes to an emergency rally point.

14.14.14. Early warning devices may be placed on avenues of approach. Weigh the value of these devices against the fact their discovery automatically alerts the enemy.

14.14.15. The TL establishes priorities of work. Security is always the first priority. The sequence of other activities must be carefully thought out and realistic. For example, if the team has had no rest for over 24 hours, sleep and rest may be high on the priority list.

14.14.16. Maintenance. Weapons and equipment are cleaned and maintained as required. Only a few members of the team clean weapons at a time.

14.14.17. Sanitation and Personal Hygiene. In daylight, expedient latrines, i.e., cat holes outside the perimeter are used. The user must be guarded. At night cat holes are inside the perimeter.

14.14.18. Messing. Men eat at staggered times. Avoid meals requiring elaborate preparation.

14.14.19. Water. TMs must travel in pairs to procure water. Visits to the source should be limited to twice per 24-hour period.

14.14.20. Rest. Permit rest and sleep in accordance with the priority of work. Stagger rest periods so security is maintained. Consistent with work and security requirements, each man must get as much sleep and rest as possible.

14.14.21. Planning and conduct of operations are as follows: details of the operations planned must be passed to each TM separately. Assembling all TMs at one time would endanger/compromise the security of the site.

14.14.22. Departure. Remove or conceal all possible signs of the team's presence. This will deny the enemy knowledge of foreign presence in the area, prevent pursuit, or deny him information of team bivouac operations. The team evacuates as a unit, when possible.

14.14.23. Sleeping Positions. TMs should sleep in a circle with their heads toward the center like the spokes of a wheel and each must be able to touch adjacent TMs. Rucks will be in the center of the circle. All personal items and team equipment will remain packed unless actually in use. This will ensure the team is ready to make an immediate move. No one will leave the circle without first notifying one of the other TMs. Anyone detected walking in the area will be considered the enemy.

14.14.24. As soon as possible after establishing the defensive position, the TL will brief the team on actions in event of an attack. The briefing should include avenues of escape, rallying points (primary and secondary) and actions at rallying points. One half of the team should have their compasses set on the primary rallying point and the other half on the alternate. If the enemy comes from the direction of the primary rallying point, the man with the azimuth of the alternate rallying point set on his compass can lead the team out. Allow no smoking in the field. The light and smell from a single cigarette can draw the enemy's attention to the team. Firearms should not be fired at night except as a last resort (the enemy will see your muzzle flash). Use grenades at night over the use of firearms.

14.15. Observation Posts For Small Elements.

14.15.1. An OP is a fixed location from which one observes and listens for the activities that occur within a particular area and provide early warning of enemy approach. They are positioned along probable avenues of enemy approach and are operated in shifts when the team remains static for more than 30 minutes. The number of OPs established depends on threat, the number of TMs available, and the degree of observation permitted by the terrain and weather. OPs are used with teams of three or more PJs if determined necessary by the TL.

14.15.2. OPs should be selected and established with the following in mind: maximum observation for the desired area, cover and concealment of the OP, concealed routes to and from the OP.

14.15.3. Normally, the best location for an OP is on or near the military crest of a hill. Ridge tops should be avoided because individuals may be skylined when occupying the OP. It may be appropriate to establish the OP well down the forward slope when observation is restricted by terrain.

14.15.4. Establishment and operation of an OP. Radio antennas must be carefully positioned and concealed so they do not disclose the OP location to the enemy. People going to and from the OP must move carefully so movement does not reveal the location to the enemy. Separate routes to and from the OP are established. When natural concealment is not adequate, the OP is camouflaged.

14.15.5. Communication between bivouac site and OPs. The system must provide for every man to be alerted quickly and quietly. Radios are good for this, but must be carefully controlled due to the possibility of an enemy radio direction finder (RDF) capability. Tug lines or pull lines may be used for signaling. They are quiet and reduce radio traffic.

14.16. Objective Area (OA) Actions.

14.16.1. After the PJ team has traversed the planned approach route, the team will establish a concealed position in the vicinity of the objective, which will be designated as the objective rallying point (ORP). The TL will conduct an initial reconnaissance of the immediate area using standard binoculars or night viewing devices, as light conditions permits. Upon completion of his initial reconnaissance, the TL will position security elements and begin a detailed reconnaissance of the objective. At night or during poor weather conditions, this reconnaissance element must move to several positions to observe the objective, because of the visibility limitations. It will be necessary to move closer to the objective at night than it will for daylight a daylight reconnaissance. The security elements displace, as required, to secure the reconnaissance element. Upon completion of the reconnaissance, survivor contact will be made, if practical. After survivor authentication has been completed the team will move back to the ORP or to an alternate rally point as pre-briefed by the TL.

14.16.2. Team Action at the Objective. Security at contact sites is very similar to security measures used for rest, meals, and comm. contact pre-planned. The major differences between the two are upon securing the objective site the TL will place the cover-man/sniper in a position to cover the contact team. The TL will direct those who are responsible for entry procedures and authentication upon return of the contact team. The TL may position himself to observe the contact procedures or conduct electronic surveillance. The RO and NAV will make up the contact team if so directed.

14.16.3. Security and an LP/OP (if team size allows) will be deployed and an observation period will begin based on TL discretion, reconnaissance/surveillance will be accomplished and a final check of plans, personnel, weapons, equipment will be conducted. Communication will be limited to those involved in the contact procedure. Time limits will be established for contact, recon, search etc. TL will deploy personnel responsible for contact. Upon return to ORP authentication will be further reviewed. Medical treatment will be conducted as thorough as possible before movement by pre-designated personnel. ATL will brief survivor on movement plan (if feasible) and responsibilities during movement. Security will be called in and RS will sweep the area prior to movement.

14.17. Danger Areas. A danger area is any place where the team may be exposed to enemy observation or fire. Examples of danger areas are roads and trails, open areas, villages, enemy positions, and obstacles such as minefields, streams, and barbed wire. A team must avoid danger areas whenever possible. If the team must pass or cross them, extreme caution will be exercised. Crossing at night is preferable.

14.17.1. The team should cross a danger area where observation is restricted, such as at a curve in a road, where vegetation comes right up to both sides of the road, and a point that would leave a minimum of foot prints or tracks (grass, hard clay, pine straw). Secure the near side of the danger area and secure flanks. Usually a visual reconnaissance and the presence of the team are enough to secure the near side. A security halt is effected at this time, looking for movement across the danger area, listening for noises or breaks in light discipline at night.

14.17.2. Designate near side and far side rallying points. The rallying point on the near side will usually be the last rallying point designated before encountering the danger area. The rallying point on the far side will be at a safe distance on the far side of the danger area along the route of march.

14.17.3. Reconnoiter and secure the far side. This may require the PT to cross the danger area, and check to see that the crossing site is safe and suitable. The team should not cross the danger area until the recon is complete.

14.17.4. If a team is split by enemy action while crossing, men who have already crossed should go to the rallying point on the far side, and men who have not crossed return to the rallying point on the near side. At the rallying point on the near side, the senior man takes command and tries to cross the danger area at another place. If, after crossing the danger area, the predetermined time limit has not expired, he tries to rejoin the remainder of the team at the rallying point on the far side. If the time limit has expired, he tries to rejoin the team at the ORP, or an alternate rallying point, based on instructions issued by the TL.

14.17.5. Remove evidence that the team has crossed, such as footprints.

14.17.6. Security During Sentry Removal. When the occasion arises that sentry neutralization must occur, the TL designates the most accurate shot along with the most experienced and qualified member to perform the action. In general, the PT (due to his position and its requirements) will provide weapon security to the combative. The TL will ensure adequate planning is involved prior to moving to the area. The team will stop short of the objective and the PT will conduct a recon. The TL will designate whether the PT is to return and report or whether the report will be by electronic means. In the case the PT reports electronically, he will establish himself in a position to cover the combative and provide protection to the team as an alert. In either case the PT will observe the area for habits, contact procedures, etc. and remain in place long enough to ensure complete success of the operation. The team will remain close to the objective and set up security using the remaining members. The PJ TL will direct the combative to enter the designated site. It is at the combative's discretion when to complete the assignment and the mode. Upon completion the PT will direct the team to move through the area, and the combative if possible will remove the body and sanitize the area. The team must move as quickly as possible through the area. Operations of this type are usually considered extensive as well as exhaustive.

14.17.7. Security and Movement Through Barriers. If it is unavoidable to avoid barriers, it should be regarded in the same respect as danger areas. After it is determined the area must be breached the area should be placed under surveillance as long as the tactical situation permits. The PT should place himself in an appropriate place in which to cover the team. The RS will ensure natural materials are gathered prior to breaching the barrier. As soon as the materials are gathered the team will start crossing through the barrier in the team position of PT through RS. Upon arrival on the opposite side the PT will set up security for the rest of the teams crossing. The PJ TL will decide the spacing based upon the situation.

14.17.8. Crossing linear danger areas (i.e., roads, railroads, and trails). When the TL is alerted to a danger area by the PT, he will go forward to see if he should proceed with his original plan or modify it. He will also decide if the tentative rallying point on the near side and rallying point on the far side are suitable. Security is then sent to the flanks and they should be able to communicate with (signal) the team. Consider terrain/visibility and put the security element out far enough to give warning of enemy approach to the remainder of the team so they will not be hit by enemy fire directed at the security element. A small team, such as four-man or less, may not be able to put a TM at each flank. When flank security is in place, send the PT across the danger area to recon and secure the far side.

14.17.8.1. There are several ways to reconnoiter the area. The PT recons the area forward far enough to allow room for the team to move back into its formation.

14.17.8.2. There are several methods for the main body of a team to cross. It may use an area of limited visibility, may cross in groups, in the modified wedge (file), or on line. The PT stays on the far side of the danger area where he is least exposed. He then signals the TL it is safe to proceed across. At the signal from the TL, flank security moves directly across the danger area and then moves diagonally to rejoin the team.

14.17.9. Bypassing small open areas. Open areas are bypassed whenever possible. As with any danger area, when the TL is alerted by the PT an open area is to the front, he will go forward to see if he should proceed on the original route or bypass. The TL directs the NAV to make a 90-degree change in azimuth to the right or left. This takes the team parallel to the base of the open area. The pace-man does not keep pace on this leg of the detour, but the compass man does. When the TL is satisfied the team has moved far enough to clear the side of the danger area, he tells the NAV to go back to his original azimuth. The pace-man once again keeps pace on this leg of the detour since it is part of the straight-line distance on the team's route. When the TL is satisfied the team has reached the far end of the open area, he has the NAV make a 90-degree turn back toward the original route. When the NAV has traveled a distance equal to the pace he covered on the first leg of the detour, he returns to his original azimuth and the team is back on its original route.

14.17.10. Crossing large open danger areas. As in the techniques used for small open areas and linear danger areas, the TL has the option of changing the original plan (i.e. consider the feasibility of bypassing). The TL directs the team to cross the danger area using the movement technique commensurate with the possibility of enemy contact (normally traveling overwatch). The movement technique is employed until the entire team has crossed the danger area. The TL ensures that, when nearing the far side, the PT is far enough in front of the team to keep the team from being hit by enemy fire directed at the point.

14.17.11. Inhabited Areas. Pass on the downwind side, well away from the village. Always avoid animals that may signal one's presence.

14.17.12. Mine fields. Be alert for mine fields and avoid them whenever possible, even if it means going a considerable distance out of the way. Routes of approach, ditches, and the banks of streams are frequently mined. If the team must pass through an area that has been mined, use extreme caution and work through slowly. For additional information on mines, see FM 20-32.

14.17.13. Barbed wire. Stay low when approaching wire. At night, silhouette the wire against the sky and figure out its design. Check for mines, boobytraps, and warning devices. In day, cross in the manner which will expose one for the shortest time. At night, follow the procedures described below:

14.17.13.1. To go over the wire grasp the first strand lightly and cautiously lift one leg over. Lower the foot to the ground, feeling carefully for sure footing. Lift the other foot over the wire. Quietly release the wire and feel for the next strand. Cross it in the same manner.

14.17.13.2. To go under the wire, go through headfirst. Slide under the bottom strands on the back, pushing forward with the heels. Carry the weapon length-wise on the body. Steady it with either hand. Lift the wires up with one hand. Do not pull or jerk on the wires. Feel ahead while moving, there may be low strands or trip wires.

14.17.13.3. If it is necessary to cut through the wire, cut only the lower strands and leave the top wire in place. This makes it less likely the enemy will discover the gap. Cut the wire near a picket. When accompanied by another TM, have them hold the wire with both hands. Wrap cloth round the wire between his hands and cut part way through the wire. Quietly bend the wire back and forth until it separates, then bend back the loose ends. When alone, wrap the wire, hold it, and then cut the bend between the hand and the picket. Carefully roll back the loose end to clear the path. Do not cut concertina if there is any way to bypass it. Most concertina is like a spring and is under tension between stakes or pickets. It is very difficult to control after cutting and may snap back noisily and reveal the team's presence. If a TM must cut through concertina, stake down two loops far enough so it is possible to crawl between them; then cut the wire as described above. The two stakes will prevent the wire from snapping back.

14.18. Team Actions at Danger Areas.

14.18.1. Linear. PT halts the team, gives danger signal, recons area then returns to report his findings to the PJ TL. TL then establishes far and near rally point and ensures the team is clear on danger area procedures while ensuring each member is clear of the RPs. At the TL's command the flankers deploy within TL site or communication and provide security in the appropriate direction. The flankers will indicate to the TL when it is safe by giving him the appropriate signal ("__XX__" during daylight, ___XX___ small flash(s) when not equipped with night vision devices, or flash(s) of infrared light when equipped with night vision devices or by electronic contact). On the flankers guidance the TL will deploy PT for far recon. Upon direction from the TL the PT crosses the danger area as appropriate and recons the area using a pattern consistent with terrain (box, heart, contour, etc.) ensuring the area is large enough for the team to remain undetected after crossing and give passive security. Upon securing the area the PT moves into position on the far side and gives the clear to cross signal ("__XX__" during daylight, ___XX___ small flash(s) when not equipped with night vision devices, or flash(s) of infra-red light when equipped with night vision devices or by electronic contact). In the case the area is not secure the signal will be given __XX__ times in rapid succession. The PT will ensure acknowledgment of signal by the same code sequence from the TL and upon receipt provide far side security or wait until it is safe to return to the team. TL will deploy team on line if terrain permits (file if otherwise) after point has crossed the area and he has received the all clear signal. On prearranged signal by PT signifying the area is secure, TL will motion to flankers for permission to cross by signal. Main element crosses area, providing security as they cross (place feet perpendicular to direction of movement and avoid banks), flankers follow main element providing rear security. PT picks up file formation and continues out of danger area. Do not allow team to bunch up on far side of danger area.

14.18.2. Open Areas. Avoid if possible. TL will decide course of action depending on size. Single file with appropriate spacing or bounding overwatches may be used.

14.18.3. Water Areas. Same technique as linear will be used, however, extensive reconnaissance may be used for determining route. For deep water, fast water, team will move to secure area, plan and prepare equipment for crossing. Strongest swimmer will cross with rope and tie off on far side. TL will send one man across on rope at a time. Last man will strike near system. On far side team will move to secure area and prepare equipment for movement.

14.18.4. Unlikely contact. PT will follow same procedure as likely contact up until returning to report findings. At this time the PT will indicate likelihood of detection. PJ TL will determine course of action. In event TL determines it is relatively safe to cross without preparation the team will arrange itself in file formation and cross one at a time with far and near security posted. Upon successful crossing, the team will move away from the area as quickly as possible.

14.19. Immediate Action Drills (IADs). A team may make contact with the enemy at any time. Contact may be through chance contact, air observation, or ambush. Contact, if unavoidable, is broken as quickly as possible and the team continues its assigned operation whenever possible. During ground movement, contacts are often unexpected. In these situations, IADs provide a means for swiftly initiating action, as appropriate.

IADs are designed to provide swift and positive small unit reaction to enemy contact. They are simple courses of action in which all individuals are so well trained that minimum signals or commands are required to initiate action. It is not feasible to attempt to design an IAD to cover every possible situation. It is better to know one IAD for each of a limited number of situations occurring in a combat area.

14.19.1. Signals. Some IADs, such as the counter-ambush IAD described below, are initiated without signals or commands, as prearranged automatic reactions to enemy contact. Others, such as the FREEZE, are initiated on silent (arm-and-hand) signals. The standard arm and hand signals are used, when appropriate. When these are not appropriate, special signals are developed and used. The drills described are examples that illustrate the application of principles and are not considered as standardized reactions to fit every situation.

14.19.2.   FREEZE. When the situation requires the immediate, in-place halt of the team, the arm-and-hand signal FREEZE is used. This is the reaction when the team detects the enemy but is not in itself detected. The first man detecting the enemy (visually or otherwise) gives the arm-and-hand signal FREEZE. Every man stops in place, weapon at the ready, and remains absolutely motionless and quiet until further signals or orders are given.

14.19.3.   Hasty Ambush. An ambush is a surprise attack from a concealed position upon a moving or temporarily halted target. Surprise must be achieved, as it is the only factor that distinguishes ambush from other attack. Camouflage, movement, light and noise discipline must be observed. Have an objective rallying point selected in event of compromise. In understanding ambush mechanics you can know what to look for and possibly avoid ambush sites. This IAD is both a defensive measure used to avoid contact and an offensive measure used to make contact. When used as a defensive measure to avoid contact, ambush is not initiated unless the team is detected. It may often be a subsequent action to FREEZE. When the hasty ambush signal is given (by PT, TL, or another authorized man), the entire team moves quickly to the right or left of the line of movement, as indicated by the signal, and takes up the best available concealed firing positions. The TL initiates the ambush if required by opening fire and shouting, "Fire." This ensures initiation of the ambush if his weapon misfires.

14.19.4.   Air Observation. The first man hearing or sighting an aircraft, which may be a threat, signals FREEZE. Every man freezes in place until the TL identifies the aircraft and gives further signals or orders.

14.19.5.   Air Attack. When an aircraft detects a team and makes a low-level attack, the IAD air attack is used. The first man sighting an attacking aircraft shouts, "Aircraft; (front left, rear, or right)." The team moves quickly into line formation well spread out, at right angles to the aircraft's direction of travel. This is to deny the attacker a linear target. As each man comes on line, he hits the ground, using available cover. He positions his body at right angles to the aircraft's direction of travel, to present the shallowest target possible. Between attacks (if the aircraft returns or if more than one aircraft attacks) seek better cover. Attacking aircraft are fired on only on command of the TL.

14.19.6.   Indirect Fire. If a team comes under indirect fire (i.e., artillery), the first man to hear the incoming rounds yells "Incoming." All TMs immediately assume a prone position. Between salvos, the team double times to a new position that provides cover and concealment. The PJ TL gives the direction/distance to move using the clock system (i.e., 3 o'clock, 200 meters. 12 o'clock is the old direction of movement). The purpose of moving to concealment is to deny the forward observer who is directing the fire on you a target.

14.19.7.   Australian Peel. This IAD is used to break chance point contact. There must be two or more individuals on the team to use this technique. The basic principles of the drill are to eliminate the immediate threat, establish fire superiority, force the enemy to take cover, and to withdraw one person at a time while providing continuous cover fire. This IAD is usually initiated when the PT of the PJ team and the PT of the enemy element come upon and see each other simultaneously. For chance contact, anybody may initiate the Australian peel. Peel right/left will be used determined by consideration for terrain/cover/concealment and likely areas that the enemy may be using for ambush. This IAD is usually initiated by the PT by virtue that it is a chance contact drill. Upon the initiation of Contact

(Point/rear) The PT/RS will shout "Contact, Front/Rear" and fire well aimed, accurate shots using the two round burst technique or two shots when using a shotgun at enemy targets. He shouts, in addition to firing, in the event of a weapon malfunction. If the enemy become non-visible the PT/RS will direct his fire toward and behind the last visual reference. Upon dispatching the enemy the PT/RS will peel in the appropriate direction (tactical or speed loading) and take a place a reasonable distance behind the last man. Upon PT/RS passing the last man the last man will call out indeed that he is the "last man". Everyone who assumes this position will repeat this. When contact is made the rest of the team will settle down off centered, on one knee, behind cover and prepare to fire. The second man will fire a 40mm (if available) in the general direction of the enemy and after the PT runs past take up coordinated two round bursts and he will also peel. The process continues until contact is broken or until the TL signals otherwise. The last man should consider smoke/gas grenades depending upon the wind and the amount of time it is requiring for the additional TMs to break contact. In the event a weapon malfunctions the TM will transition to his secondary weapon and clear his primary weapon when time permits. The peel is continued a minimum of one complete cycle. Care should be exercised when using 40mm or hand grenades when breaking contact as to the specific detonation range of the devices.

14.19.7.1. Team Consolidation. After contact is broken, the TL calls for a head count, ammo count and redistribution and gives brief orders as required. The team moves out of the contact area as soon as possible.

14.19.7.2. Peel Center. This IAD would be used if the team were traveling in a staggered file, for chance contact front or rear. Upon contact, the first two men fire on enemy then yell, "CONTACT FRONT." The rest of the team steps one pace right or left to form a clear center lane. TL yells "PEEL CENTER REAR," and everyone passes it on. The first two men peel down the center; rifles at high port, to take up positions in the rear. This IAD continues as in the Australian Peel until contact is broken. It has the advantage of two persons firing forward at all times instead of one as in the Australian Peel. The rear contact just flows toward the front instead of the rear.

14.19.8. The "clock system." The direction in which the team is moving is always considered to be 12 O'clock. When contact is made, and the TL's decision is to break contact by the clock system, he shouts a direction and a distance. For example, "Ten o'clock-two-hundred," means for the team to move in the direction of 10 o'clock for 200 meters. Each individual must be alert to move in relation to the team's direction of march, not in relation to the direction he is facing at the moment. TMs keep their same relative positions as they move so the original formation is not disrupted. Subordinate leaders must be especially alert to ensure all personnel get the word and movement is quick, correct and in an orderly manner. The command is repeated only as necessary to ensure all personnel comply. Unnecessary repetition creates confusion and noise which may help the enemy to more accurately determine the location and extent of the team.

14.19.9. Counter Ambush Drills. When a team is ambushed, the IAD used is determined by whether the ambush is near or far. A "near ambush" is one whose attack force is located within hand grenade range (approximately 40 meters or less). A "far ambush" is one where the attack force is located beyond hand grenade range.

14.19.9.1. In a near ambush (ambushes within grenade throwing distance), the killing zone is under very heavy, highly concentrated, close-range fires. There is little time or space for men to maneuver or seek cover. The longer they remain in the killing zone, the more certain is their destruction. Therefore, if attacked by a near ambush, react as follows: person spotting the ambush yells, "AMBUSH RIGHT" (or left as appropriate). Men in the killing zone, without order or signal, immediately assault directly into the ambush position, occupy it, and continue the attack or break contact as directed. The team should go to full auto, sweep the area while rushing into the enemies emplacement, pass the enemy, fire into enemy position while leaving area and continue onward, pulling into file formation and executing an Australian peel until contact is broken. This action moves them out of the killing zone, prevents other elements of the ambush from firing without firing on their own men, and provides positions from which other action may be taken and directed by the TL. Men not in the killing zone maneuver against the attack force and other elements of the ambush. The attack is continued to eliminate the ambush or to break contact as directed. As individuals you must react swiftly, violently and deadly in order to survive.

14.19.9.2. In a far ambush, (ambushes out of grenade distance), the killing zone is also under very heavy, highly concentrated fires, but from a greater range. This greater range provides men in the killing zone some space for maneuver and some opportunity to seek cover at a lesser risk of destruction. Therefore, if attacked by a far ambush, react as follows: TMs in the killing zone, without order or signal, immediately return fire, take the best available cover and lay down a base of fire until otherwise directed or indicated. TMs not in the killing zone maneuver against the ambush force, as directed. TL will call appropriate IAD, (bounding, Australian, etc.). If elements of the team become pinned in position, members who may move in relative freedom must maneuver to flank and engage the enemy to create weak spots. TMs who are trapped by fire must seek cover and concealment and lay down a well-aimed base of fire until otherwise directed. The attack is continued to eliminate the ambush or to break contact, as directed.

14.19.9.3. In an ambush situation, all TMs immediately return fire aiming at the enemy muzzle bursts. Fire is characterized by volume, violence, and accuracy. Single enemy positions are destroyed as rapidly as possible to create weak points in the ambush position. A base of fire is established and a maneuvering force is designated to assault the enemy from the flank or rear (far ambush only). All TMs on the team must realize their teammates are trapped in an ambush and will be destroyed if they do not react violently and aggressively in an immediate attempt to destroy the ambushing force.

14.19.10. Advanced Counter Ambush/Chance Contact.

14.19.10.1. When teams have worked and practiced together, a better method to counter ambush is to get "on line", keep the enemy suppressed and then maneuver the team from the kill zone or flank a weaker force.

14.19.10.2. Team Breakdown: In a formation the team moves as a single unit. When enemy contact is made the formation is broken up into two separate teams. These teams are known as Fire Teams. The separated teams are termed Fire Team "one" and Fire Team "two" or Fire Team "A" and "B".

14.19.10.3. Roles and Responsibilities: As you move in a formation there should be an appointed TL and ATL. During an IAD it is each TMs responsibility to maintain fire suppression and follow the command of the TL and ATL. Secondly, all TMs should be looking for a way out (or door) to break enemy contact. The TL is in control of one Fire Team and the ATL has control of the other. It is the fire TL's responsibility to control the movement of his particular fire team and still maintain visual contact with the other fire TL.

14.19.10.4. Verbal Commands and Movement: Upon initial engagement or contact from the enemy the first person that sees enemy fire needs to call it out. It is imperative the call be clear, loud, and echoed by all TMs. Remember, at this point confusion may be high, good communication is the key to keeping everyone on the same sheet of music. The call should be "CONTACT" and the direction from which the fire is coming from, i.e. Front, Rear, Left, Right. After the contact call every man in the formation should drop on line in the direction of enemy fire and begin picking up a sustained rate of fire. The purpose for getting on line is that it is the most effective means of putting suppressive firepower down range.

14.19.10.5. Bounding or Leapfrog: Once the team is on line and a sustained rate of fire is attained the TL of Fire Team "one" should call out "ONE'S READY". At this time all members of Fire Team "one" should be preparing to bound back and returning the call "READY". The next call will be from the TL, "MOVE". Again the call should be echoed from all members of that fire team. As the team bounds back they should be changing out low or empty magazines. The ideal time to reload is on the move when you are not firing and not while you're in position and need to be putting rounds on target. Terrain and the amount and concentration of enemy fire will depend on how far the Fire Team will travel during its bound. A good train of thought during a bounding movement is, (I'm up, they see me, I'm down). The next and last call of the bound will be from the TL. His call will be "DOWN". Again, all members of the Fire Team should echo the call. As soon as Fire Team "one" begins to pick up their rate of fire, that is the signal for the TL of Fire Team "two" to start making his calls and getting his team ready for a bound. All calls and movements should stay the same.

WARNING: Before bounding back, safe and high port the weapon.

14.19.10.6. Dead Space: Dead space is a term used to describe the space created between the two teams as they bound back. As each team bounds they should not be moving straight back. Rather each team should be moving back at a slight angle away from each other. Every time the Fire Teams bound they should be increasing the distance between themselves. The intended purpose of this is to make the enemy fight you on two fronts instead of one. Thus making the enemy have to choose between one and the other as their intended target. Another reason for dead space is to create the illusion there is more than one ground team to aggress/defend against. This may give the enemy second thoughts about the size of their opponent and cause them to stand down.

14.19.10.7. Break Enemy Contact: Once a member finds a good spot to break contact with the enemy he is to shout the call "DOOR". In addition to the "DOOR" call the TM needs to be pointing out the direction of the door. At this time the TL of the Fire Team that has found the door needs to be communicating with the TL of the other Fire Team. The call will be "CONSOLIDATE". Once the call to consolidate has been established the Fire Team farthest from the door will begin a continuous peal movement until consolidation of the two fire teams is complete. If terrain and enemy fire concentration allow, the whole team can move as one to consolidate the fire teams together. As soon as the two fire teams have linked back together the peal movement either continues or is established. Every member of the team is responsible to ensure all members are notified they are the last man on the peal. What this means, is if you're the last man in the formation and it is your turn to peal, you are to tap the person next to you and yell, "LAST MAN". This action allows the person who was tapped to know they are now the last man to peal in the formation. Just as you are required to notify the person on one end of the formation they are the last man you also need to let the person pealing know you are the last man on the other end of the formation. This will ensure the person pealing knows to stop in position at point and not keep going.

14.19.10.8. Contact Broken: After the contact has been broken a good head count needs to be taken. To start the head count the last person in the formation will tap the man in front of him and say, "I'm one, your two". The next person will do the same but say, "I'm two, your three". This will continue until all are accounted for. Next is a personnel and equipment check. The terminology is as follows, "ONE, UP, UP, FOUR". This means person number one is okay, weapon is up and running and he has four magazines of ammo left. At this point the TL will have to make a determination weather to continue the mission or not.

14.19.10.9. Conclusion: IADs are fast paced and potentially dangerous. Safety is paramount when conducting live fire IAD training. This is a need to know skill in a war time environment. Knowing the correct actions for yourself and others on your team could mean the difference between life or death.

14.19.11. Repeated Use of IADs. Some IADs may be used repeatedly with little danger the enemy will develop effective countermeasures. FREEZE and HASTY AMBUSH are examples of this category. The situations in which their use is appropriate do not lend themselves to easy conversion by the enemy into a baited trap. Any IAD must be carefully studied to detect potential dangers that may arise from frequent use. If these dangers cannot be eliminated, the drills must be varied to avoid setting patterns.

14.19.12. Prevention of Ambushes. Precautionary security measures are taken by teams to prevent an enemy surprise attack. In moving through open or broken terrain, all-around security must be maintained. In jungle terrain, security elements should be sufficiently forward to prevent a linear ambush of the main body. The main body must maintain sufficient room to maneuver once the forward element makes contact. At night, night viewing devices are very valuable. One of the best defenses for avoiding ambushes is to study the terrain ahead and avoid walking through areas that look like good ambush locations. Go out of the way to avoid any location that looks like it would be a good spot for an ambush. Remember the best defense against ambush is avoidance of potential ambush locations.

14.20. Actions Under Flares. There are two general types of flares; grounds flares which burst and burn in place; and overhead flares which burst and burn high in the air.

14.20.1. Ground Flares. Ground flares are placed in the same manner as anti-personnel mines, so you will set them off by pulling wires. The areas in which they are placed are often under enemy observation and fire. A ground flare set off nearby usually means the enemy has seen you or suspects your presence. If caught in the light of a ground flare, move quickly out of the lighted area. Keep moving until you are well away from the area, reorient yourself, and look to the TL to direct the team as to direction, speed, etc.

14.20.2. Aerial Flares. Overhead flares may be placed and set off in the same manner as ground flares or may be fired from rifles, mortars, artillery, or hand projectors, or may be dropped from aircraft. Except for those dropped from aircraft, all rise high in the air before bursting and burning.

14.20.3. If a flare is set off overhead or is rising overhead, get down and seek cover before it bursts. If caught in the light of the burst where blending into the background is possible, freeze in place until the flare burns out. If among trees, step quickly behind one. If caught in the open, and cover and concealment are not possible, crouch low or hit the ground. The burst of light is temporarily blinding and may prevent being seen. Close the dominant eye to aid in recovery of night vision and protect the eye used in sighting the weapon. If caught by a flare while crossing an obstacle, such as barbwire, crouch low and stay still until the flare burns out. As soon as the flare is extinguished the TL will direct the team as to the direction to move out of the area.

14.20.4. If the TL suspects the flare is directed directly towards the team and the team is compromised he will utilize the actions used in the event of a ground flare. Aerial flares may not indicate the enemy has seen the team, but in fact may be used only to help them illuminate random areas for the observation.

14.21. Emergency Close Air Support.

14.21.1. There are two types of Close Air Support (CAS) strikes: pre-planned and immediate. Pre-planned CAS strikes are requested, coordinated, and, if possible, confirmed during the mission preparation phase. The team sends its request through channels and is given a priority by higher headquarters. Pre-planned strikes can be used to create a diversion during a critical phase of the team's mission. Before he departs, the TL must know the location, time, and ordnance to be used on all pre-planned CAS strikes in his area of operation for the duration of his mission. Immediate strikes are used for emergency situations or for targets of opportunity not anticipated. These sorties come from the daily allocation of alert sorties or from diverted pre-planned missions. Frequently, whatever ordnance and strike aircraft are most readily available are used. Most of the air strikes used by PJ teams will be of this type.

14.21.2. A team is normally equipped with UHF/VHF/FM radios. Most Forward Air Controller (FAC) and strike aircraft have UHF/VHF or FM radios. When a team is supported by a FAC, the FAC will serve as a communication link between the team and the strike aircraft. Communication procedures, frequencies, and equipment should be coordinated during the preparation phase.

14.21.3. Air strike Request/Briefing. The elements of a request/briefing are:

14.21.3.1. Requester's call sign.

14.21.3.2. Authentication. Pilot request ground to authenticate.

14.21.3.3. Target description. This is the most important part of the request. It describes the nature of the target and permits the pilot to determine what type of ordnance to use.

14.21.4. A team reports the target's location using one of these methods:

14.21.4.1. Grid Coordinates. Coordinates are the simplest way to report target location. Include the UTM grid designator.

14.21.4.2. Shift From a Known Point. Target location can be given as a distance and direction from some known point. This known point could be a target, smoke, or a panel.

14.21.5. A prescribed Time Over Target (TOT) allows the PJ TL to ensure his team is either clear of the target or ready to mark the target. TOT may be given several different ways; as soon as possible, no later than, only time acceptable, or a time bracket/window. To reduce the chance for compromise, a team should try to be far enough from the target and in a covered position where it is not necessary to mark its location during the strike. As a rule, a mark is necessary when the team is closer to the target than 500 meters. When some obvious terrain feature, such as river, road, or cultivated field, is between the friendly troops and the target, a mark of the team's position may not be necessary, even when the strike is very close. The team must report the type of mark to be used or that no marking will be used. Marking the team's location may be visual or electronic. The distance should be included, especially if the enemy situation does not permit the team to mark its location for the FAC or strike aircraft. The direction is as important as the distance when no friendly mark is used. If a target location can be given with precision, target marking by the team may not be necessary, especially when airborne FAC is available to mark it. When a PJ team uses its own position as a reference, target marking by the team can help ensure an accurate strike. A 40mm CS round can be used to mark targets up to 400 meters away.

14.21.6. When a PJ is giving ground-to-air advisories for CAS, there are certain factors that must be considered. Do not direct the supporting aircraft to fly attack runs that:

14.21.6.1. Overfly the team's position, if possible. Runs should be aimed parallel to the team's front.

14.21.6.2. Are in line with obstacles such as towers, power lines, and hills.

14.21.6.3. Overfly enemy anti aircraft positions.

14.21.7. Escape heading is an advisory; expressed in degrees, on the direction the strike aircraft should fly out of the target area. Considerations are the same as for the attack heading. It is only given if different from the attack heading.

14.21.8. The aircraft selected to FAC the strike and make the strike will be largely dependent on the enemy AA defenses in the area. The team should report on these defenses as well as possible. The report should include type and density of weapons. Both the FAC and the strike aircraft need to know the location of enemy AA defenses in the target area to plan their strike. This direction and distance is given in respect to the primary target and should be clarified in the advisory. The distance is expressed in meters.

14.21.9. Tactical Air Request Call For Fire (Fixed Wing).

14.21.9.1. (Aircraft call sign), this is (your call sign).

14.21.9.2. I have (emergency), (priority), fire mission.

14.21.9.3. My position is (give location), marked with (?).

14.21.9.4. Targets (description).

14.21.9.5. Located at (coordinates), (chart number).

14.21.9.6. Target bears (degrees) (distance) from (landmark).

14.21.9.7. Target is (stationary/moving).

14.21.9.8. Will (not) mark with (color) smoke.

14.21.9.9. Request (bombing) (rocket) (strafing) (napalm) attack.

14.21.9.10. Run-in Heading (degrees), pull out (right) (left) (straight).

14.21.10. Example (Fixed Wing): "Manny 22, this is Eraser 02. I have an emergency fire mission. Target is an armored patrol vehicle and squad of riflemen located at MA 275943, chart number S514IVSE. Target bears 090, 1500M from hilltop 467. Target is stationary and will not be marked. Request napalm attack, heading 180, pull out left. Request two runs using one canister per run. Run mission ASAP. We have negative front line. Our position is marked with orange panels. I can observe and will not control. Over."

14.21.11.   Tactical Air Request Call For Fire (Helicopter Gunships):

14.21.11.1.   Observer's location and markings.

14.21.11.2.   Target location.

14.21.11.3.   Target description (troops, bunker, vehicles, etc.).

14.21.11.4.   Desired results (destroy, pin down, screen, etc.).

14.21.11.5.   Time on target.

14.21.12.   Example (Helicopter Gunships): "Scarface, this is Eraser 02. I'm at MA 916314. My position is marked by panels. Enemy position is 250M west of my position, one enemy tank with infantry. Request rocket and gun run to pin down troops. Request your run ASAP. Over."

14.22. Policy On Enemy Contact. The success of PJ team operations is predicated on the avoidance of enemy contact. For team and survivor safety, and to avoid mission compromise, enemy contact should be avoided, even if it requires the team to resort to a contingency plan, which may delay extraction. With the limited firepower and size of a PJ team, the cost of enemy contact could be devastating for both the team and the survivor.

14.22.1.   Small teams are not manned or equipped to handle prisoners. It is not reasonable to expect the team to bring a Prisoner of War (POW) along during an operation. The TL must guard against situations that create POWs.

14.22.2.   Prisoners. Prisoners will be bound and gagged and if possible blindfolded, and may be returned under guard to extraction point or friendly area or treated as in the same manner as seriously wounded. In the event the PJ TL decides a prisoner must be taken, the contact team is responsible for the actions. The contact team will follow the same procedures as in evader/detainee search and secure with the exception a more aggressive action will be used. The TL will stress the importance of the five "S" system of prisoner handling (silence, search, secure, segregate, and a speedy recovery to the rear). If the prisoner responds to any action with violence use only that amount of force necessary to control the situation. Do not let emotion cause unnecessary risk to the team.

14.22.3.   Non-combatants could compromise a small team. The non-combatant must be prevented from compromising the team until they are out of the area. They should not be harmed since the enemy may go out of their way to hunt you down. You could consider binding and gagging the person near a trail where they will eventually be found.

14.23. Team Casualties. In the event of a casualty, the first concern of the team after withdrawal from the danger area is care of the casualty. Quick and thorough medical treatment must be performed to ensure survivability. An element compromise message and contingency action plan code will be relayed to the mission commander as early as the tactical situation permits. After caring for the casualty, the TL will make the decision to continue or abort the mission based on the following: condition of casualty, compromise of team position/mission, availability of personnel to complete the mission and time remaining vs. time required for mission completion.

14.23.1. A non-ambulatory casualty may have to be hidden in a concealed shelter and picked up by the team after survivor contact, or he may be taken to an extraction point. An ambulatory casualty may continue with the team.

14.23.2. If a TM is killed in action, and extraction of the remains is not feasible, the remains should be buried at or near an easily identified site and the grave well concealed. Remains should be wrapped securely in a poncho or other suitable covering and buried deep enough to prevent exposure from erosion or animals. TMs should make a mental note of the grave location on a map. The following items should be removed from the remains and retained by the team: One dog tag, identification card, classified material, maps and compass, communications equipment, weapons and ammo (as needed) and any other equipment needed for mission accomplishment or survival. All other equipment will be buried with the remains. Any weapons left behind will be rendered inoperative or destroyed.

14.23.3. Methods of Handling Wounded, and Dead Personnel.

14.23.3.1. Wounded. Wounded will be removed from immediate area if possible, before applying first aid. Each TM will have secured on their body a personal medical kit, which is used to stop life threatening injuries. Personnel who treat the wounded will not utilize their own personal first aid kit. If additional treatment is required, the TL will move the team based upon the urgency of the situation to a site adequate for more definitive care. The NAV and RS are responsible for definitive treatment while the rest of the team provides security. If it is determined the injuries are too extensive and preclude movement the TL will decide whether to effect another planned recovery of the patient and who will be left to provide definitive care.

14.23.3.2. Walking Wounded. The TL will decide the method of recovery for walking wounded, (evacuation by air, accompany the team, concealment for later pickup, or return on own to friendly area).

14.23.3.3. Seriously Wounded. Seriously wounded may be evacuated by air, concealed for later pick up, or carried by team if practical.

14.23.3.4. Dead. Dead, may be handled similar to seriously wounded (no one will be left with dead personnel).

14.24. Body Searches.

14.24.1. After making initial contact with an evader, the subject must be handled very cautiously until positively identified. A brief summary of the technique involves: matching the physical appearance (body, clothing and equipment) against the pre-mission evader identification information, checking the Armed Forces Identification Card/dog tags, and asking personnel authentication questions. When searching an evader or detainee, always use assistance. Move the subject to an area where another can provide cover fire during the search. In extreme circumstances it may be necessary to make a thorough search unassisted. Methods for an unassisted search are explained in this text. Evaders who have been positively identified will not have their survival equipment taken away from them. This does not prohibit temporary removal of survival equipment to conduct a search and make a positive ID of the evader. In the event the evader becomes separated from the PJ team during the recovery phase (i.e., the team is ambushed or the rescue aircraft shot down on exfiltration), the evader must have the means to continue evasion and contact rescue forces. The one exception to this rule is the evader's weapons.

14.24.2. Rules for Searching. The rules to follow when searching an evader/detainee are:

14.24.2.1. Indicate by speech and actions you are confident of your actions and intent and will shoot if necessary.

14.24.2.2. Do not let the evader/detainee talk, look back, move, or otherwise distract you.

14.24.2.3. Never attempt to search a person until you have him in an off-balance position.

14.24.2.4. Do not move within arms reach until the subject is in an off-balance position.

14.24.2.5. If armed with a pistol, have it cocked, hold it at your hip in a ready position and keep it on the side away from him.

14.24.2.6. When you have assistance, keep out of your TM's line of fire. One TM conducts the search while the other remains far enough away to observe the evader/detainee at all times.

14.24.2.7. Do not relax your guard after completing the search.

14.24.3. The "Pat" or "Feel" Method of Searching. The "pat" or "feel" method of searching will reveal most weapons and concealed objects. Search the subject's entire body, paying particular attention to the armpits, arms, back area, and legs. Thoroughly search the clothing folds around the waist, chest and top of his boots. Knives can be concealed on a string around the neck, stuck in a boot or taped to any area of the body. Be extremely cautious when putting your hand in a subject's pocket or in the fold of the clothes. The subject may grab your arm and throw you.

14.24.4. Prone Method of Searching When Armed With a Rifle. Make the subject lie down on his stomach so the arms are extended beyond the head with the arms close together, palms facing upward. The legs are also extended with the feet close together, toes pointed out to the sides.

14.24.5. The Kneeling Method of Searching When Armed with a Rifle. Direct the subject being searched to interlock the hands behind the head, palms facing outward and kneel. Bend the subject forward until balance is maintained with difficulty.

14.24.6. The Lean-To Method of Searching When Armed With a Pistol. Have the subject being searched lean against a tree, wall, or other upright object, one hand over the other, with the feet crossed and extended as far as possible to the rear. This puts the subject in an off-balance position. In the event the subject being searched makes a threatening move, immediately kick his foot outwards, throwing him to the ground.

14.24.7. Standing Method of Searching When Armed with a Pistol. Make the subject spread the legs far apart and place the hands on top of the head, fingers interlocked, palms facing the sky. Move in close to search the front, place your foot against the heel and turn your body to the side to protect your groin.

14.25. Evader/Survivor Contact.

14.25.1. Evader/survivor contact procedures are provided by the Joint Rescue Coordination Center (JRCC) or theater guidance documents.

14.25.2. Single Ambulatory. In the event the TL or circumstances direct an evader or detainee be searched and possibly secured, the contact element of the team will conduct the operation. The contact element will move into the area in a circuitous manner and observe the contact or contact area. After it is determined applicable to proceed the contact cover-man will position himself in position to provide cover and possible help (he must stay out of the line of fire provided by the point). The contact-man will initiate the contact and authenticate if applicable. Upon contact the RO will demand the contact lay down on the ground and assume a spread eagle position with hands on top of the head and feet pointed inwards. He will indicate by speech and actions he is confident of his actions. The contact-man will not allow the contact to talk, move or otherwise distract him. In the event the prone position cannot be used he will have the contact assume an off -balance position (kneeling, lean to, or standing). When the contact has assumed an off-balance position, he will move forward and conduct a cursory search, using the pat and feel method (rifle/pistol). If articles are found which may pose a hazard he will confiscate those items. If applicable the contact-man will further authenticate the contact. If the contact is deemed dangerous whether by action or if the contact-man is suspicious, the contact will be bound and may even be gagged. After the cursory search the contact-man will move a short distance away (but still within control of the contact) and direct the contact to move in the direction he has indicated. The distance between the contact-man and the contact will not be so great that the contact may run or escape. The contact cover-man will remain behind for a short period to determine that no one is following and then will move behind the contact towards the security position. The cover-man/sniper will remain vigilant of the contact and surrounding area for any unusual occurrence. The contact-man will again move in a circuitous route towards the security position. He will pass the security position without alerting the contact that the sentry is present and move to the TL position inside the secure area where a more thorough search and authentication procedure will be conducted. The medic will render appropriate medical attention.

14.25.3. Multiple Ambulatory. Procedures remain the same except the contact-man will take more caution in the separation and observation of the contact. If needed the contact-man will indicate to the contact-cover that additional manpower/control is needed. The cover-man/sniper will ensure adequate coverage of the contact area and if possible direct the contact element by electronic means for best coverage.

14.25.4. Non-Ambulatory. In non-ambulatory situations, the PJ TL will follow standard procedures for ambulatory with the following exceptions. The time of site observation will be shortened as much as possible, depending upon the tactical situation. The contact team will report directly back to the TL by visual or electronic method as to the condition of the survivor. If site is relatively secure, the TL will direct the contact team to begin treatment. The TL will evaluate the condition of the survivor and determine if it is possible to move him. If so, the TL will direct the team to move to the survivors location and quickly begin movement towards the extraction area. Procedures for serious wounded will be followed. Litter patients will most likely require partisan assistance in moving, large team tactical assistance, long term treatment in place, or abandonment if necessary to save the lives of others.

14.26. Evader/Survivor Medical Care. A major responsibility is to provide emergency medical evaluation and treatment for the trauma patient in a combat environment. In this situation, the degree of threat is weighed against the need for initial medical evaluation and treatment. In a direct threat, the extent of evaluation and treatment performed on initial contact with a survivor is limited either to none at all or to the minimum action required for sustaining life and preventing further injury. These actions must take into consideration the well being of the team and its members, the survivability of the survivor, the immediate threat, the extraction or withdrawal requirements and time, and the environment into which the team will be entering. Medical treatment becomes secondary when the team and survivor are placed into a direct threat situation. Reinitiate medical treatment when the survivor is removed to a secure area. The TL explains to the survivor the possible delay in extraction and transport. The fact is made clear that when extraction is not possible at the time of contact, he may be hidden and returned to at an appropriate time.

If this occurs with no immediate threat, all medical treatment is accomplished prior to concealment. The survivor is also informed of typical duties while unattended. The time of the team's return should not be discussed. If contact is made and the survivor is left, he is told to stay concealed. In all instances the survivor is informed on impending actions, to prepare tactically and mentally for the situation, reducing his apprehension. Explain to the survivors that their well being is considered, as is the well being of the entire rescue team.

14.27. Security for the Survivor. The overall security of the survivor is the responsibility of the ATL. The survivor (s) will be placed between the ATL and RO in the case of a file formation. When in the line formation the survivors will remain on line between the ATL and RO. When in a wedge formation the survivors will be placed in the center of formation. After initial contact, search, and authentication, the survivor should only talk or be talked to, by the ATL/as necessary by the TL.

14.28. Exfiltration Procedures. Exfiltration responsibilities begin with security and authentication of the recovery zone. Physical security of the recovery zones rests with the team until on-board the recovery vehicle. Authentication procedures between the team and the recovery vehicle will be pre-planned. During an aircraft recovery, all team personnel will maintain their security positions until the aircraft is stabilized on the ground or in a hover and ready for pick-up. The TL will initiate radio communication and immediately inform the aircrew of any immediate threat to the aircraft. The FE or AC will give the on-load signal. The loading sequence will be pre-planned.

14.28.1. Exfiltration/Movement. The fundamentals of movement during exfiltration are exactly the same as those defined for day or night team surface operations. Specific procedures will differ depending on the degree of threat present and whether the team is dealing with an evader or survivor. The team briefs the evader/survivor on required actions and behavior. The TL considers the increased potential for enemy detection when dealing with an evader/survivor prior to mapping out a plan for movement.

14.28.2. Exfiltration/Extraction Preparation. Most often recovery is by rotary-wing aircraft. Certain criteria and procedures are necessary for successful rotary-wing recovery operations and are listed below. Alternate means, modes and methods are considered. If "air" is impracticable or impossible, don't hesitate to select a water or land mode and method.

14.28.3. Extraction Site Security. Security of the extraction site is similar to security at contact sites with the following exceptions. The contact element will serve as the individuals who ready the site for pickup. (See extraction procedures)

14.28.4. LZ Selection Criteria.

14.28.4.1. Tactical Suitability. The LZ is secure, free of enemy, and close enough to the team's route of travel.

14.28.4.2. LZ Size Criteria. The number and type of helicopters determine the size of the area required and will have a bearing on the size of the landing site. Twice the rotor diameter is good LZ size criteria. A helicopter usually requires more usable landing area at night than during the day.

14.28.4.3. Surface conditions. Surface conditions are firm enough to prevent helicopters from bogging down, creating excess dust, or blowing snow. Rotor wash on dusty, sandy, or snow-covered surfaces cause loss of visual contact with the ground and should be avoided, especially at night. Loose debris is removed from landing zone.

14.28.4.4. Ground slope. Normally, if the ground slope is greater than 15 percent, helicopters cannot land safely. This percentage will vary depending upon type of helicopter and angle of approach.

14.28.5. Extraction Procedures. Extraction responsibilities begin with security and authentication of the extraction zone (EZ). Physical security of the EZ rests with the team until on-board the helicopter. Authentication procedures between the team and the helicopter are mutually dependent and pre-briefed depending on type of authentication. Some examples may be: authentication by radio, TOT/covert/overt LZ lighting/strobe configurations. TM authentication is also (if possible) pre-briefed. I.e. All TMs are wearing an IR armband or all TMs will have an active strobe light on in their chest cargo pockets or IR strobe turned on in the chest area. All non-equipped survivors or personnel will be in physical contact with a TM who is properly equipped. Pre-brief such items to the extraction crew that will either allow them to be "weapons free, weapons hold, or weapons tight". All team personnel maintain their security positions until the helicopter is stabilized on the ground or in a hover. The TL initiates radio communication and immediately informs the pilot of any immediate threat to the aircraft. Loading sequence and position in the aircraft is briefed in advance. All personal weapons are cleared and all equipment secured as soon as feasible. The TL is the last to load and is responsible to inform the extraction crew of "all on-board".

14.28.6. Aerial Movement Responsibilities (Exfiltration). The TL's first responsibility on-board the aircraft is to establish intercom with the aircrew and confirm they are briefed on any known threats in the area. The remaining TMs will provide care for the survivors, if required, strap in and safe weapons.

14.29. Debriefing. Provide a thorough record of medical treatment provided to the survivors when transferring them to definitive medical care. A thorough and complete intelligence debriefing is mandatory after returning to friendly forces. TMs are cautioned to treat all information regarding the operation as sensitive even if not officially classified.

14.30. Team and Individual Patrol Tips.

14.30.1. Make a detail map study. Know the terrain and prominent land marks which will aid you in navigation.

14.30.2. Consider the use of difficult terrain in planning your route.

14.30.3. In mountainous terrain plan to use ridgelines for easy movement whenever possible but avoid skylining.

14.30.4. Plan your route along easily recognizable key terrain features, rather than along direct compass headings.

14.30.5. When navigating to linear terrain features (rivers, mountain ranges, etc.) use deliberate offset either to the left or right of the point you are going to. Each degree offset will move you 17 meters left/right, for every 1km.

14.30.6. Refer to your maps at halts.

14.30.7. Keep team informed of their position from one key point to another.

14.30.8. At night follow your compass from one key terrain point to another.

14.30.9. Roads and intersections are not terrain features you can count on. Do not plan your route counting on intersections, however, if time dictates travel by road, be sure the road is traveling in the same direction you wish to move and check your compass frequently. You can be sure the enemy will see your footprints so be sure that extraction is close.

14.30.10. Noise and movement are the two biggest giveaways. In most cases movement can be detected before noise. Fast movement can be seen before slow movement. Take advantage of background noises. Weapons banging against equipment make the most common form of noise infractions. Clean, check, and live fire your weapon prior to departing. Don't forget your weapon cleaning equipment and ensure your oil bottle and cleaning fluid is clean.

14.30.11. When crossing danger areas select far and near RPs.

14.30.12. When close to the enemies main battle position, avoid lateral movement across his front.

14.30.13. During an airborne assault, parachutist will remain close together in the air.

14.30.14. Carry gloves to protect hands.

14.30.15. Use friction tape to secure rifle swivels, sling points and other items that may rattle.

14.30.16. Perform the bounce test with all equipment to detect noise.

14.30.17. Consider replacing the rifle sling with a single point attachment of 550 cord.

14.30.18. Tape over the end of the weapon being sure to leave a small side opening to prevent accumulation of dirt in the barrel and facilitate water draining. The tape will not interfere with firing.

14.30.19. Weapons are always carried at the ready position.

14.30.20. Provide every man with an area of responsibility.

14.30.21. Designate at least two pace men and use the average for the count.

14.30.22. Use the KISS principle (keep it simple stupid).

14.30.23. Prearrange and rehearse all signals to be used.

14.30.24. Send up the count after every halt.

14.30.25. Use the PT as that and not as a NAV.

14.30.26. TL is ultimately responsible for navigation.

14.30.27. On long patrols, change PT and NAV frequently to reduce fatigue and increase distance.

14.30.28. Know your location at all times.

14.30.29. Do not jeopardize security with headgear that impairs hearing.

14.30.30. Keep talking to a minimum.

14.30.31. Never throw trash on the ground; carry it with you, or bury it so it will not be unearthed by animals.

14.30.32. Inclement weather is best for patrols.

14.30.33. Use bungee cords instead of 550 cord when it is necessary to set up a shelter.

14.30.34. Make cold camps whenever possible.

14.30.35. Flashlights should have red lens. If necessary to use white light, use a poncho as cover and use one eye.

14.30.36. Technical and non-technical terrain that risks exposure should be negotiated at night in one continuous pitch.

14.30.37. If you have to cough, open your mouth and cough into your hat or press into the hollow point of your throat with your fingers.

14.30.38. Ensure your maps are not marked with friendly information or information that may aid the enemy.

14.30.39. Each member should have an escape and evasion (E & E) map.

14.30.40. All-important papers should be kept in one location and be easily accessible even in the dark.

14.30.41. Keep your map folded in its original condition, special folding could give away important information.

14.31. General Tips of the Trade.

14.31.1. While on a mission minimize fatigue because tired men become careless.

14.31.2. If you show confidence your team will.

14.31.3. Do not lose your temper, it will affect your judgment. Take guidance from your team and make decisions based upon them. Always keep an alternate plan in mind.

14.31.4. Never lose sight that teamwork is the key to success. Use live training scenarios and constant practice to hone skills.

14.31.5. Teams that have a good physical training program have fewer health problems.

14.31.6. Make sure TMs take proper precautions for health care, do not wait until they requires special attention.

14.31.7. All personnel should wear loose and un-tailored clothing in the field. Tight fitting clothing allows for tearing and insects to bite/sting through the clothing.

14.31.8. Each TL and TM should have checklists to ensure nothing is left behind.

14.31.9. Use tact when reprimanding personnel, especially indigenous members. If possible take the man to the side to criticize. This allows him to respond positively and not feel ridiculed or lose self-confidence.

14.31.10. Do not hang clothing on foliage that will cause itching later on (such as green bamboo).

14.31.11. Carry Crystalline Sterate (CS) powder in a small vial and sprinkle it on food containers. This keeps animals from digging them up.

14.32. Weapon Tips.

14.32.1. If CAS is expected on insert/extract keep a magazine full of tracers; they can be used to identify enemy positions.

14.32.2. The last three rounds in the magazine should be tracers. This reminds you that you are empty.

14.32.3. Replace the cartridge in the chamber each morning as condensation may cause a malfunction.

14.32.4. Oil the selector switch daily and work the function of the weapon, especially during rainy season.

14.32.5. Always carry your weapon on safe, the time it takes to move the selector switch is weighed against the more common occurrence of shooting yourself or a teammate.

14.32.6. During extraction due not fire from the airframe unless pre-briefed or directed by the AC.

14.32.7. Do not retrieve your first magazine on contact.

14.32.8. Check all magazines for cycling prior to assuming the mission.

14.32.9. Ensure the magazines are placed so they transition smoothly to the weapon.

14.32.10. Practice speed and tactical loading, as it may save your life.

14.32.11. Never assume your weapon is clean enough. Clean it daily.

14.32.12. Consider placing magazines upside down with bullets away from the body. This keeps dirt and water from contaminating the rounds and if hit by enemy fire the rounds will not hit your body.

14.33. LBE Tips.

14.33.1. Ensure all buckles and straps are secured. Do not use paper tape.

14.33.2. Consider using triangular bandages in wrapping the bottom of magazine carriers to facilitate easy removal of individual magazines and increase the first aid capability of the team.

14.33.3. Cut the front corners of the ammo pouches one half to three quarters of an inch to make it easier to remove magazines during the rainy season. Consider using canteen pouches for holding magazines as they are easier to open, carry more magazines and you will not need as many pouches.

14.33.4. Always carry a strong knife on patrol.

14.33.5. Snap links should be secured around the harness and not in the cloth loops.

14.33.6. Consider carrying no more than one smoke grenade on the harness (this allows breaking of contact). In general you don't fight with smoke grenades, and if you need one, chances are you don't have time to remove it from your pack.

14.33.7. Fold paper tape through the rings of the grenade and secure to the body of the grenade. Paper will tear fast for use, plastic or cloth tape will not. Also, it stops noise and prevents snapping while keeping the ring open.

14.33.8. Camouflage equipment that will be exposed.

14.33.9. Do not bend the pins on the grenades flat, the rings are to hard too pull when needed. Inversely, do not straighten them as the may fall out.

14.33.10. Make a daily check to ensure grenades are safe and operational. (Fuses may become unscrewed)

14.33.11. Each team should carry one thermite minimum for destruction of equipment.

14.33.12. Do not secure grenades by the rings to the harness or place them in an area that makes them a target for snipers (killing several with one shot).

14.33.13. Ensure a snap link is snapped through the frame and ruck at the top so you won't lose the ruck during extraction if you must secure it to a ladder, maguire rig, etc.

14.33.14. Insect repellent spills easily, therefore isolate it from other equipment. Also, squeeze air from the container and screw cap on firmly.

14.33.15. Always use water from the ruck prior to that on the LBE. This will ensure a water supply in the event your ruck must be ditched.

14.33.16. Always test the ruck prior to the mission and carry a sail needle or awl for repair.

14.33.17. Waterproof essential equipment prior to mission execution and carry a waterproof bag in the ruck to allow for flotation during water crossings.

14.34. Recon Tips.

14.34.1. Base the number of canteens per man upon weather, water sites and availability in the AO. Plan for water points when planning the route of march. (Beware of poisoned water supplies)

14.34.2. Check all TMs for anything that may provide intelligence. TMs should only carry ID and tags.

14.34.3. Always carry maps and notebooks in waterproof containers.

14.34.4. Use a pencil or grease pencil for taking notes, ink smears when wet. Also, grease pencils may be erased.

14.34.5. Inspect all team and individual equipment for completeness and function.

14.34.6. All survival/essential equipment should be ranger corded.

14.34.7. Matches should be kept in waterproof containers.

14.34.8. Never take a picture of members on patrol; use the camera for intelligence purposes only. In addition, remove film after mission completion and place with other valuables.

14.34.9. Each team should take at least two penlights.

14.34.10. While on patrol move for 20 minutes and halt/listen for 10. Listen half the amount of time you move. Move and halt at irregular intervals.

14.34.11. Stay alert at all times, you are never safe until after the debrief.

14.34.12. Never break foliage and try to remove any trail that the enemy may follow.

14.34.13. Put insect/leech repellent around areas which may allow insects to move next to body (waist, boot tops, etc.).

14.34.14. Do most of your moving during the morning hours and at night to conserve water.

14.34.15. Continually check the PT to ensure he remains moving towards the objectives. Make irregular legs and do not run a compass course unless absolutely necessary.

14.34.16. Do not ask for a "fix" from support aircraft unless absolutely necessary.

14.34.17. Force yourself to cough whenever external noise permits. This will clear your throat, ease tension, and cannot be heard.

14.34.18. When removing or adding clothing is necessary no more than two members at a time should do so, and the others should provide cover.

14.34.19. If you change socks try to wait until the remain over night (RON) site. Never remove both boots at the same time.

14.34.20. When a TM starts to get immersion foot, stop in a secure position, remove the boot, dry the foot, powder and allow foot to dry out. Do not continue, as this will cause the member to become a burden on the team rather than an asset.

14.34.21. Do not throw away batteries when on patrol, warming them up may aid in getting a crucial transmission from them.

14.34.22. Always carry spare batteries in original containers as these aid in battery life.

14.34.23. Avoid over-confidence as it leads to carelessness. Because you have not seen the enemy does not mean he has not seen you.

14.34.24. Correct all team and individual errors as they occur.

14.34.25. All TMs should take notes while on the operation and compare them nightly. Each man should keep a list of lessons learned and add to them after the operation.

14.34.26. Each man must continually observe the man ahead and behind and is responsible for all hand signals. Remember you are responsible for the team's welfare.

14.34.27. During the dry season do not urinate on rocks or leaves but rather in holes and crevices. The wet spot may be seen and the odor may carry.

14.34.28. Carry an extra pair of socks and foot powder. Consider carrying an extra large set of socks that may be worn over the boots for crossing roads and trails/streams.

14.34.29. During rest breaks do not leave your weapon alone or remove the ruck.

14.34.30. In most areas, the enemy will send patrols along roads and major trails between the hrs. of 0700-1000 and from 1500-1900. Since most enemy vehicular movement is at night, the team should stay no closer then 200 meters from the road network. Usually roads are swept twice a week no further then 200 meters. Road crossing should be considered just prior to last light.

14.34.31. A dead enemy's shirt, contents of pockets, or pack are more valuable than his weapon.

14.34.32. If the enemy is pursuing you, delay grenades/claymores of 60-120 seconds. In addition throw gas to your rear and flanks, give the enemy reason to quit.

14.35. Forward Air Control (FAC) Tips.

14.35.1. The FAC is second in importance to your weapon while on an operation. Learn all you can about FAC operations and procedures. Proper use of a FAC could mean the difference whether you return or not.

14.35.2. When making a FAC VR, make a map that covers the AO from the FOB to your OA.

14.35.3. Whenever you hear an aircraft, ensure your radio is turned on, they may be trying to contact you.

14.35.4. The FAC is weather limited, plan for this.

14.35.5. Average time for reaction IAW his mission profile.

14.35.6. Tactical aircraft may have mixed ordnance, or if it is a diverted aircraft, ordnance someone else has requested.

14.35.7. If on patrol, request ordnance appropriate to the target.

14.35.8. Do not use the PRC-90 as a homing station (beacon). Instead use the radio to direct the FAC to your position. If pre-planned, use the appropriate frequency.

14.35.9. The FAC must know your position before he will clear the strike, plan for this.

14.35.10. A signal mirror is the best way of signaling the FAC to your position. If the mirror cannot be used use your panels.

14.35.11. If the sun is obscured, a strobe light placed against the mirror may allow the pilot to locate your position.

14.35.12. Do not cut your signal panel if it will make it difficult to see from the air.

14.35.13. Use smokes, flares, tracers, etc., as a last resort for marking position.

14.35.14. If contact is made in a dense area, White Phosphorous (WP) grenades may help in marking position. Caution must be taken whenever using WP. In dense jungle, smokes are not sufficient.

14.35.15. At night use lights in addition to other devices. If using flares do not fire at the aircraft and let the pilot know. If using a strobe light use it directionally and cover.

14.35.16. When directing a FAC to your position use the clock position from the aircraft's nose.

14.35.17. Do not use azimuth readings until the FAC has your position. Once located direct the FAC using azimuth in degrees and distance in meters.

14.35.18. Always give the FAC a complete description of the target and target area.

14.35.19. Make adjustments for the FAC after each round and pass.

14.35.20. Given the track that you request is flown, always try to put the strike across your front. Do not call air in with its strike coming across your position from front to rear.

14.35.21. A combat sky-spot can be used for immediate as well as pre-planned strikes. You must give an eight-digit coordinate and a track for the aircraft. If possible, have the FAC determine the patrol location before the sky-spot makes the strike.

14.35.22. Whenever possible, try to give the FAC a BDA (bomb damage assessment) to the FAC.

14.35.23. A FAC can be used effectively to direct a team in contact to LZs. A FAC can also provide an airstrike to prep an exfil LZ for a team before it reaches the LZ. This is a good technique to employ in dangerous areas.

14.35.24. A FAC can be used to break off contact while a patrol is waiting for strike aircraft. A low pass or a pass firing a marking round may make the enemy think they are being attacked, causing them to withdraw.

14.35.25. When directing gun ships over your target do not let him fly over the target.

14.35.26. Ask the gun ship to drop a flare and direct him to the target from that flare. Make adjustments from his tracer impact area to ensure that you get full coverage.

14.36. Breaking Out of Encirclement Tips.

14.36.1. When encircled the sooner you attempt to break out the better chance you will have with a minimum of casualties. The longer you wait the stronger the enemy becomes.

14.36.2. Plans should be made prior to the break out attempt.

14.36.2.1. Equipment left behind must be destroyed.

14.36.2.2. Dead must be left behind and all personal articles/classified removed.

14.36.2.3. RS will help wounded who fall behind and sanitize casualties.

14.36.2.4. All-important information must be reported to HQ or controlling agency.

14.36.3. The wedge formation or bounding overwatch provide the best defense for movement.

14.36.4. Upon deciding the direction to be moved, the area should be prepped with heavy fire and explosive devices.

14.36.5. Continue to move rapidly, do not run, and do not stop until completely out of the encirclement.

14.36.6. Use artillery, Tactical CAS (TCAS), ECAS, and gunships as much as possible for direct aid.

14.37. Remain Over Night (RON) Tips.

14.37.1. Practice RON procedures when the team is in training, even if the training is routine (take advantage of all training opportunities). Many training areas are not in "safe zones".

14.37.2. Select opportune RON sites from the map, at least two hours in advance.

14.37.3. Deviate from the route of march often, never moving in a straight line unless unavoidable.

14.37.4. After passing the RON site "button hook" and move into position so you may observe your own trail.

14.37.5. When in position, personnel should remain on alert status until the perimeter can be checked 360 degrees at a distance of 40-60 meters.

14.37.6. Rucks should not be removed until it is your turn to rest. If the area is considered unsecured, consideration should be given to sleeping in full equipment.

14.37.7. Before rest, each person should memorize the azimuth and distance to escape routes and alternate rally points.

14.37.8. When deploying the team from a RON, the PT should be positioned opposite the likely avenue of approach in order he may lead the team out in emergency. The maximum amount of firepower should be directed towards the most likely avenue of approach.

14.37.9. If a team is within range of friendly artillery, and has pre-planned concentrations, azimuths should be taken (OT lines) to the concentrations, noting distances prior to rest. Obvious landmarks should be measured to aid in calling artillery for day/night.

14.37.10. Keep all transmissions to a minimum. If required by the controlling agency, send your location prior to moving from the RON site. Do not send messages from the RON unless absolutely necessary.

14.37.11. Prior to rest the TL should ensure each man knows both the primary and alternate rally points in the event of an emergency.

14.37.12. One half of the team should have their compass set to the primary RP and the other the alternate RP. Teams should be designated by the TL to ensure no matter which direction the enemy advances at least one team will be able to lead the team out.

14.37.13. Buddy teams should be designated, as stated above, in the event casualties are taken. Each man will take care of another and his equipment if one is injured, wounded, or killed.

14.37.14. The ruck may be used as a pillow, however, the carrying straps should remain in the up position in event rapid withdrawal is required.

14.37.15. It is permissible to remove part of the LBE, but it should not be removed in its entirety at night or any time in the field.

14.37.16. If a person coughs or talks in his sleep, make him sleep with a gag in his mouth.

14.37.17. TMs should not bunch up or sleep next to one another if possible to avoid the entire team being destroyed at on time. In hasty RONs TMs should be able to touch one another without moving from position.

14.37.18. Know what your next day's plans are before settling in to rest.

14.37.19. When placing claymores around the RON they should be placed by two persons at a time if possible, one man placing the mine while the other stands guard. Never place claymores in a position that prevents you from having visual contact with them (electrical detonated).

14.37.20. Claymores should be placed so the blast parallels the team, ensuring the firing wire does not lead straight back to the team. If the enemy turns around the claymores they will not face the team.

14.37.21. Determine in advance who will fire each claymore and who will give the command or signal.

14.37.22. In most instances it is better not to put claymores around the RON but rather to rely upon the use of CS grenades for the following reasons;

14.37.22.1. When claymores have been put out, and the enemy is discovered to be moving in on the team, the tendency is to remain to long in the site, waiting for the enemy to get within the killing zone.

14.37.22.2. If the team discovers the enemy moving in, the enemy will normally be "on line" not knowing the exact location of the team. If no claymores are out, pre-designated TMs throw CS grenades in the direction of the enemy force. After the gas begins to disperse the team can withdraw. When the enemy hits the CS he will normally panic, when coming upon claymores he has a general location to the team and if quiet enough may be able to flank the mine and follow the movement directly to the team. If he has gas masks it restricts his vision, he may fire indiscriminately causing confusion and panic and the team has a good chance of escaping unharmed or unseen.

14.37.22.3. Self-detonating claymores are used more for a pursuing enemy than a static position. You would not want your own weapons used against you.

14.37.22.4. If a claymore is fired, a grenade thrown, or a rifle fired, the enemy may flank the team and box it in.

14.37.23. All TMs should be awake, alert, and ready to move prior to first light or complete darkness.

14.37.24. Another check of the perimeter, for 360 degrees, at a distance of 40-60 meters should be made prior to moving from the RON or retrieving the claymores.

14.37.25. A thorough check should be made of the RON site to ensure nothing is left behind and the site is sterile.

14.37.26. The TL must make sure that any medications that are required are taken prior to movement.

14.37.27. Never eat or smoke in your RON position. Odors may give your position away.

14.37.28. Be alert when leaving the RON. If you have been seen, you will probably be attacked or ambushed within 300 meters.

14.37.29. TLs should check themselves to ensure they are not forming common habits when setting up RONs. If the enemy observes some sort of pattern it makes it easier to plan an ambush upon the team.

Chapter 15

COMBAT SEARCH AND RESCUE (CSAR) OPERATIONS MISSION PLANNING

15.1. GENERAL . During wartime/contingency operations, any search and rescue operation will be referred to as "CSAR operations". In peacetime environments, search and rescue coverage is referred to as "SAR". As CSAR covers and expands on conventional SAR techniques and procedures, information contained in this chapter can be modified to meet SAR requirements. CSAR is a specific task performed by designated forces to effect the recovery of personnel or equipment during wartime or contingency operations. CSAR is one part of Personnel Recovery. Personnel Recovery is the aggregation of military, civil, and political efforts to recover captured, detained, evading, isolated or missing personnel from uncertain or hostile environments and denied areas. Personnel recovery may occur through military action, action by non-governmental organizations, other U.S. Government (USG)-approved action, and diplomatic initiatives, or through any combination of these options. Though personnel recovery may occur during non-combatant evacuation operations (NEO), NEO is not a subset of personnel recovery. Pararescue personnel are involved in aspects of PR other than CSAR. This chapter will mainly deal with CSAR , future revisions will include PR to include assisted recovery.

The successful conduct of CSAR operations requires meticulous planning, preparation, and training. CSAR procedures will be initiated as soon as awareness and notification is received the position of the survivor(s) is known, it is verified the survivor(s) is still alive, and the threat will allow or can be reduced to affect a successful recovery.

15.1.1. CSAR is a basic aerospace power function. Each service is tasked with, and is responsible for, conducting CSAR in support of their own operations. Theater commanders implement and direct theater CSAR actions during wartime and contingencies. This includes the condition of the survivor, the ability of the survivor to continuing surviving, equipment to be recovered, meteorological and specialized recovery equipment and personnel. It is critical that CSAR planners do not rely on the survivor's ability to assist in the recovery and plan the mission accordingly.

Figure 15.1. General Stages of CSAR.

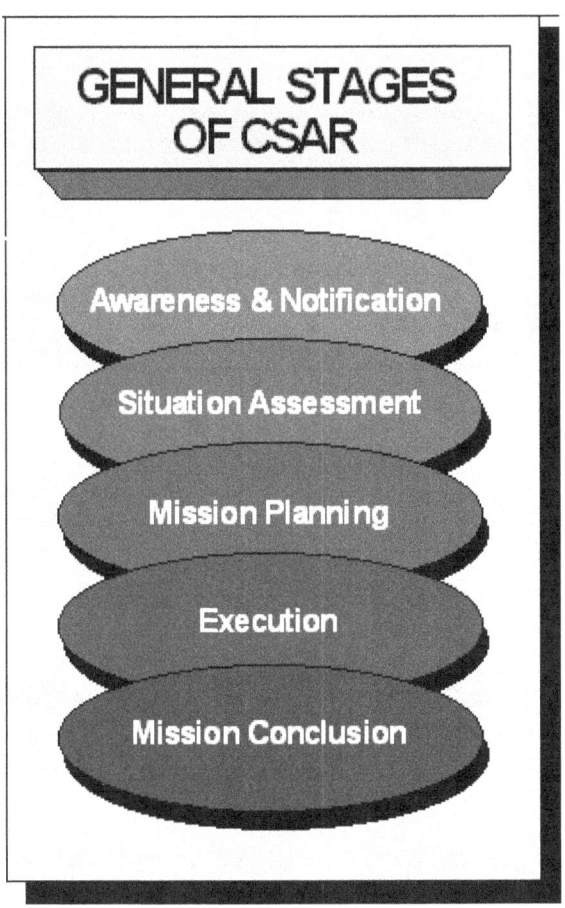

15.1.2. The best chance of success is immediately after the need for CSAR has been declared. Extensive mission planning may be required for objectives. CSAR by its very nature implies justification of risk. CSAR planning should focus on a single catastrophic event conducted under worst case circumstances. CSAR coverage is defined by the capability and risk involved in the delivery and recovery of the CSAR force in a reasonable period. For casualties with severe medical complications or located in high risk environments of urban, water, extreme weather and non-permissive environments, the response time should be less than one hour if possible.

15.1.3. Control/Coordination Agencies. The theater unified commander delegates responsibilities for coordinating rescue and recovery to the Rescue Coordination Center (RCC) or the Joint Service Rescue Center (JSRC) when the center is a combined service operation. The RCC is a collateral function and requests needed Air Force resources from approving authority. When other service resources are needed, the RCC has the authority to coordinate directly with the army Tactical Operations Center (TOC), marine Tactical Air Control Center, and the navy Combat Information Center (CIC) or the Joint Operations Center (JOC). The rescue unit's operations staff and Pararescue (PJ) Team Leader (TL) direct all requests for coordination and support through command channels to the RCC/JSRC.

15.1.4. Air Force rescue forces will receive notification of isolated personnel via the theater or joint task force command and control structure. A rescue could involve an aircrew bailout over hostile territory, crash landing, ditching at sea, foundering naval vessels, or ground forces cut off from friendly lines. Typical rescue operations might include:

15.1.4.1. Awareness and notification

15.1.4.2. Assessing the situation

15.1.4.3. Planning the mission

15.1.4.4. Launching the recovery vehicles

15.1.4.5. Refueling at a forward operating location or air refueling prior to ingress

15.1.4.6. Ingressing enemy territory to locate isolated personnel

15.1.4.7. Locating the isolated personnel

15.1.4.8. Authenticating the isolated personnel

15.1.4.9. Recovering the isolated personnel

15.1.4.10. Egressing enemy territory

15.1.4.11. Conducting air refueling, as required

15.1.4.12. Recovering at a suitable friendly base

15.1.5. The CSAR Force. Forces should be selected, and CSAR and E & R plans implemented, well before the need. This reduces confusion and increases response/recovery times. Planning should include ground teams to recover survivors, treat injuries, destroy sensitive equipment, provide evader assistance, crash site security, or provide a Ready Reaction Force (RRF).

15.1.6. Rotary wing assets should reflect a lift capability for delivering the CSAR forces to the objective area (OA) and recovering the survivor/equipment. Rotary wing assets are limited by altitude, heat, and weight capability. Fixed wing aircraft should be capable of delivering the CSAR forces to the OA and inserting the force and their equipment by landing or by air (i.e. Freefall or static-line parachuting). During immediate response missions, any mission aircraft may be used in a secondary role in the CSAR effort.

15.1.7. The specific method of recovery will be driven by terrain, threat, condition of surviving personnel, ability of survivor(s) to continue to survive, equipment to be recovered, specialized equipment required, time available, and insertion/extraction vehicles availability and capability. Because increasingly sophisticated weapons are available to a wider variety of military forces, para-military forces, and insurgents, the use of all CSAR assets must be planned carefully and used appropriately.

15.1.8. Location of the survivor should be passed as described in the theater Special Instructions (SPINS). CSAR should be initiated over the pre-briefed mission frequency when communications with the survivor permit.

15.1.9. Prior to insertion, authentication of personnel and threat will be verified. On-scene aircraft will normally conduct this authentication. Authentication will be initiated using the authenticator card or using theater SPINS. Once the proper answers/actions are received and confirmed, recovery procedures will continue. When utilizing rotary wing aircraft, the primary insertion/extraction method should be air landing. If terrain does not permit landing, other methods of insertion/extraction should be available for use.

15.1.10. Evacuation and exfiltration of the CSAR force should be initiated as soon as possible. If necessary, the CSAR force may be required to change location to expedite extraction or avoid threats. If the recovery force is delayed, the CSAR force should follow pre-briefed procedures to minimize confusion during the recovery phase. During exfiltration, contact the CSAR coordinating authority. Transmit special requirements to include additional medical intervention needs, security or force requirements, re-supply requirements for follow-on operations, and critical intelligence data.

15.1.11. Close the mission only after survivor(s)/equipment are delivered to a competent authority, debriefing has occurred, and the CSAR team has began the reconstitution process.

15.2. Mission Planning. Any employment of PJs into a hostile or potentially hostile surface environment, for however brief a period, is considered a tactical employment and must be trained for, planned, and executed as such. The responsibility for operations planning and preparation is shared jointly by the operations staff, intelligence, applicable aircrew members and PJs. Tactical employment refers to delivery and recovery of PJs to conduct a combat rescue operation. Decisions concerning employment feasibility and duration must consider the worst probable circumstances and be mutually understood by both the commander and the deploying PJs. Long before mobility actions, and before combat operations are conducted, the PJ NCOIC will establish the requirements necessary for safe and effective operations.

15.2.1. The PJ TL should use a checklist (see Figure 15.2.) in planning and preparing for a mission. The TL considers all the checklist items but accomplishes only those items, which the operational situation requires.

Figure 15.2. Team Leader (TL) Checklist (Example).

TL CHECKLIST
(Consider all: accomplish those necessary: order may vary)
1. Study the Mission.
2. Plan Use of Time.
3. Study Terrain and Situation.
4. Organize the Team.
5. Select Men, Weapons, and Equipment.
6. Issue Warning Order.
7. Coordination (continuous throughout).
8. Request Reconnaissance/Study Intelligence.
9. Complete Detailed Plans.
10. Issue Operation Order.
11. Brief-back (to the tasking authority)
12. Supervise (at all times), Inspect, Rehearse.
13. Execute the Mission.

15.2.2. Receive and Study the Operation:

15.2.2.1. The overall outline for the tasking and planning for an operation is titled the PJ Combat Rescue Operation Order. When completed, the operation order provides in sequence, information, instructions and guidance followed by a complete detailed plan on how to accomplish the assigned objective. The tasking order contains the necessary information and instructions from which to develop a comprehensive plan for execution. When initial tasking is set forth by the tasking authority, the intelligence section and operations section are responsible for compiling the information necessary to complete the Operations Order. The Operations Officer will ensure sufficient copies are available in the operations section. These standard outlines provide concise and standardized information for issuance of the tasking order to the PJ team leader.

15.2.2.2. When operations are beyond the ability of the aircraft, or the threat conditions exceed aircraft capabilities, PJs may be tasked to perform ground operations necessary to extract the survivor. Another concept is employed when mechanized rescue is impracticable or impossible. The primary considerations for this type of employment are that the transportation resource must be afforded ample standoff in order to avoid an enemy threat/that the geographic and climatological features in the OA create a situation that is beyond the capability of the rescue vehicle. Depth and duration for the later concept of operations is limited only by the transportation resources used to deliver the PJ team to the operational objective.

15.2.2.3. The type of situational information about the enemy that the intelligence section and operations section must attempt to provide for the team leader is listed below.

15.2.2.3.1. Terrain. Detailed knowledge of the terrain and climatology of the area of operations is essential. The location of the existing road net and railroads, if any, must be determined. Information regarding soil trafficability, vegetation, water routes and expected ice thickness, snow conditions, wind velocity and direction, and average snow depth should be available to the TL. The TL should also know the general features of the terrain from the viewpoint of cross-country movement. For summer operations in barren lands, it will be necessary to determine water routes suitable for transportation and dry ground routes. Occasionally, maps may be unreliable or even nonexistent. Therefore, the requirement for timely aerial photographs must be utilized as a source of terrain information. Does the terrain offer passive security due to its ruggedness? How would the area lend itself to a survival situation? Are there any cultivated areas?

15.2.2.3.2. Identification. A description of physical features, mannerisms, and types of clothing is essential for both civilian and military. Special unit recognition by attire and function should be addressed.

15.2.2.3.3. Location. The TL needs to be briefed about the location of enemy within the periphery of the designated area of operations (AO) and the expected response time and type of support the enemy may have from contingents outside the AO. In particular, the TL needs an assessment of enemy strength within close proximity to the OA (OA).

15.2.2.3.4. Activity. The assessment of activity must address whether the enemy is mobile or static and the type of enemy force; conventional, unconventional or guerrillas. What is the enemy known to be doing in the AO? Does the enemy patrol the AO regularly and what routes are usually taken? Are there any established observation posts or secured areas?

15.2.2.3.5. Strength. Strength includes both population density and Military Order of Battle for troop strength. Relative quantities of loyalists, conventional, unconventional and specialized search and destroy elements must be identified.

15.2.2.3.6. Sociological Summary. Outline any significant political, economical and cultural aspects of the indigenous enemy within the periphery of the AO to include the overall influence of the military and the possibility of indigenous sympathizers. State of health and especially the possibility of incapacitating disease affecting those within the AO should be noted.

15.2.2.3.7. Equipment Types/Abilities.

15.2.2.3.7.1. Air Forces. Fixed/rotary wing aircraft? Night and weather capabilities? General air defense?

15.2.2.3.7.2. Ground forces. AAA, SAM, and small arms; size, range, mobility, engagement parameters, optics/radar capabilities and Radar Warning Receiver (RWR) indications?

15.2.2.3.7.3. Communications jamming and direction finding capabilities?

15.2.2.3.7.4. Infrared, night vision, antipersonnel radar capabilities?

15.2.2.4. The tasking order is not to be confused with the operations or warning order. During issuance of the order, the TL listens carefully to ensure he clearly understands all information, instructions, and guidance; makes notes for later use in planning and asks questions if any points are not clear.

15.2.2.5. The TL carefully studies the operation. Through study of the terrain and situation, the TL identifies the essential tasks to be accomplished in executing the mission. These essential tasks become submissions of the team for which organization, personnel, and equipment must be considered.

15.2.3. Plan Use of Time. Combat situations seldom allow the TL as much time for planning and preparation as desired. Proper use of available time must be planned.

15.2.3.1. As soon as the TL completes a study of the mission, he quickly makes a mental or written time schedule (see Tables 15.3. and 15.4.), which allots time for each action of the team.

15.2.3.2. Plan the TL time schedule around times (if any) specified in the tasking order, such as time of departure, time to make reconnaissance, or time of return. Use a planning sequence called "reverse planning," meaning; plan from the last action for which a time is specified and works back to the receipt of tasking orders. This allocates time for all necessary actions. In planning use of time, the TL ensures subordinate leaders and team members are allowed time necessary to prepare for the mission.

Table 15.1. TL Time Schedule, Part 1 (Example).

TL TIME SCHEDULE EXTRACTION (EXAMPLE)		
DATE/TIME (ZULU)		**ACTIVITY**
19/0200		RETURN FRIENDLY AREA
18/2330 -	0200	MOVEMENT EN ROUTE
18/2300 -	2330	ACCOMPLISH OPERATION, REORGANIZE
18/2230 -	2300	LEADER'S RECON
18/2000 -	2230	MOVEMENT EN ROUTE
18/2000		DEPART FRIENDLY AREA/INSERTION
18/1945 -	2000	MOVEMENT TO DEPARTURE AREA
18/1930 -	1945	FINAL INSPECTION
18/1845 -	1930	NIGHT REHEARSALS
18/1800 -	1845	DAY REHEARSALS
18/1745 -	1800	INSPECTION
18/1700 -	1745	SUPPER MEAL
18/1630 -	1700	ISSUE OPERATION ORDER
18/1530 -	1630	COMPLETE DETAILED PLANS
18/1430 -	1530	MAKE RECONNAISSANCE
18/1415 -	1430	ISSUE WARNING ORDER
18/1330 -	1415	PRELIMINARY PLANNING
		COORDINATE
		SELECT TEAM, WEAPONS, EQUIPMENT
		ORGANIZE THE TEAM
		STUDY TERRAIN AND SITUATION
		PLAN USE OF TIME
		STUDY THE OPERATIONAL TASKING
18/	1330	TASKING ORDER RECEIVED
NOTE: USE "REVERSE PLANNING" TECHNIQUE		

Table 15.2. TL Time Schedule, Part 2 (Example)

TL TIME SCHEDULE EXTRACTION (EXAMPLE)		
DATE/TIME (ZULU)		**ACTIVITY**
18/	0900	WARNING ORDER COMPLETED
18/0900	1230	TL REQUESTS RECONNAISSANCE/STUDIES INTELLIGENCE: MAKES COORDINATION: COMPLETES DETAILED PLANS
		-ASST. TL SUPERVISES DRAWING, ISSUE, PREPARATION OF EQUIP-MENT, AMMUNITION, RATIONS
		-ASST TL SUPERVISES PRACTICE OF IMMEDIATE ACTION DRILLS
		-SPECIAL ELEMENTS REHEARSE (STREAM CROSSING, AERIAL RESUPPLY)
		-TEAM MEMBERS PREPARE INDIVIDUAL EQUIPMENT
		-SUBORDINATE LEADERS INSPECT
18/1230	1300	NOON MEAL
18/1300	1330	OPERATION ORDER
18/1330	1430	TEAM MEMBERS COMPLETE PREPARATION
18/1430	1630	TL INSPECTS
		DAYLIGHT REHEARSALS
		ELEMENT REHEARSALS
		TEAM REHEARSALS
18/1630	1730	REST
18/1730	1800	EVENING MEAL
18/1800	1900	FINAL INSPECTION
		BY SUBORDINATE LEADERS
		SPOT CHECKS BY TL
		QUESTIONS ON PLANS, SIGNALS, USE OF EQUIPMENT
18/2000	2030	AIRCRAFT BRIEFING
18/2030	2100	AIRCRAFT ON LOAD
18/2100	2130	DARK ADAPTATION OF EYES
18/2200		DEPART
NOTE: USE "REVERSE PLANNING" TECHNIQUE		

15.2.4. Study Terrain and Situation. The TL studies the terrain over which the team will operate and the friendly and enemy situations, relating these to the study of the operation and identification of essential tasks to be accomplished.

15.2.4.1. Terrain. Make a detailed study of the map and of aerial photos, if available. Note fields of fire and observation, cover, concealment, obstacles, key terrain features, and avenues of approach and withdrawal. Study the OA very closely. Consider the influence of terrain on execution of the operation. Terrain may influence the team's size, organization, and equipment. For example, a stream or lake to be crossed may require personnel/equipment floatation. Team formations while moving depend on the terrain; that is, for difficult terrain - close formations, for open terrain - extended formations. Terrain will effect speed of movement. Terrain in the OA helps determine security needed, positioning of fire support, manner of conducting the leaders' reconnaissance, and the plan of action at the objective.

15.2.4.2. Situation. Study the strengths, locations, dispositions, and capabilities of both friendly and enemy forces that may affect the team's operation.

15.2.5. Make Tentative Plan. From the study of the operation, terrain, and situation, the TL formulates a tentative plan of action for accomplishing the operation. This plan includes the number of people needed and how they will be organized, the weapons and equipment needed, and the manner in which they will be employed. Manner of employment, or scheme of maneuver, is the concept of operation. The tentative plan is later developed into the complete and detailed plan of operation.

15.2.6. Select and Organize the Team, Weapons, and Equipment.

15.2.6.1. Select the Team. Selection of team members should be based on knowledge of the individual's performance as certified in the AF Form 623, On the Job Training Record. More personnel than necessary are not taken merely to maintain unit integrity.

15.2.6.1.1. Personnel with poor health/physical condition are not taken. For example, an individual with a cold may endanger security by coughing; a person with foot trouble may slow-down the team.

15.2.6.1.2. Establish a "grub down" period, this is essential to team survivability. For PJ combat operations this period begins approximately 72 hours prior to deployment but may be longer as the operational situation dictates. "Grub down" is the reduction and control of shaving, haircuts, using scented soaps, after shaves, shampoos, lotions, colognes, deodorants, mouthwashes and toothpaste; and, wearing clothing that has been starched or scented by softeners. During periods of perpetual immediate response in the combat environment, PJs will maintain a continuous state of "grub down." Good hygiene is still essential. This will be achieved using an unscented cleaning agent for bathing, i.e., Ivory soap, Phisoderm, and sodium chloride (table salt) for brushing teeth. Shaving waivers and haircut waivers (not necessary for most mission situations) will be coordinated with the host base commander by the rescue mission commander. Under normal "grub down" circumstances, beard length will not exceed one quarter inch and hair length will be per established Air Force standards.

15.2.6.2. Organize the Team. Organization consists of determining the individual responsibilities required to accomplish essential tasks, selecting the right person for each responsibility, and determining the weapons and equipment, the team will need. Organization is a two step process: general organization and special organization.

15.2.6.2.1. General Organization. A two, three, or four man movement, with a simple operation, is not organized into elements. Instead, the entire team becomes a single reconnaissance and security element. A larger team, with a more complex operation, requires a reconnaissance element and a security element or a combination reconnaissance and security element.

15.2.6.2.2. Special Organization. The team is further organized when needed to perform essential tasks.

15.2.6.2.2.1. The PJ team should be organized into smaller elements corresponding to unique duties such as; communication, search, survivor contact, and medical.

15.2.6.2.2.2. More than one support element may be required when the support element leader, or the TL cannot directly control the weapons of the support element. This may be the case when there are too many supporting weapons for direct control or when weapons are positioned too far apart for direct control.

15.2.6.3. Weapons. Selection of weapons and ammunition is based on this question: "What is needed to do the job?" The difficulty of transporting some weapons, because of bulk or weight, must be considered but is seldom a decisive factor. Personnel should be knowledgeable in the weapons they are using. Aerial re-supply of ammunition is considered for operations extended in time or distance.

15.2.6.4. Equipment. When possible, the same equipment is used for more than one purpose or in more than one area. A unit operating instruction prescribing routine uniform and equipment saves the TL and the team valuable time in planning and preparing.

15.2.7. Issue a Warning Order. The time a team needs to prepare depends on such factors as the nature of the operation, the proficiency of the team, and the preparations made (if any) when the TL received the tasking order and made a tentative plan. The TL provides team members the maximum preparation time possible by issuing a warning order as soon as a tentative plan is made. It is desirable for the warning order to be issued to all team members. When this is not feasible, it is issued to subordinate leaders, in turn, they issue warning orders to their elements.

15.2.7.1. Situation. Minimum details are given to include only the information the team needs to prepare while the TL plans in detail. The complete situation is given in the operation order.

15.2.7.2. Mission. This is a brief but clear statement of what the team is to accomplish and the location or area in which it is to be done.

15.2.7.3. Organization. General and special organization are prescribed and explained.

15.2.7.4. Uniform and equipment common to all. This includes clothing, personal equipment, rations and water to be carried, camouflage measures to be taken, and the means of identification the team will carry. Prohibited items are also stated, such as wallets, letters, and personal papers, which might reveal information if lost or captured.

15.2.7.5. Chain of command. Individuals are assigned a place in the chain of command. In larger teams, subordinate leaders are assigned relative positions and required to establish chains of command within their elements.

15.2.7.6. Times and places for inspection and rehearsal. The TL announces the times and places to inspect the team. The time(s) of rehearsal(s) by the full team is given and the place, if known at the time. Complete uniform and equipment are worn and carried at all such inspections and rehearsals.

15.2.7.7. Specific Instructions. Specific instructions are given to/for:

15.2.7.7.1. Subordinate leaders for obtaining, checking, and distributing rations, water, weapons, ammunition, and equipment.

15.2.7.7.2. Preparation of team members for the operation.

15.2.7.7.3. Initiating and supervising other activities to be accomplished. This may include practice of immediate action drills, rest and sleep periods, or the practice of hazard crossing procedures. Reconnaissance, coordination, inspections, and rehearsals require all key individuals for their preparation, such as function checks of radios and specialized recovery equipment. Map study by point and compass personnel is mandatory, regardless whether electronic means (i.e. GPS) is used or not.

15.2.7.7.4. Safeguarding of Information. In all situations, precautions must be taken to prevent compromising the team or other operations. All information is given on a strict "need to know" basis observing all the rules of COMSEC and OPSEC. Other security measures must include isolation of the team from non-essential personnel, withholding of information until the latest feasible time and continuos security education. When filled in, the operations order and its annexes are classified "SECRET" or higher.

15.2.8. Coordination. Coordination is a continuous, joint effort by all tasked and tasking agencies, never assume anything. It is imperative to mission accomplishment that the TL posses; detailed knowledge of the various organizational structures and their contacts and the skills required to assess each is working toward the same goal. All activities requiring coordination should be documented. Coordinating frequently overlaps to ensure that coordination is continuous, complete, and properly accomplished. This is particularly true of extended operations since the dispatching unit's areas of influence and interest may overlap those of others.

15.2.8.1. Coordination must continue throughout planning, preparation, and conduct of the operation. The TL makes or arranges for all coordination possible before leaving the place where he first receives the tasking order. There, communications are better and the advice and assistance of trained and interested personnel are most readily available.

15.2.8.2. Examples of coordination, which must be made, are:

15.2.8.2.1. Movements in friendly areas. Units in whose areas the team will operate must be informed so the team will not be endangered or unnecessarily be restricted.

15.2.8.2.2. Departure and re-entry of friendly areas. Guides may be necessary, especially if the team must pass friendly obstacles such as mines or wire.

15.2.8.2.3. Fire support. Carefully planned and properly coordinated fire support can decrease the potential for fratricide and can help in six ways.

15.2.8.2.4. Destroy. Destroy enemy opposing the team en route, at danger areas, and at the objective.

15.2.8.2.5. Deceive. Deceive the enemy as to the true location or direction of movement of the team by cloaking withdrawal or other routes upon breaking contact.

15.2.8.2.6. Deny. Deny the enemy use and access of roads, trails and other terrain features from which they may detect or bring action against the team. The enemy can also be denied the use of approaches into the OA.

15.2.8.2.7. Defend. Defend the team against attack en route, at danger areas, and at the objective.

15.2.8.2.8. Direct. Assist in location of objectives.

15.2.8.2.9. Detect. Detect the enemy by firing on likely positions.

15.2.9. Make Reconnaissance. Visual reconnaissance confirms, clarifies, and supplements information provided by maps, aerial photos, and other sources.

15.2.9.1. When possible, an aerial reconnaissance is made of the OA and of the terrain. This is the only useful means of reconnoitering a large area.

15.2.9.2. A ground reconnaissance would be desirable of the team's area of operations, but is generally impossible. The TL should attempt to gather information from units who operated in these areas.

15.2.10. Complete Detailed Plan. The warning order has been issued; reconnaissance has been made; team members are preparing themselves and their equipment. The TL now develops the tentative plan into a detailed plan for accomplishing the operation. The tactical situation and designated mission objective provides the substance from which the TL draws on to build the detailed plan of execution.

15.2.10.1. The TL first assigns essential tasks to be accomplished by individual team members. The TL then plans other phases of the mission in the sequence most convenient under the circumstances. The sequence in which planning is discussed below may be followed or modified, as appropriate.

15.2.10.2. Execution Plan. This plan is a complete outline of the actions necessary to accomplish the assigned objective and should be included in the operation order.

15.2.10.2.1. Concept of Operations. In the execution plan the "Concept of Operation" is stated in the lead paragraph. This is a concise statement summarizing the method to be used to achieve the objective.

15.2.10.2.2. Coordinating Instructions. To the extent required by the situation, the TL plans when and how the team, its elements and the individual team members are to accomplish assigned responsibilities.

15.2.10.2.3. Critical Times/Dates. Critical times and dates are addressed throughout the TL's Time Schedule, and the Team Time Schedule. Times of departure and return require special attention and are addressed in detail in the following paragraphs.

15.2.10.2.3.1. Times of departure and return are based on careful consideration of the times required to:

15.2.10.2.3.1.1. Reach the objective. Considerations include; distance, terrain, anticipated speed of movement, the friendly and enemy situation, and (if applicable) the time at or by which the operation must be accomplished.

15.2.10.2.3.1.2. Accomplish essential tasks in the OA; i.e. reconnaissance, movement of elements and individuals, and actual accomplishment of the operation.

15.2.10.2.3.1.3. Return to friendly areas/extraction point. This may differ from time required to reach the objective. Survivors may slow the team. The use of a different return route may change the time required.

15.2.10.2.3.2. Advantage is taken of light and weather conditions which will aid departure and return; for example, the greater darkness before moonrise and after moonset, and the darkness and noise of wind and rain during stormy periods.

15.2.10.2.4. Specific Individual Responsibilities. Essential tasks are identified and assigned. These are the tasks whose successful performance enables the team to reach the objective and return. Such tasks as navigation, team security, security during halts, survivor contacts, as well as the authentication procedures are to mention a few.

15.2.10.2.5. Organization for Movement. Formations must be planned for movement of the team to and from the OA. Location of elements and individuals in the various formations used must be planned.

15.2.10.2.5.1. Ground movement formations should be adaptable to any size team. Each formation has its advantages and disadvantages. They may be varied to fit the terrain and the situation. For example, a situation may require some sacrifice of control in order to achieve greater dispersion; another situation may require great stealth at the expense of speed in movement.

15.2.10.2.5.2. Factors influencing movement.

15.2.10.2.5.2.1. Enemy contact. The most important consideration is the plan of action to take if the team makes enemy contact.

15.2.10.2.5.2.2. Tactical integrity. As far as possible, organization for movement maintains element and team integrity. This helps in control, security, employment at the objective, and on enemy contact.

15.2.10.2.5.2.3. Employment at objective. Consistent with other considerations, organization for movement permits quick and easy employment at the objective.

15.2.10.2.5.2.4. Control. How important is control in relation to other factors? The size of the team is always an important consideration.

15.2.10.2.5.2.5. The enemy situation. Where is the enemy? How strong is he? What/where are ambush dangers?

15.2.10.2.5.2.6. Speed of movement. When must the team reach the objective? When must it return? Rate of movement is governed by the threat, terrain, mission equipment, and security. A pace consideration is where to place the slowest team member.

15.2.10.2.5.2.7. Stealth. Can the team move quietly? Does the formation force the flanks to move through noisy underbrush? Which is most important, stealth or speed?

15.2.10.2.5.2.8. Security. From which direction is contact with the enemy most likely to come? Will the team have a 360-degree security? Will speed or stealth provide the best security? A carefully controlled combination of speed and stealth is usually best.

15.2.10.2.5.2.9. Dispersion. Consistent with control, the team is dispersed so that a sudden burst of fire will cause the fewest casualties.

15.2.10.2.5.2.10. Terrain. How does terrain affect movement? Is it wooded or open? Are there roads or streams to cross?

15.2.10.2.5.2.11. Visibility. Is visibility good or poor? Can the enemy see the team? Can the team be seen and controlled?

15.2.10.2.5.2.12. Weather. How will the weather affect the ground, streams, and visibility and equipment requirements? The operation order should provide a detailed synopsis of meteorological, celestial, nautical and atmospherics data as it affects the mission.

15.2.10.2.6. Primary and Alternate Routes.

15.2.10.2.6.1. A primary route and one or more alternate routes of return are selected.

15.2.10.2.6.2. Routes are divided into "legs" with each leg starting, if possible, at a point which can be recognized on the ground and a pace count is used between each point. This makes it easier to stay oriented at all times. When it is not possible to start and stop "legs" at recognizable points, a continuous pace count can be used.

15.2.10.2.7. "Delta" reference points. This is a pre-determined point used for secure reference of locations. The reference points are; significant landmarks or geographic features and pre-designated rallying points. Pre-planned ground fire support as with fire suppression for pre-designated targets should not be designated as a reference point but should be referred to by target number. However, aerial ordnance delivery can be directed based on bearing/direction from a reference point when the aircraft, reference point and target are within view of the person directing the strike. The TL selects enough of these reference points so that during most of the route of travel he maintains a reference point within line of sight except when impossible in heavily forested or desert terrain.

15.2.10.2.8. Support utilization. Based on the objective the TL assesses the information from the situation report to determine what support is available and what is necessary in order to achieve the mission objective. Before determining support requirements, the TL must develop a thorough understanding of the enemy situation. Then he incorporates the necessary support into the team's plan of execution. Types of support to consider are:

15.2.10.2.8.1. Aircraft Support.

15.2.10.2.8.1.1. Reconnaissance. Visual, photo, Tactical Electronic Reconnaissance, Strike Control and Reconnaissance.

15.2.10.2.8.1.2. Insertion operations. Airlanding, rappelling, freefall swimmer, hoist, parachute, vehicle etc.

15.2.10.2.8.1.3. Electronic warfare. Area jamming for insertion and extraction operations.

15.2.10.2.8.1.4. Defense suppression. "Hunter/ killer," interdiction for destruction of radiation emitters (SAM, AAA, GCI, etc.).

15.2.10.2.8.1.5. Airborne command and control communications. Communications relay, TACAIR coordination, air/ground threat advisories, and friendly aircraft vectoring.

15.2.10.2.8.1.6. Ordnance delivery. TACAIR bombs, rockets, bullets, harassment/ incapacitation ordnance, and smoke screening.

15.2.10.2.8.1.7. Re-supply. Freefall bundle drop, parachute bundle drop, parachute cargo delivery system, container delivery system (CDS), low altitude parachute extraction system (LAPES), high altitude low opening (HALO), SUU21/22 re-supply pods.

15.2.10.2.8.1.8. Extraction operations. Airlanding, rope (STABO/SPIES), hoist, rope ladder, surface to-air recovery system (STAR), and vehicle.

15.2.10.2.8.2. Ground Support.

15.2.10.2.8.2.1. Fire support (artillery ordnance delivery). Destroy, deceive, deny, defend, direct and detect.

15.2.10.2.8.2.2. Fire support (infantry). Raid patrols, ambush patrols, security patrols, contact patrols, search and attack patrols, motorized patrols, and airmobile and water-borne patrols.

15.2.10.2.8.3. Logistics and re-supply support. Caches for unconventional warfare (UW) operations, or direct support from UW forces and forward operating indigenous forces.

15.2.10.2.8.4. Maritime Support

15.2.10.2.8.4.1. Insertion/extraction operations. Swift boat, inflatable boats, swimmer deployment vehicle (SDV), and submarine wet deck operations.

15.2.10.2.8.4.2. Naval gunfire support.

15.2.10.2.9. Departure and Re-entry of Friendly Areas. These actions must be coordinated with the units near or through whose areas the team will move. Methods for accounting for personnel during departure and re-entry must be thoroughly planned. These may be used or any method which, under the circumstances, least endangers the team and other friendly forces.

15.2.10.2.10. Annexes. Actions not included in other parts of the detailed plan are planned as "other actions." This includes plans for stream crossing, adverse terrain rescue, and aerial re-supply of ammunition or rations, etc. These are the plans which, in a written operation order, would be placed in specific attachments.

15.2.10.2.10.1. Insertion Plan. The insertion plan is included with the operation order and contains only the necessary details required for the insertion phase of the operation. A copy of this plan with a large scale map identifying all critical points and known threat locations will be presented to the operation's staff or TL to the person in charge of the insertion vehicle.

15.2.10.2.10.2. Collateral Unit Coordination Plan. The collateral unit coordination plan is included with the operation order and contains the information necessary to link-up with a collateral clandestine ground element in order to accomplish a common assigned objective. If necessary, a copy of this plan is presented to the command authority in direct control of the collateral unit.

15.2.10.2.10.3. Re-supply Plan. The re-supply plan is included with the operation order and contains only a basic outline of the necessary details required for pre-planned re-supply during a mission. A copy of this plan with a large scale map identifying primary and alternate re-supply drop zones and known threat locations will be presented by the RCC/ JSRC/JOC or operations staff to the agency or person in charge of re-supply transportation.

15.2.10.2.10.4. Extraction Plan. The extraction plan is included with the operation order and contains only the necessary details required for the extraction phase of the operation. A copy of this plan with a large scale map identifying all critical points, "Delta" points and known threat locations is presented by the operations staff or the TL to the person in charge of extraction. The alternate extraction point is included in this plan only if the primary extraction vehicle is expected to divert to the secondary point. Otherwise, another attachment must be developed for the alternate extraction point in order to maintain operations security.

15.2.10.2.10.5. Master Maps. These maps become attachments to the operation order.

15.2.10.2.10.5.1. A large-scale map of 1:50,000 or larger scale will show the OA and if possible, the complete area of operations. The TL uses this map to outline the complete plan of execution in the area of operations. Required entries are; the primary and alternate routes of travel, the primary and alternate insertion points, initial rallying point, "Delta" points, fire suppression of pre-designated targets, survivor's probable location, primary and alternate objective rallying points, primary and alternate link-up points, primary and alternate extraction points, safe areas, designated areas for recovery, emergency recovery points, and known threat locations. This map is classified "SECRET" or above and remains with the operation order in a classified file.

15.2.10.2.10.5.2. A medium scale map of 1:250,000 scale will show the complete area of operations. The TL should plot the area covered by the large-scale map onto this map, and thereby develop a total perspective for the area surrounding the area of operations and the OA. This map is classified "SECRET" or above and the disposition is the same as the previous paragraph.

15.2.10.2.10.6. Evasion Plan of Action. The TL develops this plan based on guidance and information contained in the SPINS and extracted from intelligence. This plan is absolutely essential in order to cover the contingencies that would develop when the integrity of the team is disrupted to the point that the operational objective is no longer paramount and the primary objective becomes survival. For example; fifty or more percent of the team members are casualties in a chance enemy contact, failure of scheduled re-supply in extreme cold weather operations, or a PJ element is temporarily abandoned during "immediate response" combat rescue operations.

15.2.10.3. Logistics and Administration. Logistics and administration should be part of the operation order. Use unit standard operating procedures as much as possible to streamline the equipment preparation process. For the immediate response scenario, sufficient quantity and types of equipment must be pre-packaged and pre-positioned onboard the mission alert aircraft to cover a variety of contingencies. The pre-planned surface operation will require only the quantity and types of equipment necessary for that operation alone. Special consideration must be given to the impact that shortages of essential equipment items would have on successful operation accomplishment.

15.2.10.3.1. Rations and Water. The amount of water and rations that must be carried varies with the environment. All natural water sources must be considered un-potable. The quantity of chemical purification agent carried or filters for mechanical purifiers should be sufficient to cover the duration of an evasion plan of action. If the threat of NBC agents is a possibility, the team must carry enough water for the duration of the mission. Aerial re-supply is considered for extended operations.

15.2.10.3.2. Arms, Ammunition and Pyrotechnics. The warning order specifies the arms, ammunition and pyrotechnics needed to support the tentative plan.

15.2.10.3.3. Individual Uniform and Bivouac Equipment. Unit Standard Operating Procedures (SOPs) should address variations required by the environment. The TL must determine in the detailed plan, if any additions, deletions, or other changes to the uniform and equipment are required based on what is specified in the warning order.

15.2.10.3.4. Communications Equipment. Communications equipment is grouped into two basic categories: electronic and visual. The TL must determine the types of radios and beacons required.

15.2.10.3.5. Medical Equipment. What is the known condition of the operational objective? The TL must include enough medical equipment to cover any known or suspected requirements. Additional equipment must be available to provide treatment for team members who become injured or wounded. Special medical equipment items like pole/poleless litters, stokes litters and litter accessories are determined based on the plan of action for survivor treatment and survivor movement should be identified in the operation order.

15.2.10.3.6. Special Equipment. Areas of special significance are wet operations, parachute operations, adverse terrain operations, and specialized crash egress equipment requirements. Each of these areas requires special consideration based on the type of insertion and extraction planned and the type of terrain within the area of operations.

15.2.10.3.7. Color Topographic Maps and Aerial Photos. Maps of both large and medium scale are necessary for planning and executing the operation. Through the assessment, the TL decides what mapping is essential and if available mapping is sufficient. It may require reconnaissance in order to effectively plan and execute.

15.2.10.3.8. Administration. Handling of wounded, dead and prisoners is usually addressed in this section. In PJ operations, these problems become an integral part of the execution plan. Other administrative items the TL should consider are as follows:

15.2.10.3.8.1. Physical and mental condition of individual team members.

15.2.10.3.8.2. Immunization and preventative medicine requirements.

15.2.10.3.8.3. Personal affairs and emergency data records, i.e., Last Will and Testament, financial arrangements, etc.

15.2.10.3.8.4. Identification requirements, i.e., ID card, dog tags and passport (as required).

15.2.10.3.8.5. Facilities available, i.e., messing, billeting, isolation, etc.

15.2.10.3.8.6. Code of conduct review.

15.2.10.3.8.7. Sterilization of personal effects.

15.2.10.3.8.8. Standardized location of all sensitive items, i.e., classified documents, manual and electrical encryption devices, etc.

15.2.10.3.8.9. General and unique rules of conduct and engagement.

15.2.10.3.8.10. Handling of victim's effects.

15.2.10.4. Command and Signal.

15.2.10.4.1. Chain of Command.

15.2.10.4.2. Locations of Leaders. The location and communications requirements of the TL and assistant TL are planned for all phases of the operation, during movement, at danger areas, and at the objective. The TL plans to be where he anticipates he can best control and direct the team at each phase. The assistant TL maybe assigned specific duties in a sensitive location during any phase of the operation or may assist the TL in control of the entire team by locating himself where he can best assume command, if required.

15.2.10.4.3. Communications. When communication with outside command and control and support elements is required or anticipated, the plan must include radio call signs, frequencies, times to transmit or monitor, and when appropriate, the special codes to be used.

15.2.10.4.4. Signals. Signals break down into three basic areas. These are; signals for team movement, recognition symbols, and Evasion and Escape signals.

15.2.10.4.4.1. Signals for team movement. When and where will signals be needed to control the team? These signals must be planned and rehearsed. Some instances where they may be needed are to signal "freeze" or "take cover, enemy in sight," to order withdrawal from the objective, to signal "all clear," and to stop and start the team. Visual and audible signals such as arm and hand signals, pyrotechnics, voice, radios, and infrared equipment may be used. All team members must know any signals planned.

15.2.10.4.4.2. The photo recognition symbol is a simple signal, i.e., a dash and dot that can be positioned through photo-reconnaissance to track long-range ground movement.

15.2.10.4.4.3. Evasion and escape signals (letters and colors) are assigned by intelligence and usually published in the SPINS. The PJ team will only use these signals when the basic plan of execution has reverted to the "evasion plan of action."

15.2.11. Issue the Operations Order. From the planning done in the previous step, the TL should have all the information to brief the team on the operation (Issue the operations order).

15.2.12. Brief-back.

15.2.12.1. A good method is for the team to assemble for a short conference before the brief-back. Notes, thoughts, and observations are compared so complete, concise, and accurate information can be quickly given at the brief back.

15.2.12.2. Brief-back the command releasing authority. This is where you "sell" the intended operation. Approval or disapproval with a recommendation to scrub the entire mission, amend/re-do the plan, or put the operation on hold as is, should occur at this point.

15.2.13. Supervise (at all times), Inspect, Rehearse.

15.2.13.1. Inspections and Rehearsals. Inspections and rehearsals are vital to proper preparation. They must be carefully planned and conducted even though a team may be experienced in PJ combat operations. Use a rehearsal area resembling the OA. Plans must provide for inspections by subordinate leaders as well as the TL, when required.

15.2.13.2. Include provisions for test firing all weapons. A functional check is not enough. Conduct live test firing in all modes. Limit test firing to as few rounds as possible. Ensure the weapons are clean and lubricated as required by the environment.

Chapter 16

MEDICAL

16.1. General. Medical operations, kit packing, and use are covered in the pararescue medical specific AFIs and publications. However some operational guidance is provided here.

16.2. Use of the Flight Surgeon. In operations involving personnel confirmed to have serious or life-threatening injuries, the team leader (TL) will request the assistance of the flight surgeon early in the alert/notification phase of the mission. This allows the flight surgeon time to consult with the TL and obtain additional supplies and equipment that may be needed for the treatment of the seriously injured. A deployment aircraft must not be delayed for the arrival of the flight surgeon to the detriment of the survivor. However, every effort will be made to ensure the flight surgeon has sufficient time to meet with the TL. Combat operations may preclude the use of a flight surgeon aboard rescue aircraft due to their medical AFSC used in a combat aircraft. Flight surgeon assistants and medical technicians will not be taken over other available Pararescuemen (PJs) on space limited helicopters.

16.3. On-Scene Mission Commander (OMC) Aircraft. If the flight surgeon cannot be placed on the deployment aircraft, every effort must be made to place him aboard a second aircraft and deployed to the operational area. Ideally, he should be placed on-board the designated On-Scene Mission Commander (OMC) aircraft to ensure his position within the Search and Rescue (SAR) effort. This allows immediate consultation and a source of medical advice for the TL. If the situation warrants continuous medical coverage by the flight surgeon, the TL should state so and request rotational flight surgeon assistance as each OMC is replaced by another.

16.4. Recovery Aircraft. In situations where the deployment aircraft is fixed wing and the recovery of the PJ team and survivor is by rotary wing aircraft, consideration should be given to deploying the flight surgeon on the recovery aircraft so as to be of assistance to the PJ team once the survivor is aboard. Under no circumstances should a flight surgeon replace a PJ on the recovery aircraft if there are not at least two PJs on board. This is a safety measure to ensure successful deployment, ground operations, and recovery of PJs and survivor/s. Having a flight surgeon on board the recovery aircraft is especially useful when the survivor's condition necessitates the flight surgeon's personal assistance as rapidly as possible.

16.5. Relayed Communications. The least desired method of flight surgeon-PJ interface entails the use of go-betweens or third-parties (usually two or more), of personnel or stations who must relay radio messages back and fourth. Known as relayed communications, this method is subject to misinterpretation, time lapse, and general degradation of the communicative process. If the method must be used, transmissions must be made as clear and concise as possible to be handled by the relays. Medical terminology must be carefully considered and phrased to minimize the possibilities of misinterpretation. A direct line with the flight surgeon is the optimum means of communication due to his/her ability to reference and confer with other specialists. Every attempt must be made to establish good communication schedules and stick to them.

16.6. Medical After Action Report . A log must be maintained on every aspect of an operational mission which includes patient care. This is especially important since the medical care provided is often performed under adverse conditions which complicate or hamper procedures. This log is used during the patient care debriefings between the PJ team and squadron medical element flight surgeon which is conducted within 10 duty days after the mission. The debriefing will be documented.

Chapter 17

COMMUNICATIONS PROCEDURES

17.1. Safety Considerations . Communications are an essential part of every operation. The diversity of Pararescue (PJ) employment requires a communications capability. The importance of being able to communicate quickly, efficiently, and effectively becomes apparent in a situation requiring rapid rescue. In combat, communications become critical for command and control of deployed assets. The primary source document for communications is Army TC 24-19 (Radio Operator's Handbook), applicable equipment technical orders, and equipment owner's manuals.

17.2. Types of Communication. Generally there are two types of communication used by Pararescuemen (PJs) when normal verbal communications are not possible. They are electronic communication and visual communication. Electronic communication techniques encompass the use of radios. Visual communications techniques encompass the use of pyrotechnics, panels, mirrors, lights, and hand or arm signals.

17.3. Radio Employment.

17.3.1. Lost communications can result from equipment failure or terrain features blocking normal transmission. Lost communications procedures must be prearranged and understood by all personnel. Each man must know the correct signal codes and where the applicable pyrotechnics, lights or panels are located. Signal codes must be coordinated with all support elements before employment.

17.3.2. Combat intra-team communications are maintained using a radio with a minimum of VHF Lo FM (Fox Mike) or UHF AM (Uniform) as these are the commonly used military frequencies ranges and are compatible with military aircraft. These radios should be able to use US Type I Comsec with variable wattage output to keep transmissions range short.

17.4. Radio Communications. The radio will normally be used as the primary method of communications. The frequency of contacts, if feasible, should be at least three times a day for non-tactical operations. Night contacts will be scheduled when circumstances dictate.

17.4.1. Routine Radio Care. Each radio is designed to perform specific tasks under varying conditions. Capabilities and limitations of assigned radios should be known. Although designed for rugged use, radios are treated and maintained with care. Radios not specifically designed for water immersion are kept dry and free of condensation. Those designed for water are rinsed in fresh running water as soon as possible to reduce corrosion. T.O.s and manufactures instructions are reviewed periodically to ensure proper operations and care.

17.4.2. Radio Power Source. Radio batteries are susceptible to both hot and cold weather conditions, and their life span is affected accordingly. Batteries are stored IAW manufacturer's instructions/applicable directives.

17.4.2.1. While in the field, the climatic conditions become uncontrollable factors; however, the following procedures aid in extending battery life:

17.4.2.1.1. Do not expose the battery/radio unit to direct sunlight or heat for long periods of time.

17.4.2.1.2. Frequently inspect the battery and battery chamber for accumulating condensation during high humidity conditions. Wipe dry when condensation is present.

17.4.2.2. In cold weather environments, the battery life span is preserved by:

17.4.2.2.1. Keeping the battery next to the body when not in use to prevent drainage of battery power due to exposure to freezing or below freezing temperatures.

17.4.2.2.2. Keeping transmissions to a minimum.

17.4.2.2.3. Use digital verses voice transmission.

CAUTION: Do not attempt to extend battery life by placing batteries next to direct heat sources, i.e., catalytic heater, fire, cook stove. Serious injuries can result from possible explosion. Additionally, lithium batteries can explode when they come in contact with water.

17.4.3. Inherent Limitations.

17.4.3.1. Antenna Orientation. For maximum signal reception, the antenna should not be pointed directly at the receiving station. When the radio set is in use, the antenna should not come in contact with the body or any foreign object. Contact with foreign objects will cause dampening of the signal.

17.4.3.2. Line-of-Sight Communications. The reliability of radio communication depends largely on the selection of a good radio site. Hold the radio set so the antenna is essentially vertical when transmitting. This helps to assure maximum transmitting range. Hills and mountains between stations normally limit the range of radio sets. In mountainous or hilly terrain, select positions relatively high on the slopes. Avoid locations at the base of cliffs, in deep ravines, or valleys. For operational frequencies above 30 MHz, and whenever possible, select a location that allows line of sight (LOS) communications. Avoid locations that provide the enemy with jamming capability, visual sighting, or easy reception. Dry ground has high resistance and limits the range of the radio set. If possible, locate the station near moist ground, which has much less resistance. Water, and in particular salt water, greatly increases the instances that can be covered by RF (radio frequency) radiation.

17.5. Radio Frequencies.

17.5.1. Available radio communications operate in different frequency ranges - High Frequency (HF), Very High Frequency (VHF), Ultra High Frequency (UHF); and modulations - Frequency Modulation (FM) and Amplitude Modulation (AM). The numbers before the decimal in the frequency are the Megahertz and the numbers after the decimal are the Kilohertz.

17.5.1.1. High Frequency - 2.000 to 29.999 MHz

17.5.1.2. HF is used for long range communications when satellite communications is not available because of crowded frequencies or high latitude (satellites orbit the equator).

17.5.2. Very High Frequency

17.5.2.1. VHF has two different bandwidths, VHF Lo (30.000 to 89.995 MHz) and VHF Hi (116.000 to 173.995 MHz).

17.5.2.1.1. VHF Lo is referred to as "Fox Mike" is only FM and is used for ground to ground transmission. Some tactical aircraft also use this frequency range.

17.5.2.1.2. VHF Hi has two different modulations, AM and FM.

17.5.2.1.2.1. VHF Hi AM is referred to as "Victor" and is primarily used for civilian air-to-air or ground-to-air communication such as civilian air traffic control.

17.5.2.1.2.2. VHF Hi FM is primarily a civilian band used by law enforcement and civilian Search and Rescue assets. Motorola Sabers, Astros, and MX 300s use this frequency range. Most military aircraft do not have VHF Hi FM.

17.5.3. Ultra High Frequency - 225.000 to 512.000 MHz.

17.5.3.1. UHF has two different modulations, AM and FM.

17.5.3.1.1. UHF AM is referred to as "Uniform". It is the primary line-of-sight military air-to-air and ground-to-air frequency range.

17.5.3.1.2. UHF FM is primarily used for military satellite communications. The radio must be secure and have different transmit (uplink) and receive (downlink) frequencies.

17.5.4. Rescue has UHF, VHF and FM frequencies specifically assigned for operational and training use within the continental United States. These include:

17.5.4.1. UHF AM: 282.8 MHz, 236.0 MHz, 243.0 MHz, 251.9 MHz, 252.8 MHz, 259.0 MHz, and 381.0 MHz.

17.5.4.2. VHF AM High: 121.5 MHz.

17.5.4.3. VHF FM Low: 46.85 MHz.

17.5.4.4. These frequencies are cleared for use through each unit's base frequency monitor prior to conducting operations, even though they have been authorized for rescue units.

17.6. Radio Compatibility.

17.6.1. All radios transmit and receive the same thing - Radio waves. The manipulation of these waves may cause problems for two radios to communicate. Different things that may affect two radios being able to communicate are: squelch, frequency range and modulation, frequency spacing, frequency hopping, and comsec (refer to Secure Communications). The team leader (TL) ensures compatibility between his team's radios and aircraft assigned.

17.6.2. Squelch is adjusted on the receiving radio by blocking weaker, unwanted, signals from being received. As an example, the PRC-117 D's squelch settings are OFF, NOISE, and TONE (VHF Lo range only). If squelch is OFF, a weak signal can be heard, but may also be full of static. In NOISE there must be a strong signal to break squelch. TONE squelch is different in that there is a subcarrier tone that is transmitted in conjunction with the radio frequency. If the transmitting radio's tone doesn't match the receiving radio's tone, it may be impossible to communicate. On some radios (Motorola Saber or PRC-139), the subcarrier tone can be adjusted either through a computer program or a separate radio programmer. If radio A can receive radio B, but radio B can't receive radio A; this is probably the problem.

17.6.2.1. Many radios have only partial bandwidths in their frequency range (VHF, UHF) or only single modulation (AM, FM). Each operator should know the capabilities of both his and the other agencies' equipment before mission planning to ensure compatibility between radios. While considering the communications plan, it is very important to know both the frequency and the modulation (AM or FM) as that is one of the most common problems and usually the easiest to fix. Most tactical radios can also transmit and receive different frequencies on the same channel (called half-duplex). If the transmit frequency is different than the receive frequency, it will cause problems.

17.6.2.2. Frequency spacing for VHF Lo is 25 KHz, VHF Hi is 5 KHz, and UHF is 5 KHz. Some radios have a VHF Hi spacing of 6.25 KHz spacing (use by some Motorola Sabers) and unless the radio is designed to accept that spacing, they will not be able to accept certain frequencies.

17.6.2.3. Frequency hopping is also referred as electronic counter counter measure (ECCM). They include SINCGARS, used by Army and Marines; and HAVEQUICK, used by the Air Force. The basic concept of both is to hop between different frequencies at the same time to limit the enemy's ability to jam frequencies. The most common reason for communication problems is improper set up/timing.

17.7. Antennas. A major factor in the quality and range of radio communications is antenna selection. Consult the applicable radio technical orders for modified or improved antenna capabilities.

17.8. Voice Procedures.

17.8.1. Use standard pro-words and the phonetic alphabet.

17.8.2. Use call signs assigned in the AFKAI-1 (S), USAF Voice Call sign List. Included in the AFKAI-1 is a list of changing call signs that are classified and static call signs (i.e. GONDOLA) that are unclassified.

17.9. Secure Communication.

17.9.1. Secure communications are a prime concern for the military. There are presently two accepted methods for encrypting transmissions, electrical and manual. Basic cryptography is essential to provide interim security of information during transmission, but it is important to note no system is absolutely secure and the primary function is to gain time on the enemy.

17.9.1.1. Electrical encryption. Scrambles the signal being transmitted with a Comsec "key". This makes it unable for anybody to understand the transmission unless they have the same Comsec key installed in their receiver to unscramble the transmission. The Comsec key is transcribed electrically from a tape through the KOI-18 into the encryption device or a portable storage device called the KYK-13 or ANCYZ-10. The operator can then uses one of these devices to transfer the Comsec key into the encryption device. All encryption devices used to secure military communications must be approved through the National Security Agency and use Type-1 Comsec encryption.

17.9.1.1.1. The two ways to electrically encrypt a radio are with encryption hardware or with embedded encryption software. Most newer radios such as the PRC-117D/F and the PRC-148 have embedded encryption software. Older radios such as the PRC-113 need encryption hardware. These include the KY-57, and KY-99.

17.9.1.1.2. The KY-99, which is replacing the KY-57, is used to secure all radios without embedded encryption software. It also digitizes transmissions to allow narrow band Satcom communications.

17.9.1.2. STU-3 Telephone. A secure telephone allowing both voice and digital encryption transfer using regular telephone lines.

17.9.2. Manual Encoding. Involves brevity codes or secret words and phrases.

17.9.2.1. Brevity codes. These codes are designed solely for condensing messages rather than the concealment of the content. They may be developed from abbreviations, numbers, letters, or phrases, which are shorter than the information to be transmitted. They must be used in conjunction with secure codes. The primary brevity code used is the Communications Electronic Operating Instruction (CEOI).

17.9.2.2. Secret words and phrases. Designed to conceal the meaning of the transmission by using non-literal terms or by using a matrix sheet which both use to encode and decode the message.

17.10. Security Considerations. Security considerations influencing electronic communications include:

17.10.1. Radio Direction Finder (RDF) capability. Enemy's RDF can obtain a "lock on" in very short periods of time and may lead personnel or artillery fire in the direction of radio transmissions.

17.10.2. When using manual encryption procedures, transmissions are prepared in advance and made as short as possible.

17.10.3. Radio transmissions are not made from bivouac sites. RDF receivers may locate the transmission site and direct an enemy patrol to the transmitter coordinates.

17.10.4. Move out of the transmission area immediately following any radio transmission.

17.10.5. Forms Adopted. AF Form 623, On-the-Job Training Record, AF Form 803, Report of Task Evaluations, and AF Form 922, Individual Jump Record.

ROBERT H. FOGLESONG,   Lt Gen, USAF
DCS/Air & Space Operations

Attachment 1

GLOSSARY OF REFERENCES AND SUPPORTING INFORMATION

References

NOTE: Required minimum hard copy sectional publications are denoted by an "#". Required minimum hard copy individual publications are denoted by an "*".

GENERAL:

JOINT PUB 3-50, *NATIONAL SEARCH AND RESCUE MANUAL VOL I: NATIONAL SEARCH AND RESCUE SYSTEM*

JOINT PUB 3-50.1, *NATIONAL SEARCH AND RESCUE MANUAL VOL II: PLANNING HANDBOOK*

JOINT PUB 3-50.2, *DOCTRINE FOR JOINT COMBAT SEARCH AND RESCUE*

JOINT PUB 3-50.3, *JOINT DOCTRINE FOR EVASION AND RECOVERY*

AFDD 2-1.6, *COMBAT SEARCH AND RESCUE OPERATIONS*

#AFPD 16-12, *PARARESCUE*

AFI 10-216, *EVACUATING AND REPATRIATING AIR FORCE FAMILY MEMBERS AND OTHER US NONCOMBATANTS*

AFI 11-402, *AVIATION AND PARACHUTIST SERVICE, AERONAUTICAL RATINGS AND BADGES*

AFI 13-208, *RESCUE COORDINATION CENTER COMBAT SEARCH AND RESCUE OPERATING PROCEDURES*

*AFI 16-1201, *PARARESCUE RESOURCE MANAGEMENT*

*AFI 16-1202, *PARARESCUE OPERATIONS TECHNIQUES AND PROCEDURES*

*AFI 16-1203, *PARARESCUE TRAINING AND EVALUATION PROGRAM*

AFI 36-2108, *AIRMAN CLASSIFICATION*

AFMAN 10-206, *OPERATIONAL REPORTING*

AFMAN 37-139, *RECORDS DISPOSITION SCHEDULE*

AFP 3-20/FM 100-20, *MILITARY OPERATIONS IN LOW INTENSITY CONFLICT*

AFTTP(I) 3-2.21/FM 90-41, *JTF LIAISON HANDBOOK - MULTISERVICE TACTICS, TECHNIQUES, AND PROCEDURES FOR JOINT TASK FORCE (JTF) LIAISON OPERATIONS*

PACAFP 50-56, *MULTISERVICE PROCEDURES FOR HUMANITARIAN ASSISTANCE OPERATIONS*

#MACR 64-2, *PJ TACTICAL CHECKLIST*

ARMY FM 1-108, *DOCTRINE FOR ARMY SPECIAL OPERATIONS AVIATION FORCES*

ARMY FM 90-29, *NONCOMBATANT EVACUATION OPERATIONS*

FLYING:

AFI 11-2C-130v1 thru 5 *C-130 AIRCREW TRAINING*

AFI 11-2HC-130v1 thru 5 HC-130 AIRCREW TRAINING

#AFI 11-2HH-60v1 thru 5 HH-60 AIRCREW TRAINING

#AFI 11-401, *FLIGHT MANAGEMENT*

*AFI 11-202V3, *GENERAL FLIGHT RULES*

AFTO 00-105E-9, *AIRCRAFT EMERGENCY RESCUE INFORMATION*

AFTO 1C-130A-9, *CARGO LOADING MANUAL*

#AFTO 1H-60(U)A-1, *FLIGHT MANUAL USAF SERIES UH-60A, UH-60L, MH-60G, HH-60G AND HH-60L HELICOPTERS*

*AFTO 1H-60(U)A-1CL-2, *GUNNER HOIST OPERATORS FLIGHT CREW CHECKLIST*

OJT:

#AFI 16-1203, *PARARESCUE TRAINING AND EVALUATION PROGRAM*

AFMAN 36-2108, *AIRMAN CLASSIFICATION*

#AFI 36-2201, *DEVELOPING, MANAGING, AND CONDUCTING TRAINING*

#AFMAN 36-2245, *MANAGING CAREER FIELD EDUCATION AND TRAINING*

#AFMAN 36-2247, *PLANNING, CONDUCTING, ADMINISTERING, AND EVALUATING TRAINING*

PARACHUTE:

#AFJI 13-210, *JOINT AIRDROP INSPECTION RECORDS, MALFUNCTION INVESTIGATIONS, AND ACTIVITY REPORTING*

#AFI 13-217, *ASSAULT ZONE PROCEDURES*

#AFI 11-231, *COMPUTED AIR RELEASE POINT PROCEDURES*

AFI 11-403, *AEROSPACE PHYSIOLOGICAL TRAINING PROGRAM*

AFI 11-409, *HIGH ALTITUDE AIRDROP MISSION SUPPORT PROGRAM*

#AFI 11-410, *PERSONNEL PARACHUTE OPERATIONS*

#AFI 11-410/PACAF1, *PERSONNEL PARACHUTE OPERATIONS*

AFTO 13C5-1-31, *PARACHUTE, AERIAL DELIVERY TYPE G-8 AND M390A/B*

AFTO 13C5-14-12, *PARACHUTE CARGO, 28 FT DIAMETER, NYLON CANOPY, T-7A CONVERTED*

AFTO 13C7-1-11, *AIRDROP OF SUPPLIES AND EQUIPMENT: RIGGING CONTAINERS*

#AFTO 13C7-51-21, *AIRDROP OF SUPPLIES AND EQUIPMENT: RIGGING FOR SPEC OPS (RAMZ)*

AFTO 13C7-55-1, *AIRDROP OF SUPPLIES AND EQUIPMENT: RIGGING MOTORCLYLE*

#AFTO 14D1-2-1-121/FM 57-220, *STATIC LINE PARACHUTING TECHNIQUES AND TRAINING*

AFTO 14D1-2-181, *WIND DRIFT DETN PARACHUTE, TYPE AF/B28J-1*

AFTO 14D1-2-396, *PERSONNEL PARACHUTE, TYPE A/P28S-17, -18*

AFTO 14D1-2-451, *MC-3, FREEFALL PERSONNEL PARACHUTE SYSTEM* (MAINT MNL FOR FF2)

AFTO 14D1-2-463-2, *PARACHUTE, PERSONNEL TYPE, 35 FT DIAMETER, MC1-1B*

AFTO 14D1-2-465-2, *INTERIM RAM AIR PRCHT (IRAPS) MODELS MT1-XX, MT1-XR AND MT1-XCCT*

AFTO 14D1-2-466-2, *PARACHUTE, PERSONNEL, TYPE 35 FT DIAMETER, MC1-1C*

AFTO 14D1-2-468-2, *PARACHUTE, RAM AIR, FREEFALL, PERSONNEL, MODEL MC-4*

#ARMY FM 31-19, *MILITARY FREEFALL PARACHUTING*

ARMY FM 57-38, *PATHFINDER OPERATIONS*

#USMC TM 09770A-12&P-1, *USE AND MAINTENANCE OF MC-5 PARARCHUTE*

FIELD:

*AFMAN 36-2216, *SURVIVAL TRAINING* (SUPERSEDED AFR 64-4), (UNDER REVISION)

ARMY FM 20-3, *CAMOUFLAGE*

ARMY FM 21-10, *FIELD HYGIENE AND SANITATION*

ARMY FM 21-26, *MAP READING AND LAND NAVIGATION*

ARMY FM 21-60, *VISUAL SIGNALS*

ARMY FM 21-75, *COMBAT SKILLS OF THE SOLDIER*

ARMY FM 21-76, *SURVIVAL*

ARMY FM 23-10, *SNIPER TRAINING*

ARMY FM 23-23, *ANTIPERSONNEL MINE M18A1 AND M18 (CLAYMORE)*

ARMY FM 23-30, *GRENADES AND PYROTECHNIC SIGNALS*

ARMY FM 23-31, *40-MM GRENADE LAUNCHER, M203*

ARMY FM 24-19, *RADIO OPERATOR'S HANDBOOK*

ARMY FM 31-70, *BASIC COLD WEATHER MANUAL* (AKIO SCOW SLED)

ARMY FM 31-71, *NORTHERN OPERATIONS*

ARMY FM 90-3, *DESERT OPERATIONS*

ARMY FM 90-5, *JUNGLE OPERATIONS*

ARMY FM 90-10, *MILITARY OPERATIONS ON URBANIZED TERRAIN*

ARMY FM 90-10-1, *AN INFANTRYMAN'S GUIDE TO COMBAT IN BUILT-UP AREAS*

ARMY TC 90-11-1, *MILITARY SKIING*

MEDICAL:

#AFI-16-1204, *ADMINISTRATION OF PJ MEDICAL MATERIAL ACTIVITY* (WHEN PUBLISHED)

*AFI 16-1205, *PJ MEDICATIONS AND PROCEDURES* (WHEN PUBLISHED)

ARMY FM 8-40, *MANAGEMENT OF SKIN DISEASES IN THE TROPICS AT UNIT LEVEL*

PARAMEDIC EMERGENCY CARE, SECOND OR THIRD EDITION

PJ MEDICATION AND PROCEDURE HANDBOOK

DIVING:

AFTO 42B-1-22, *QUALITY CONTROL OF COMPRESSED AND LIQUID BREATHING AIR*

#AFTO 42B5-1-2, *USE, HANDLING AND MAINTENANCE OF GAS CYLINDERS*

#US NAVY NAVSEA 0994-LP001-9010, VOL 1, *US NAVY DIVING MANUAL*

US NAVY NAVSEAINST 1056O.2B, *DIVING EQUIPMENT AUTHORIZED FOR NAVY USE*

US NAVY OPNAVINST 3150.27A, *NAVY DIVING PROGRAM*

US NAVY OPNAVINST 3150.28A, *DIVING LOG*

#ARMY FM 20-11-1, VOL 1, *MILITARY DIVING* (ACCURACY REQ FOR NAVY DEPTH GAGES)

ARMY FM 20-11-2, VOL 2, *MILITARY DIVING* (MIXED GAS DIVING)

FEDERAL SPECIFICATION BB-A-1034B(1) NOT 1, *COMPRESSED AIR BREATHING* (PURE AIR BREATHING SPECIFICATION)

Abbreviations and Acronyms

AC—Aircraft Commander

AFI—Air Force Instruction

AFJI—Air Force Joint Instruction

AFMAN—Air Force Manual

AFPD—Air Force Policy Directive

AFR—Air Force Regulation

AFRC—Air Force Reserve Command

AGL—Above Ground Level

AJM—Assistant Jumpmaster

AMVERS—Automated Mutual Vessel Emergency Rescue System

AO—Area of Operations, Area Objective

ARP—Alternate Rallying Points

ARR—Automatic Ripcord Release

ASL—Above Sea Level

ATA—Atmosphere Absolute

ATAR—Air-To-Air Recovery System

ATL—Assistant Team Leader

AWADS—Adverse Weather Aerial Delivery System

AWL—Above Water Level

AZ—Azimuth

CADS—Computers Aerial Delivery System

CAF—Combat Air Forces

CARP—Computed Air Release Point

CAS—Close Air Support

CDC—Career Development Course

CDS—Container Delivery Systems

CEOI—Communications Electronic Operating Instruction

CSAR—Combat Search and Rescue

CS—Crystalline Sterate (Riot Agent)

CSO—Communications Systems Operator (Radio Operator)

DZ—Drop Zone

DZC—Drop Zone Controller

DZSO—Drop Zone Safety Officer

DZSTL—Drop Zone Support Team Leader

ECAS—Emergency Close Air Support

E & E—Escape and Evasion

EL—Electro-Luminescent

EPA—Emergency Plan of Action

ERP—Enroute Rallying Points

EXRP—Extraction Rallying Point

EZ—Extraction Zone

F—Fahrenheit

FAC—Forward Air Controller

FCB—Flight Crew Bulletin

FCIF—Flight Crew Information File

FE—Flight Engineer

FEBA—Forward Edge of the Battle Area

FM—Field Manual, Functional Manager

FOB—Forward Operating Base

FOIA—Freedom of Information Act

FS—Flight Station

FSW—Feet of Salt Water

GCA—Ground Control Approach

GMRS—Ground Marking Release System

GPS—Global Positioning System

GRADS—Ground Radar Aerial Delivery System

HAHO—High Altitude High Opening

HALO—High Altitude Low Opening

HARP—High Altitude Release Point

HF—High Frequency

HGRP—High Glide Ratio Parachute

IAD—Immediate Action Drill

IAW—In Accordance With

IMC—Instrument Meteorological Conditions

IR—Infrared

IRP—Initial Rally Point

JFC—Joint Force Commander

JM—Jumpmaster

JMDD—Jumpmaster Directed Drop

JMPI—Jumpmaster Personnel Inspection

JRRC—Joint Rescue and Recovery Center

KIAS—Knots Indicated Air Speed

LBE—Load Bearing Equipment

LM—Loadmaster

LP—Listening Post

LPU—Life Preserver Unit

LZ—Landing Zone

MCI—Multi-Command Instruction

MDS—Mission Design Series

MFF—Military Freefall

MOA—Military Operations Area

MRE—Meal, Ready to Eat

MSL—Mean Sea Level

METT-T—Mission, Enemy, Terrain, Troops, - Time Available

NAV—Navigator

NCOIC-—Non-Commissioned Officer In Charge

NOTAM—Notice to Airmen

NVD—Night Vision Device

NVG—Night Vision Goggle

OA—Objective Area

OD—Olive Drab

ODS—Overhead Delivery System

OMC—On-Scene Mission Commander

OP—Opening Point, Observation Post

ORP—Objective Rallying Point

PAX—Passenger/s

PD—Policy Directive

PDO—Publishing Distribution Office

PI—Point of Impact

PJM—Primary Jumpmaster

PJTL—PJ Team Leader

PLF—Parachute Landing Fall

PRP—Preliminary Release Point

PT—Point Man, Physical Training, Physiological Technician

RAMZ—Rigging Alternate Method-Zodiac

RDF—Radio Direction Finder

ROE—Rules of Engagement

RO—Radio Operator

RON—Remain Over Night

RP—Release Point

RS—Rear Security

RTB—Return to Base

SA—Situational Awareness

SCNS—Self Contained Navigation System

SCUBA—Self-Contained Underwater Breathing Apparatus

SKE—Station Keeping Equipment

SOP—Standard Operating Procedures

SPUDS—Single Para Scuba Deployment System

TALO—Tactical Air Liaison Officer

TL—Team Leader

TM—Team Member

T.O—.-Technical Order

TOT—Time Over Target

UHF—Ultra High Frequency

USAFR—US Air Force Reserve

USMC—United States Marine Corps

VHF—Very High Frequency

VIRS—Verbally Initiated Release System

VMC—Visual Meteorological Conditions

VOX—Voice Operated Circuits

WDI—Wind Drift Indicator

WP—White Phosphorous

WSVC—Wind Streamer Vector Count

WX—Weather

ZM—Zone Marker

Attachment 2

D-RING THREADING

Figure A2.1. D-Ring Threading.

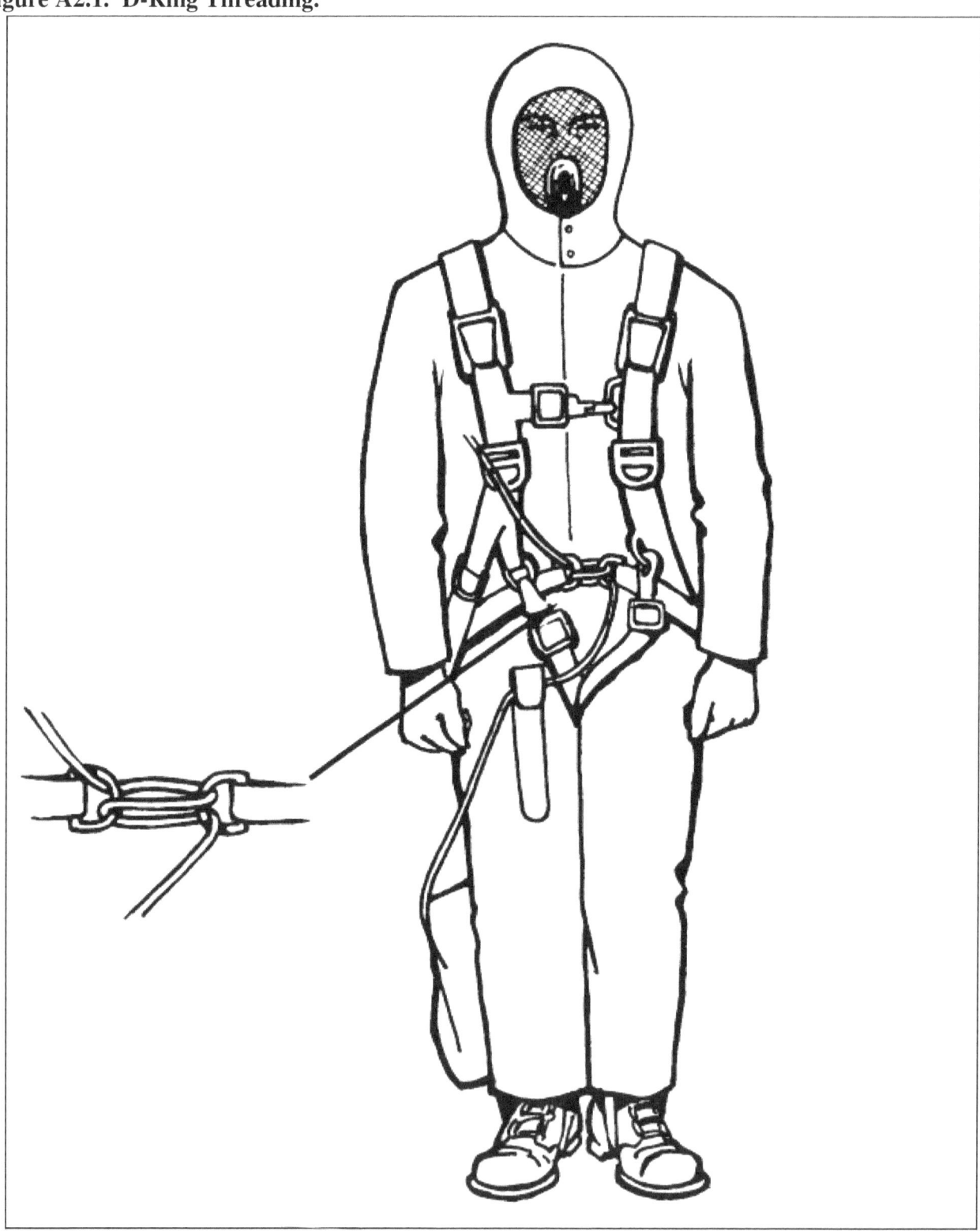

Attachment 3

RISER TIE-OFF

Figure A3.1. Riser Tie-Off.

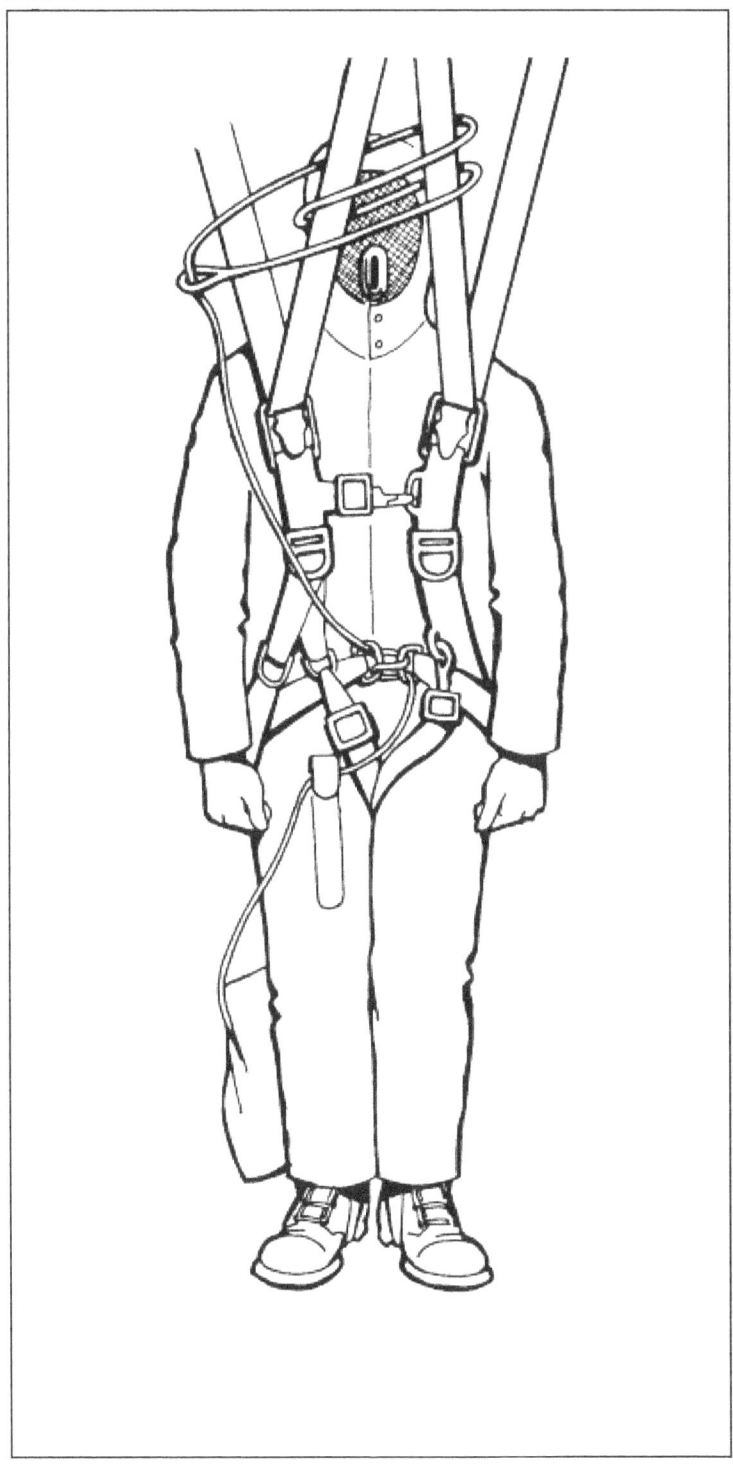

Attachment 4

FIXED TARGET PROCEDURES

Figure A4.1. Fixed Target Procedures.

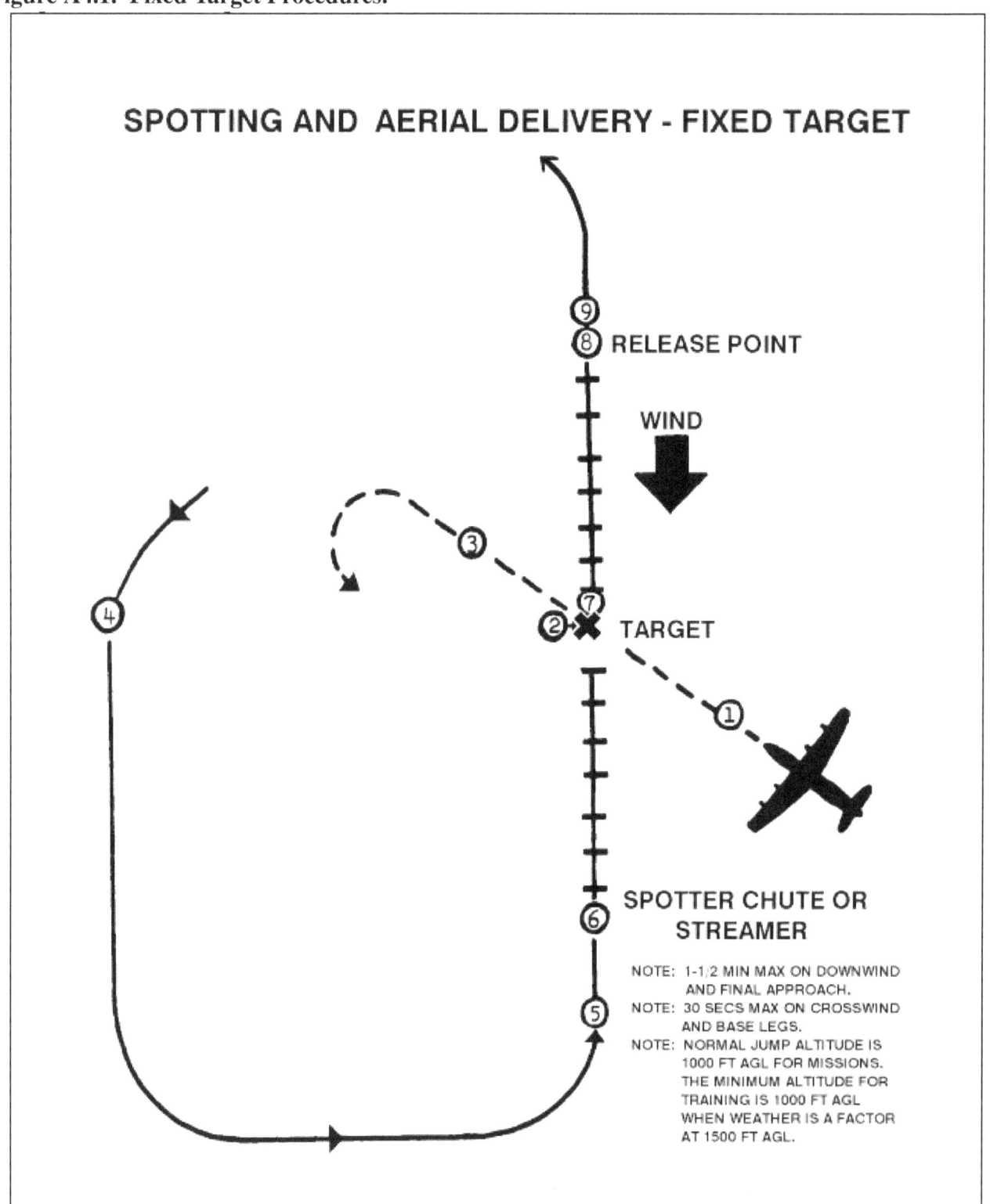

Figure A4.2. Figure Explanation - Fixed Target Procedures.

1.Head directly toward the target, regardless of the wind direction.

2.Release the spotter chute/streamer directly over the target.

3.Immediately upon release, make left/right turn to observe descent and position of spotter chute/ streamer.

4.Establish rectangular drop pattern oriented so that the final approach will be aligned with the spotter chute/streamer and the target, respectively.

5.Turn on approach. Make minor changes in heading to pass over the spotter chute and the target on a direct line. Aircraft drift correction should be established prior to passing over the spotter chute.

6.Initiate uniform count over the spotter chute/streamer.

7.Reverse count over the target.

8.Deploy the second spotter chute/streamer or PJ at last digit of reverse count

9.After the jumper clears the aircraft, turn to observe the accuracy of the drop.

(a) The normal flight pattern will be a rectangular or racetrack pattern with the final approach from WDI to target. Each leg of the pattern must be long enough to allow the JM and jumpers the preparation needed prior to deployment.

(1) For high performance aircraft, the turn to the crosswind leg will be made as soon as possible after the WDI is released. A pattern with crosswind and base legs of not over one half minute and with downwind and final legs of 1 to 1 ½ minutes will allow time for heading corrections on final. This allows the JM time to observe the descent of WDI device or jumpers. If a delay is expected, another full pattern should be flown, as opposed to extending the downwind leg, this maintains the aircraft close to the area for continued evaluation. This pattern will place the aircraft a maximum of 5 minutes from the site at any one time.

(2) The aircraft will be flown over the target at a predetermined altitude and airspeed. When directly over the target a minimum of one WDI will be dropped. The JM and aircrew will make every effort to keep the WDI in sight from release to impact. Over land, the pilot may have to circle over the WDI to ensure the definite location of , or orientation to the impact point to the target. After the first WDI has reached the ground and its position noted, the aircraft will return to the normal pattern. The final approach should pass directly over the WDI and the intended target, in that order. This pattern automatically aligns the final approach into the wind.

(3)A right or left hand pattern may be flown depending on terrain and aircraft configuration. The aircraft will be flown in this pattern with minor course corrections on final. As the aircraft passes directly over the first WDI, the JM will start a uniform count to measure the time from the WDI to the target. When the aircraft is over the target, the count will be stopped and immediately a new count will begin, when that count equals the first, the second WDI or jumper will be deployed. The increasing count will measure the same distance past the target with the accuracy of the deployment dependent upon the JMs alignment and count.

Attachment 5

MOVING TARGET PROCEDURES

Figure A5.1. Moving Target Procedures.

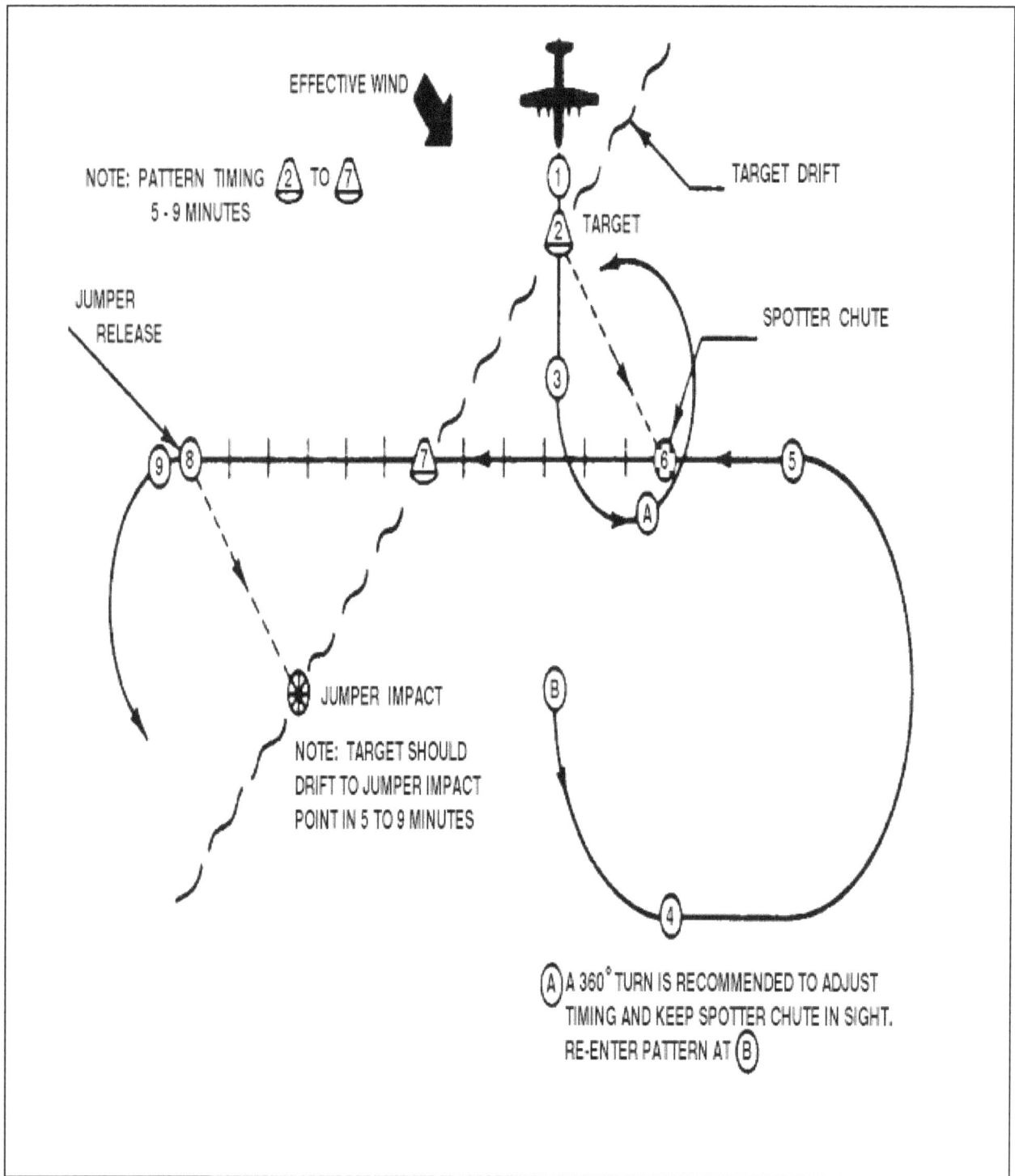

Figure A5.2. Figure Explanation - Moving Target Procedures.

1. MOVING TARGET PROCEDURES

a) Head directly toward the target, regardless of the wind direction.

b) Release the spotter chute directly over the target.

c) Immediately upon release, make a left/right hand turn to observe the descent and position of the spotter chute.

d) Establish rectangular drop pattern oriented so the final approach will be aligned with the spotter chute and the target, respectively. The pattern should be adjusted so that the aircraft will be over the target five to nine minutes after the spotter chute is deployed.

e) Turn on approach. Make minor changes in heading to pass over the spotter chute and the target on a direct line. Aircraft drift correction should be established prior to passing over the spotter chute. Initiate a uniform count over the spotter chute.

f) Reverse count over the target.

g) Deploy PJs when the last digit in reverse count is reached.

h) After the jumper clears the aircraft, turn to observe the accuracy of the drop.

i) Deploy additional jumpers using the drop heading and count established in steps 5, 6, and 7.

j) Disregard the spotter chute for subsequent passes.

k) When the target drift rate is changed (drogue chute is installed on target, know wind shift occurs, etc.) the entire spotter chute procedure must be re-accomplished and a new drop heading and count established starting with step 1.

2 MOVING TARGET PATTERN. Deployment procedures to a moving target are similar to those employed for a stationary target. The moving target procedures takes into consideration target drift and will place the team on the downdrift line of the moving target and not necessarily on target. Special attention should be paid to the following items:

(a) The pattern must be adjusted so that the initial pass over the target after WDI deployment is not less than 5 minutes and not more than 9 minutes, 7 minutes being ideal. If the initial pattern requires more than 9 minutes, the team will be too far downdrift/downwind and with a high target drift rate may not be able to locate the target visually.

(b) On the initial pass after the WDI deployment, an accurate count can be obtained by the JM and the heading noted by both the JM and pilot. All subsequent passes will be made on this initial heading using the count obtained on the first pass. No attempt should be made to recheck the count or change the initial heading because the target will have drifted.

NOTE: On subsequent passes requiring a change of heading to place the aircraft over the target, ensure the pilot corrects back to original heading. Moving target procedures are normally conducted from fixed-wing aircraft.

Attachment 6

CROSSWIND PROCEDURES

Figure A6.1. Crosswind Procedures.

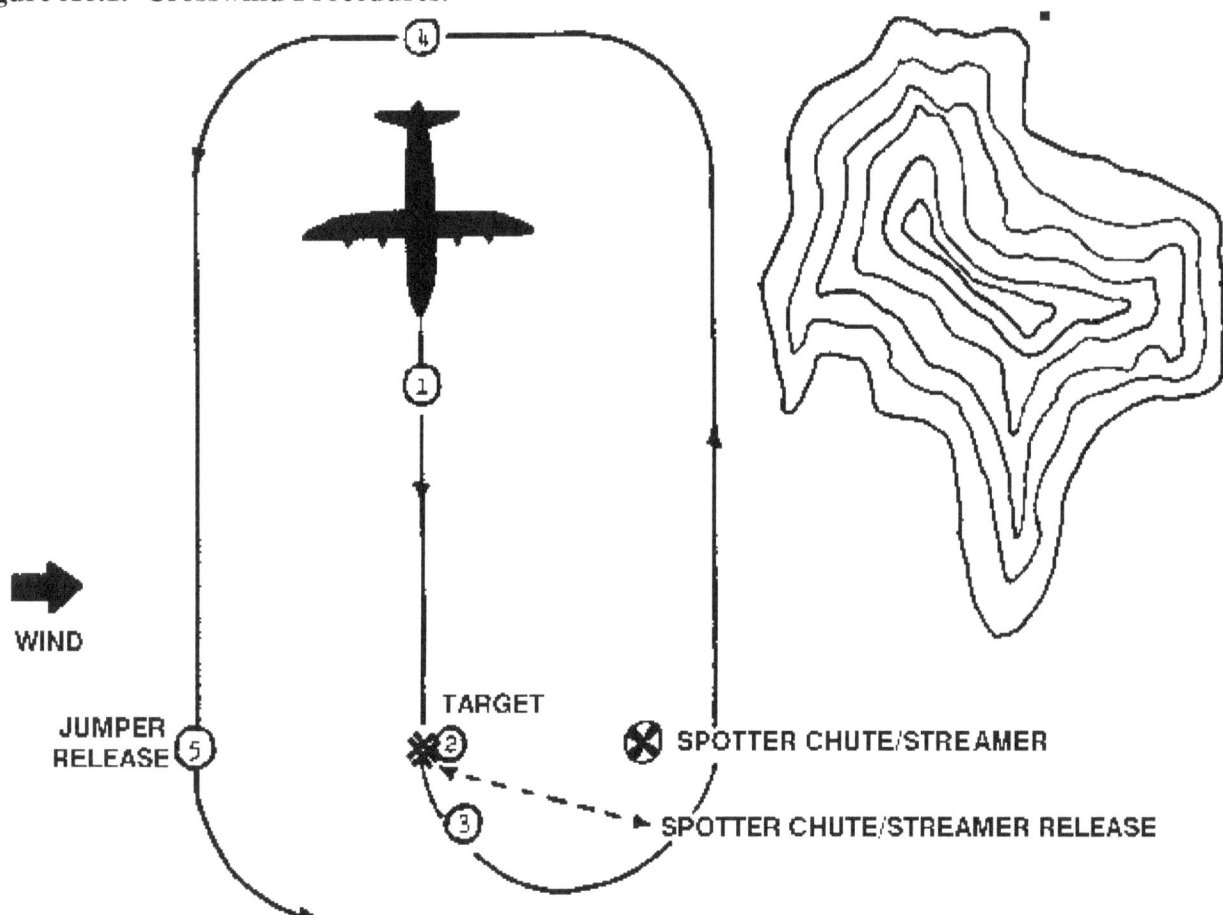

Figure A6.2. Figure Explanation - Crosswind Procedures.

1.   Spotting and Aerial Delivery - Crosswind Procedures.

a. Fly over target on heading in a direction to permit a left/right hand pattern.

b. Release the spotter chute/streamer directly over target.

c. Accomplish a 180 degree turn (terrain permitting) in direction of drift and observe distance of spotter chute/streamer from target.

d. Make another 180 degree turn to place the aircraft on the approach leg the same distance upwind from the target as the spotter chute is downwind.

e. Deploy PJs, equipment or additional spotters chutes/streamers (as required) just prior to when the aircraft is in direct line with the target and spotter chute/streamer.

2. Crosswind pattern. A crosswind pattern may be required by terrain conditions or possible sun reflection on the waters surface. The pilot and JM must accurately judge the upwind distance from the target in order for this technique to be effective. The easiest method for obtaining an accurate upwind distance is the utilization of a reference/release point. It is imperative that the jumpers be deployed prior to reaching the reference point due to the forward ballistics of the parachute as opening occurs. The objective is to place the reference point at the center of the stick after forward throw is considered.

3. Spotting techniques. Reference points may be used on all JMD land deployments. The utilization of reference points will increase the JMs accuracy in determining the proper release point. Also an established reference/release point will allow the aircraft to be flown in any direction as long as it will pass over the reference/release point. These points are a necessity when accomplishing a crosswind or downwind deployment pattern. The correct method for establishing e reference/release point is:

(a) Upon completion of the initial over the target WDI deployment, establish the impact location of the WDI.

(b) Pick out a spot that is an equal distance on the opposite side of the target as the WDI. This spot can be any readily identifiable feature, i.e. discolored ground, bushes, trees, etc.

NOTE: The JM should pass the reference/release point to the pilot to assure that both are utilizing the same point of reference.

www.ingramcontent.com/pod-product-compliance
Lightning Source LLC
Chambersburg PA
CBHW081206280526
45787CB00006B/2350